EDUCATION AND THE IDEA OF MANKIND

EDUCATION

AND

THE IDEA

OF

MANKIND

EDITED BY ROBERT ULICH, *1890 -*

Under the Auspices of the Council for the Study of Mankind

HARCOURT, BRACE & WORLD, INC. 〈HB〉 NEW YORK

GERHARD HIRSCHFELD

Foreword: The Council for the Study of Mankind

I HAVE been invited to give the reader a brief account of the history of the Council for the Study of Mankind, under whose auspices this book is published, and of the motivations that led up to its organization. Its history goes back five thousand miles and nearly fifty years.

I was born and raised in Berlin, Germany, the youngest of six brothers, but I grew up in a far greater world, the world of Socrates and Horace, Spinoza and Kant, Beethoven and Tolstoi, not to forget Walther Rathenau and Theodor Herzl. The environment may have been confusing for its richness, depth, and variety, but I found it interesting and challenging.

Though I had many questions to ask about this fascinating world, the teachers in the gymnasium did not share my enthusiasm for asking questions, and I therefore did not want to go on to the university. While I was still arguing with my parents about the matter, World War I swept our placid world, severely testing my dreams and ideals. I was badly shaken by the experience of being witness to the wholesale massacre, witness to a mother's grief over the loss of two sons. I came out of

v

the war with a determination to work for the abolition of war.

Times changed, but not hostility. Tolerated during the war, Jews again were discriminated against, and so I left for Peru, combining the offer of a job with the opportunity to visit the relics of the cultures of the Incas, the Quechuas, and adjacent tribes. In search of wider horizons, I went to New York, where, after a round of odd jobs, I began to write on the subjects that I thought bore on the causes of war—international relations, economic interests, social conflict. At night I studied the causes of war. Still, I did not seem to make any progress toward greater knowledge or enlightenment, and after about fifteen years, I switched my search to the principles of conflict, in and outside the human world. Another fifteen years passed during which the search seemed hopeless, but my determination remained. World War II came as no surprise. I lost another brother.

Year after year I had been trying to do something to help create an orderly mankind, one in which armed conflict among nations would no longer be possible. But what did I mean by "mankind"? I put the question to eminent scholars at the University of Chicago—Herbert Blumer in sociology, Richard P. McKeon and Charles Morris in philosophy, Quincy Wright in international relations, and the late Robert Redfield in anthropology. They were not agreed on the meaning of "mankind," but they were interested in exploring the question. In the spring of 1952, I invited these and other scholars, among them Adolf A. Berle, Jr., of Columbia University, to participate in informal talks on the subject of mankind.

Like many others throughout the world, we were concerned with finding answers to such questions as: What brought about this frightful state of world affairs? What specifically are our problems? What can we do about them? What kind of knowledge do we need and what kind of education? Obviously, there was need for inquiry. But before we started on a program of inquiry, we wanted to find out what scholars at other institutions here and abroad, who no doubt were similarly concerned, were doing about these questions. Perhaps they knew some of the answers.

On an extended tour through the United States and Western Europe, I discussed the problem of mankind at academic institutions. I found studies in progress that had some relation to our question. But the idea of mankind was usually relegated to and submerged in whatever other subject was under consideration—usually DEMOCRACY and mankind, FREEDOM and mankind, or CHRISTIANITY and mankind. Mankind was considered the secondary rather than the primary concern. In contrast, our group of scholars thought it indispensable to the understanding of mankind that we see mankind as the primary concept. It would rather put the inquiry the other way: MANKIND and democracy, MANKIND and freedom, MANKIND and Christianity.

Upon hearing my report, the group decided to go ahead with a program of inquiry: What is mankind? There was no lack of answers. Mankind is that which is different from the tulip and the crocodile. Mankind is nearly three billion people. Mankind is that which is different from any living thing anywhere in the universe. Mankind is different from the angels and the spirits. These are really meaningless definitions. In seeking to abolish war what help is it to know that man is different from the insects, the rocks, and the planets? The members of the group asked whether one has to define mankind in order to do something about its problems. Can we define the atom, nature, life, or even the individual person? Yet we do a great deal about these and many other things without benefit of definition.

With this question disposed of, another arose: How do we make this inquiry meaningful? It also became obvious that an inquiry based on the trial-and-error method would be wasteful and ineffective. Generally, things become meaningful to us as we attach values. Family, community, church, nation are meaningful to us because they represent certain values. Would this be equally true of mankind? Is not mankind meaningless to most of us because we do not attach any particular value to it? This may be a matter of indifference rather than intent. Some may also question whether the survival of mankind is worth the effort involved. But suppose we had determined that civilization must not perish, that we want to make a better world for our children if not for ourselves, that through education we must try to create a better understanding of our world. Would mankind not then become meaningful? The group agreed that it would.

Concern is fine, but how do you rationalize it? The advance of science and technology has created conditions that have produced vast opportunities along with urgent problems. However, the opportunities and the problems are not of the same importance. There is no urgent need to melt down the polar icecaps or to irrigate the Sahara. You can also take one at a time. Not so the problems that face man everywhere—nuclear war, the need for food, overpopulation, automation, the loss of values, and many others. Not only do they require an urgent solution but a solution that, if it is to be effective, must embrace all the major problems. For example, war cannot be permanently abolished without abolishing hunger, illiteracy, and overpopulation.

The problems are universal; they concern men everywhere. The proposed solutions, however, are colored by the influence of specific environments and interests. They are American,

French, Chinese, Christian, Buddhist, democratic, communist, capitalist, socialist—i.e., sectional or segmental solutions. The basic question emerges: Can we realistically hope to find solutions for the universal interests of man by way of partisan approaches? The scholars who initially looked at the problem did not think so. The need was to understand mankind as a universal quality. Without realizing it at the time, the group was approaching what turned out to be the final question in its search for a new way of thinking, namely: How does one go about understanding mankind?

We say we must understand other cultures. But how can we grasp the intrinsic values of Bulgarians and Indonesians if the whites find it difficult to understand the colored, or the haves the have-nots? We must understand world history. Agreed, but how do we teach world history? What *is* world history? If these and similar questions are important in the microcosm of education, they become decisive in the macrocosm of mankind. One can apply diversionary tactics in explaining conditions and events in the classroom, but one cannot avoid the full impact of problems facing mankind.

We realized then that looking at things from a parochial viewpoint and again from the viewpoint of mankind involved a basic difference. Education in the American perspective emphasizes problems such as overcrowded classes, underpaid teachers, federal subsidies, desegregation. Education in the perspective of mankind stresses the vast differences in levels of education between, say, the United States and Central Africa or the interior of Latin America, with all the problems of poverty, illiteracy, disease, exploitation, discontent. The needs of American education do not at all resemble the needs of world education; nor would the course of action demanded by the one resemble the course of action demanded by the other.

The mankind conception of freedom would differ greatly from that held by a citizen of the United States; or the concept of peace from the official interpretation of the Chinese government. Freedom under a mankind system would embrace all kinds of freedom, as mankind peace would consider all kinds of peace. In a pluralistic society—which a mankind system by its very nature would have to be—there is more than one interpretation of values, rights, institutions.

The danger is that we misinterpret mankind problems and thus arrive at false conclusions. We call universal problems like hunger mankind problems, but we evaluate them as agricultural surplus problems of the United States, and try to find a solution on that basis. We evaluate disarmament in terms of tax reduction and seek a solution in the national interest. We stress the need for world law but seek to develop international agreements on the sole basis of existing—i.e., parochial—systems. We see technology as a world force but proceed to refine and to elaborate it on the basis of national or regional considerations. Obviously, an effective solution of these and other problems cannot be found as long as a situation exists in which the problems operate on a universal level while the solutions are constructed on a sectional level. The members of the group were agreed on the need to find a basis upon which mankind problems can be evaluated as transsegmental problems, i.e., upon a world-wide basis.

The search for the idea of mankind had extended over several years of frequent discussion meetings. It had left us with the conviction that awareness of mankind and action oriented toward meeting the needs and assessing the values of mankind rather than of some segmental group were essential instruments to our solution of the problems of a world facing a deep crisis. In order to use these instruments we needed to understand their development and application. We did not seek a concept of mankind in the sense of ideological agreement on a doctrine or philosophy, but in the sense of a framework within which to discuss common actions, associations, attitudes, and values. We did not want to become a pressure group, at one extreme advocating a program of world society or government, or at the other, a sect promulgating a dogma of salvation. We wanted to advance the discussion of common ends and to explore the possibilities of associated action.

The unity of mankind in co-operative action does not depend on a unity in ideas and beliefs. On the contrary, it depends on a pluralism that would provide the energy and diversity of ideas to constitute an active and ever-growing unity. Indeed, unity in ideas and beliefs is contrary to the human personality; except in special circumstances, it is usually forced and therefore artificial. Pluralism is the mark of the advancing organization. Totalitarian dogmata notwithstanding, free organizations prosper because there is a diversity of identities and interests. Their progress would be hindered by a unity in beliefs and ideas.

The group developed a program in which the concept of mankind was one pole, and disciplines, institutions, nations, cultures, the individual person the other. The first meeting in 1952 was followed by many others, in the United States and in other countries. Five years later, the informal group became an official organization. The number of participants in the academic world grew; they were later joined by persons in business and the professions. Views and opinions developed into research and education programs, evolving through conferences and discussion groups and crystallizing into seminars, lectures, and books, made possible by growing foundation support. Dr. Clarence Faust, President of the Fund for the Advancement of Education; Dr. Frederick Burkhardt, President of the American

Council of Learned Societies; Dr. Leslie Paffrath, President of the Johnson Foundation; Professor Adolf A. Berle, Chairman of the Twentieth Century Fund, were among the first to encourage and to support the work of the Council.

Initial grants enabled the Council to invite noted scholars to a series of two-day conferences. Thus, the Johnson Foundation sponsored conferences on science, law, and history, held at the University of Chicago, the University of Virginia, and Wingspread, Racine, Wisconsin, respectively; the Twentieth Century Fund, a conference on economics held at the Massachusetts Institute of Technology: the Rockefeller Foundation, on nationalism (six days), held at the Villa Serbelloni, on Lake Como, Italy; the Corning Glass Works Foundation and Armour Research Foundation, on technology, held at the Illinois Institute of Technology; the Fund for the Advancement of Education, on education, held at Teachers College, Columbia University.

As the work of the Council developed, grants were provided by the Fund for the Advancement of Education for a series of seminars and lectures at the University of Chicago, Boston University, and other institutions. Still later, foundation funds were provided for a series of books related to the idea of mankind. A special grant was obtained for administrative expenses, to enable the Council to continue its basic operations independently of special projects.

When the first conferences were held, the scholars came— some fascinated, some curious, some doubtful, some highly skeptical. However, many of those who came, if not to scoff, at least to smile, remained to take up the problems presented by the Council as worthy of the careful attention of the ablest minds.

Conferences have served as the first step in a series of

activities: lectures, seminars, books. The members had agreed from the early days that, if in our existing framework of interests, loyalties, commitments in special areas, some space is to be cleared in the mind of man for the idea of mankind as a newly emerging social, political, economic concept, it would have to be done primarily through education. They also knew that many people are convinced they already have global awareness. Rarely do people realize the extent and depth of counter-indoctrination they have undergone since birth—psychological or spiritual, political or social.

How can a group consisting of a small staff, an executive committee, a board of directors and advisers, and hundreds of scholars around the globe—fewer than are found in any medium-sized university—be expected to make an impact on any of the major problems confronting mankind? It seems presumptuous that, with the world on fire, one should consider the most urgent need to think, to study, to teach. How can we afford precious time if we are not sure we shall be alive tomorrow?

Efforts to create an orderly world have been going on for a long time. Although supported by millions of devoted people, by very large sums of money, by intelligent leadership, they have not succeeded in creating that world or even in bringing society closer to it. By concentrating upon the idea of mankind, a group, however small, *can* help to bring about a new way of thinking. The Council confines itself to stimulating interest in the idea and to designing methods by which it may be studied and taught. Other institutions, better equipped than the Council, have and will aid the further development and dissemination of the material.

If this, the first in the series of books on the idea of mankind, deals with education, this is as it should be. Has it not always been the task of educators to interpret the meaning and the challenge of their particular age? In doing so they have been faced with the opposition of reactionary groups and of those who wanted clear-cut definitions before they would be willing to act. Fortunately, the deep resources of the human spirit have always been available to match the influence of the temporal. It is these resources of the human spirit that helped the great educators of the past and will help the educators of today.

Looking back, it seems that the search has been successful. The Council has found profitable questions to ask and has been able to clarify many of the questions. In developing its inquiry it has also laid the groundwork for an organized attack upon today's widespread ignorance of the idea of mankind as a newly emerging social, political, and economic concept. If successful, this effort will result not only in creating a more general awareness of mankind but in expanding the horizon of knowledge to a point at which the fundamental problems of mankind could be approached upon the basis of world-wide discussion of universal values and the formulation of policies. Specific problems could then be considered in the framework of the concept of mankind. The resolution of such problems must constitute the ultimate test.

ROBERT ULICH

Introduction: Purpose of the Book

OUR LITERATURE is replete with books on liberal education, on new programs and methods of studies at the various stages of schooling, and on the desirability of acquainting our youth with the new demands of the international situation. All this will, so we hope, make the minds of the new generation richer, more methodical, and more world-minded.

But we have also to face the danger that all these educational activities will merely mean a further increase in our busy emphasis on means unless we provide at the same time some sense of inner unity through a continuous attempt at clarifying their human ends. If the liberal arts, or what we now often call "general education," remain a mere accumulation of segments of knowledge without direction toward their depth, they will inform, but not form a person. If we stuff our curricula with more and more subjects, they may lose the inner organization that the young mind needs for its steady and methodical development. And a mere horizontal acquaintance with foreign cultures may, as we all know, lead to alienation instead of cooperation.

Here is the reason for this new book, planned under the auspices of the Council for the Study of Mankind. We would like to make educators as well as laymen aware of the fact that all the great teachers of mankind aimed at something more profound than mere instruction, acquisition of knowledge, usefulness, and efficiency. Rather, they believed that education, through widening man's intellectual horizon, should at the same time lead him deeper into his own self, and this not merely for the purpose of developing his individuality—which, when leading to isolation, may even lead to catastrophe—but for the purpose of helping him to discover the unity of his own striving with the strivings, hopes, and ideals, and also the loneliness, the sins, sufferings, and the aggressive tendencies, of all mankind. We do not want to create illusions and delusions but constructive realism. There should be a continual mutual fertilization between knowledge, self-knowledge, and understanding of humanity. None can develop to its fullest without the help of the others.

We know that every good teacher does exactly that: through teaching competently and devotedly—i.e., through identifying himself with his topic as a gathering point of significant ideas— he transcends the limits of mere "subject matter" toward meaningful and universal concepts. And through doing this he evokes in his pupils a sense of personal participation in the enterprise of civilization. Far from asserting that every subject of teaching is just as good as any other, we nevertheless believe that the teacher who knows the inner secret of his work can give life and color to subjects that under the treatment of a mediocre and unimaginative instructor would be boring or trifling. And we also believe firmly that, if there was any time in human history when the younger generation had to be taught how to connect their learning to the future of mankind as a whole, it is ours.

The essays in this book are partly of theoretical and partly of practical nature; some, so we hope, will stimulate thinking about the nature and mission of learning in our time of re-evaluation of values, while others should inform the reader about the experiences and actual work of outstanding teachers concerned with interesting their pupils, young and old, in the common concerns of humanity. But we warn the reader. The task of using our present forms of education for the emergence of an international conscience, or for the idea of mankind, is too complicated to be solved by panaceas. What we need first of all is fundamental thinking—not only about our schools and our world, but also about ourselves.

CONTENTS

PART ONE

Basic Considerations

1.

ROBERT ULICH

The Ambiguities in the Great Movements of Thought

IN 1921 Rabindranath wrote an essay, "The Unity of Education." It began with the statement "It must be admitted on all
hands that the world today belongs to the Europeans. It is their
milk-cow, and it fills their pail to overflowing."[1] History has now
reversed the process. Who is now milking whom? But, in its
essence, the essay speaks to us today even more vividly than
four decades ago.

Why, Tagore asks, could the West conquer the world? His
answer is: because the European used systematic and empirical
thinking instead of outmoded magic, and thus created the
"science of life" that, at the present, is "the most important
branch of secular knowledge." Only a turn of mind that would
unite old intuitional wisdom with modern methods of thinking
and research could create an independent Indian nation.

But while Tagore acknowledged without prejudice the
reasons for the material and intellectual superiority of the West,
he also perceived its inner weakness. The dreadful war of 1914-
18 had ended, only to "recommence under the mask of peace";

1. Rabindranath Tagore, *Towards Universal Man* (New York: Asia Publishing
House, 1961).

3

nationalism was rampant, greed had crept into the heart of the European civilization, and one listened in vain for some inner music within the noisy "stone-and-brick jungle of the other side of the Atlantic. . . . Its machines have no message for us. They do not respond to any tune of the universe, they answer no call of the heart."

Obviously, so Tagore said, modern traffic will bring the nations of the world ever closer to each other, but the closeness will not create unity. The only remedy Tagore can conceive of is education toward an understanding of life, which, with due regard for the truth in nature, searches also for the truth in men. This was known by the authors of the Upanishads when they said, "And he who sees all beings in his own self and his own self in all beings, he does not remain unrevealed."

But, so far, Tagore continues, education has been used mainly by the mighty for increasing their power, and by the modern states for fanning the fires of nationalism. Only when education helps a man to recognize the deep and common interests of humanity can it change the inevitable internationalism from a physical and even dangerous fact into a new "universality," or, we could say, make man aware of mankind.

THE AMBIVALENCE IN RELIGION

We would misinterpret Tagore's hopes for a new "science of life" if we did not recognize in them a profoundly religious— though entirely undogmatic—element. Humans have always been yearning for universal meaning beyond merely detailed knowledge. In ancient times they expressed their hopes and fears in the form of myths that emerged in astounding similarity on the most distant lands and continents of the earth. But whereas these intuitional creations accepted the will of the gods and the eruptions of irrational forces in the lives of men as unalterable facts—we still sense this attitude in the plays of Aeschylus—the great religious and cosmological systems tried to detect in the history of the world not only fate but also grace, not only law but also freedom, not only suffering but also salvation.

The answer to man's quest for communion with the Ultimate enabled the world religions to unite the pious in worship and in associations wider and more lasting than even the most mighty political organizations. We do not know what came first—the person's longing for solidarity with a meaningful universe, or the desire for solidarity with one's equals. Probably the two enforced each other in common growth. The so-called Golden Rule, expressed by all great religions in very similar wording, was probably conceived as both a pragmatic device and a reflection of the cosmic order on the level of human society.

At that amazing period of awakening of man's ethical consciousness, connected in the Western mind mainly with the appearance of the Jewish prophets, Confucius replied to the question of a disciple, whether there was no word that could serve as a rule for all life, "Yes. Is not reciprocity such a word?"[2] He also said, "Within the four seas, all men are brothers." And whether, of the great Chinese sages, we read Confucius, or Laotse, or Chuang-tsu, there is always before us the vision of a co-operative society within a co-operative cosmos.

Among the Indians, Buddha recommended to his followers the Noble Eightfold Path of right views, right attention, right speech, right action, right livelihood, right effort, right mindfulness, and right concentration. Like his contemporaries, Confucius believed that by following such practices men would discover the inner sources of world unity. King Asoka, who ascended to the throne of India in 273 B.C. and became a convert

2. David Rhys Williams, *World Religions and the Hope for Peace* (Boston: The Beacon Press, 1951), p. 9.

to Buddhism, declared in his Twelfth Edict, ". . . there ought to be no exaltation of one's religion and finding fault with others. . . . On the contrary, others' religions should be honored in every way. By so doing one exalts one's own religion and does service to another's religion."[3]

About two hundred years later Jesus delivered to his disciples the Sermon on the Mount and St. Paul proclaimed the superiority of charity over all the other virtues of the world. In spite of all their early dogmatic differences, the early Christians believed that through the coming of Christ the whole of humanity, or "the world," would be saved ("For God so loved the world"). Through his belief in God, who was "the Truth," each person was related to all other persons; mankind was one.

Even the historian who rejects the supernatural premises of the Judeo-Christian doctrine will have to admit that the new faith, while contributing to the disintegration of one of the greatest achievements of humanity, the *Civitas Romana,* helped the newly emerging medieval civilization to establish a code of conduct, more often disobeyed than obeyed, but nevertheless providing a standard. Since this code is one of the elements of the Western heritage, and since there are so many similarities between its postulates and those of other cultures, we may refer here to its history as to a symbolic illustration of the relationship between the ideal demands and the actual practice in human society.

It is idle to argue whether, after the migration of the nations, some such ideal standard would have come about without Christianity. Perhaps the missionary zeal of the Church arrested the gradual maturing of a cosmic metaphysics, the seeds of which we find in the old Germanic myths. Nevertheless,

3. Handas T. Muzumdar, *The United Nations of the World* (New York: Universal Publishing Co., 1942), pp. 166-67.

certain it is that Charlemagne and Alfred the Great could avail themselves of nothing else besides their arms, but the Christian Church set out to reorder the European continent and England. Also, on other continents, reorganization and reintegration were generally connected with some kind of religious revival.

Since during the Middle Ages the theology of the Church was able to absorb more and more of the Greek-Roman and Jewish-Arabic philosophical heritage, it became the primary intellectual force of the time, providing a frame of reference even for heretical sects such as the Waldenses and Albigenses, which it persecuted. Although against its will, it prepared the intellectual groundwork of the Renaissance and the thought of one of the first liberal and democratic men of Western history, Erasmus of Rotterdam. On the Protestant side, the opening of the leaves of the Bible, so far jealously guarded by the hierarchy, stimulated Christian laymen to inquire into the meaning of one of the most profound and enigmatic books of mankind and to develop that philosophical urge that gave rise to the internationally influential systems of Germany during the decades around the eighteen hundreds.

Before the flowering of philosophical idealism, at the period of the Thirty Years' War, the Moravian Bishop John Amos Comenius could say in his *Way of Light*:

For there is inborn in human nature a love of liberty—for liberty man's mind is convinced that it was made—And this love can by no means be driven out; so that wherever and whatever means it feels that it is being hemmed in and impeded, it cannot but seek a way out and declare its own liberty.[4]

In conformity with the idea of Christian freedom Comenius demanded public schools and the mutual co-operation of

4. *The Way of Light* (via Lucis), trans. by E. T. Campagnac (Liverpool: University of Liverpool Press, 1939), p. 18.

science, politics, and religion, and he asked for a league of nations that should promote "universal books, universal schools, a universal college and a universal language."

When Comenius wrote these lines, it had become clear that the hierarchy which, in spite of all political and intellectual warfare, had given some semblance of unity to medieval Europe had fallen apart. No one could hope any more for a continent under one empire, one church, and one ideal of learning. The time had become ripe for new orientations, but as to the ways to go, there were still many differences within the Christian nations and denominations.

However great the difficulties in evaluating the effect on mankind of a historical event of such complexity as Christianity, within an environment dominated by the brutal battle for survival it has deepened man's conscience and charity, civilized retarded parts of the world, and is still a source of strength for millions.

But one might also contend that that which Christianty has given with one hand it has taken away with the other. Perhaps less than other religions it has understood how to solve one of the most difficult predicaments of the human mind, namely, that without some belief in things ultimate, called "truth," man cannot establish firm principles of thought and conduct. But if he takes his beliefs absolutely, to the degree of negating the necessity of continuous development and the respect for honest differences, he turns belief into a totalitarian doctrine. How much harm and discord has been created out of falsely placed loyalties! Actually, this tendency toward totalitarian fanaticism results from a misplaced desire for an all-embracing unity of minds (unless it is, as also happens, motivated by a combination of fear and lust for power). If frustrated, this desire for conformity tries to achieve its goal by cruelty and persecution or, at least, by intolerant forms of argument. Too many of the writings of the church fathers breathe the spirit of "contra."

To what degree, we may ask, did the teaching of Jesus, or of Confucius, Buddha, and Mohammed, really change the morality of natural men? Certainly, it changed the lives of many. Saints and martyrs appeared and were venerated as examples of Christian virtue. The persecutions of Christians by the Roman rulers were unable to crush the new faith. But hardly had Cyril (376-444), declared a saint by the Church, entered his holy duties at Alexandria, than he closed and plundered the churches of a dissenting Christian sect, expelled thousands of Jews, and did apparently nothing to stop a series of antipagan riots, during one of which the mob killed the famous Neoplatonist woman philosopher Hypathia. All this happened in the most famous international center of ancient learning, where Philo the Jew had attempted a synthesis between the Hebrew and Hellenic traditions, and where the enlightened church fathers Clement and Origen had tried to reconcile the Christian gospel with the Greek concept of Logos, an act of thought without which Christianity could never have become a world religion.

The finally established Christian orthodoxy suppressed its pagan opponents as well as the dissenters within the Church itself as far as its power permitted. Some centuries later the Crusaders, with the cross on their armor, celebrated the conquest of Jerusalem with a ghastly orgy of bloodshed, followed by prayer in the Church of the Holy Sepulcher. At the same time, there began the wholesale persecution of Jews, based on prejudices that even today have not entirely lost their diabolical power, and the Inquisition gave to the worldly arm the task of burning witches and heretics. Woe to the princes who would not have obeyed!

The contrast between charity and fanaticism strikes one especially in the person of one of the famous medieval theologians, John Gerson, chancellor of the University of Paris. This leader of the Christian reform movement before the Reformation wrote a touching pamphlet, "On Leading the Children to Christ," in which he defended his concern for the souls of the poor and declared that, in his role as father confessor, "there has never, with my will, remained in my heart a trace of revenge or hatred during someone's confession of sin, were it even with the murder of his own parents."[5]

Yet, the same Gerson was influential in the condemnation and burning of the pious Czech reformer, John Huss, at the Council of Constance, and thus helped to touch off the cruel war of the revenging Hussites against the House of Hapsburg. He wanted reform, but brought a reformer to the stake; he wanted unity of the Church, but disunited Christians against Christians.

Unbaptized children, so parents were told, and are still told, were considered to be doomed to eternal damnation; furies of hatred were raging during the period of the Reformation, and almost a century after the Treaty of Westphalia, which had guaranteed religious liberty, the Archbishop Firmian of Salzburg —to mention only one of several—felt the extirpation of Protestantism in his realm to be his most sacred duty. In 1732, not many years before the birth of Goethe, he forced twenty-two thousand of his subjects to leave their homes. In England, the Protestants persecuted the Catholics, and in New England the Puritans persecuted the Quakers. At the present, the schools of many countries suffer from denominational interferences.

5. See Robert Ulich, *Three Thousand Years of Educational Wisdom* (Cambridge: Harvard University Press, 1959), pp. 188 *ff.*

THE AMBIVALENCE OF SECULARISM

After the Renaissance, Christendom's picture of itself and of mankind began to change. In course of time, this change has influenced the whole of humanity. With the discovery of new continents the curtain went up, and so-far-unknown peoples moved on the surprising stage. With the Reformation even the semblance of a unified Christian theology broke down. Literacy spread among the masses, and the wisdom of the Greeks and Romans was no longer regarded as the propylaeum to the temple of Christianity but as a stimulus to independent thinking. Finally, the disciples surpassed the masters. The old Christian cosmology and anthropology were shaken by Copernicus, and the Christian thinkers found themselves side by side with various forms of secularism, from a humanism that still retained much of the old metaphysical heritage, though in an undogmatic mode, to rather rebellious forms of atheist materialism.

By secularism, I mean here man's attempt to learn about himself and his world, not by the medium of propositions derived from supernatural premises, but by means of rational inquiry. Let us assume that it began with the Socratic postulate of "Know thyself," but "Know thyself" not merely as an isolated individual but as a member of mankind and as a participant in an overarching "cosmos" (which originally meant "order"). Actually, even the materialist did not think to be a micro-*chaos* within a macro-*chaos;* he also assumed blithely to be a micro-*cosm* within a macro-*cosm.*

Of course, the hope that man can find his own intellectual endeavors reflected by an encompassing world system is based on a faith that one may or may not share. It is however not only at the base of all great religions, though there supernaturally explained, but it is also the unconscious or conscious belief of every scientist who works in the assurance that his research may provide some insight into the gigantic workshop of life. Historically, the conviction of the participation of the human person in a higher order of being has been the most powerful challenge to ancient tribalism, fears, and idolatries. Without it, the concept of mankind as an inner unity of souls would make no sense.

As we did in regard to the mankind idea in religion, let us show the development and the failures of a sense of universality in relation to our secular-humanist tradition.

Whereas Plato and Socrates had taken the institutions of slavery for granted, the Stoic philosopher Epictetus, living at the time of Christ, protested against human exploitation with the following words:

Do you not remember what you are and over whom you rule—that they are kinsmen, that they are brothers by nature, that they are the offspring of Zeus? . . . Do you see whither you bend your gaze, that it is to the earth, that it is to the pit, that it is to these wretched laws of ours, the laws of the dead, and that it is not to the laws of God that you look.[6]

Finally, Epictetus develops the vision of a great international and rational society:

If what is said by the philosophers regarding the kinship of God and men be true, what other course remains for men but that which Socrates took when asked to which country he belonged, never to say "I am an Athenian," or a "Corinthian," but "I am a citizen of the universe." . . . Well, then, anyone who has attentively studied the administration of the universe and has learned that the greatest and most authoritative and most comprehensive of all govern-

6. Epictetus, *Discourses*, trans. by W. A. Oldfather (Cambridge: The Loeb Classical Library, Harvard University Press, 1956), Vol. 1, pp. 99 *ff*.

ments is this one which is composed of men and God, and that from Him have descended the seeds of being, not merely to my father and to my grandfather, but to all things that are begotten and that grow upon earth, and chiefly to rational beings, seeing that by nature it is theirs alone to have communion in the society of God, being intertwined with Him through reason—why should not such a man call himself a citizen of the universe? Why should he not call himself a son of God?[7]

The stoic concept of *humanitas* as embedded in an all-embracing Logos had a decisive influence on the legal thought and practice of Rome. In his *Treatise on Law* (*De Legibus*) Cicero wrote that "the whole world may once become one community [*una civitas*] equally respected by the gods and men." Stoic and Ciceronian thought became absorbed by Christianity to such a degree that we may call its theology a fusion of pagan and Christian elements. Unfortunately, the Christian thinkers turned the monism of the Stoics into a dualistic interpretation of the world. Thus, it was a hostile environment to which, in the seventeenth century, Spinoza presented again a unified world outlook, rational as well as humanistic. It expressed confidence in man's capacity to build the house of mankind in a planned and systematic fashion instead of living forever with a sense of helplessness in self-inflicted ruins. Spinoza, in turn, inspired many of the great thinkers, educators, and poets, such as Goethe, during the following centuries. It does not matter here whether Spinoza's pantheism, just as Rousseau's concept of nature, were always correctly understood. What matters is that both men belonged to the leaders of a movement that created, within certain parts of the Western world, a new feeling of universality and human togetherness, or of belongingness to mankind. It drove Christian men out of a sense of separation from both the rest

7. *Ibid.*

of mankind (because it was not Christian) and from nature (because man was supposed to overcome it). And, as always when a new level of self-consciousness is reached, there emerged a sense of independence, optimism, and of wider horizons with regard to the purpose of education. Thus Kant wrote, in his *Notes on Pedagogy,* that "the peculiarity of a truly human life lies in the fact that man has to create himself by his own voluntary efforts. He has to make himself a truly moral, rational, and free being."[8] In other words, so Kant says, "education is the process by which man becomes man." By this formula Kant, like Goethe, combines the individualistic ideal of self-development with the cosmopolitan ideals of his time. The same combination of self and mankind we find also in Wilhelm von Humboldt, the reformer of the classical gymnasium. He too had in mind classical languages, not as a specialty but as a gate to the humanities, not the well-drilled individual but the person enriched by a universal tradition. Hence, he defined education *(Bildung)* as an ever-deepening and widening process of enrichment by the great thoughts of humanity, from the Bhagavad-Gita and Homer up to the works of the modern nations.

In spite of all divergence, Goethe, Kant, and Humboldt would be unthinkable without that great intellectual movement that, more than any other in modern times, has inundated our present culture—the era of Rationalism, or the Enlightenment. Its practical effects on a better self-understanding of mankind have been momentous. It fought physical torture and vicious legal procedure, witch trials, and the Inquisition. From the

8. *Immanuel Kant über Pädagogik,* Hg. F. Th. Rink. (Königsberg, 1803). There Kant says also: "An educational principle that those should have in mind who determine educational policy is this—children ought to be educated, not merely for the present, but for the improvement of the conditions of the human race, that is—the idea and the mission of humanity in its totality." There exists an English edition: Immanuel Kant, *Education* (Ann Arbor Paperbacks, University of Michigan Press, 1960).

Enlightenment we have inherited the idea of tolerance and the understanding of non-Christian cultures. It fostered the ascendance of methodical and empirical inquiry over theological systems; it has turned the gaze of men from the past to the future, and it has taught us to look at the world at large and within ourselves without magical fears.

There can be no change in spirit that is not at the same time a change in politics, for as we think of ourselves, so we try to organize our community. Reason needs freedom, and thus it came about that during the flowering of rationalism, democracy was born, as it will die when man despairs of reason and is forbidden to use it freely. Beginning with the eighteenth century the previously theoretical concept of the "natural rights of man" became transferred into political reality, and it became the mark of a civilized nation to insist on habeas-corpus, impartial justice, freedom of speech and assembly, freedom of faith, the right to own personal property, and the privilege to move and vote. All these rights are indispensable for one of the main requisites of human survival, i.e., the right to search for truth, to hear the truth, and to apply it in practical life. The Constitution of the United States applies the spirit of rationalism to the political order, and though the French Revolution, which followed, in 1789, was a failure in many respects, it was nevertheless, like the German Reformation, one of those great experiments that open the way toward new human accomplishments.

Intimately connected with the spirit of the eighteenth century was the rise of our modern public, universal, and tax-supported school system. For only a country that can rely on a certain knowledge and maturity of its citizens can trust them to use their freedom in harmony with the laws and interests of the community. Such a country will also strive to free its schools from the strife of denominations. Only in a combination of political liberty with freedom of conscience in matters of faith can the walls be broken that separate man from man and which prevent the gradual unification of the nations of the world.

Together with the growth of rational humanism—as a matter of fact, as an integral part of it—modern science developed, to be understood here not merely as natural science but as the methodical pursuit of the study of man, or the humanities.

Every great philosopher of the age of reason wrote on "method," that is, the right way of procedure. This passionate interest in valid forms of research would not have emerged without the pioneering work of Galileo, Kepler, Huygens, and Newton. It meant, for their contemporaries, the lifting of man and nature out of inscrutable powers into an order still full of mysteries, but nevertheless open to systematic inquiry. The concept of causality replaced the concept of inherent tendencies in things, which was essentially a transfer of the inner experiences of man into the realm of nature. No other achievement brought man to mankind so effectively as science. Through biology and related studies the human being began to understand his place in the evolving continuity of nature. Medicine taught him how to fight disease. Technology freed him from the exhausting fight for food and shelter. Every new nation wants engineers. In contrast to theology and many humanistic disciplines, science has a clear and unambiguous vocabulary that can be understood by trained men in every nation. It has brought into our schools subjects that excite the imagination of intelligent youth, invite them to accept the rigors of methodical discipline, and force them to look over the borders of their own people toward the work of other nations. Science now transcends even the boundaries of our globe. If there is any future in mankind, it will depend largely on the development of science;

while it has expanded its frontiers over so-far-unknown areas of the outer world, it has helped the human person to probe the depths of his inner self. Certainly, the religious prophets and the great thinkers fathomed the human soul, and our poets and artists listened to its finest vibrations. Nevertheless, it is the result of the scientific temper that we try to approach the hidden areas of the soul with as little prejudice as possible. It remains to be seen whether the judgment of the future will place Freud beside Darwin and Einstein. Nevertheless, whether in agreement or disagreement, whether for truth or for error, people have been aroused by him to inquire anew, "What is man?"

We may now ask the same question we asked in relation to the role of religion in the education of man toward mankind. Have all the humanistic and scientific achievements since the Renaissance really helped the human society to grow more closely together? The answer will be: Just as religion is beneficial if it meets men whose souls are prepared for its wisdom, so humanism and science are beneficial if they meet men of good will. Otherwise, they may be turned into evil.

Humanism and its historical companion, liberalism, have often created a self-centered individualism that forgot the roots of the person in the common ground of life. Hence it has caused as much segmentation as religious institutionalism. Men can become the victims of their freedom if they do not know what to do with it, as they can become the slaves of their tradition if they have lost courage and perspective. Freedom without common goals creates a state of alienation within each person and within the community. Eventually disenchantment and fear of chaos may drive them into shameful surrender to totalitarian powers. The French Revolution produced the mob tyranny of Paris, and all the humanism of the German gymnasium did not prevent thousands of its disciples from welcoming the rise of national-socialist materialism.

Certainly, illiteracy today means backwardness. The shrewdness in the proverbs of the Russian peasant, the fascination of old epic poetry, and the profoundness of ancient myths are not substitutes for self-information by means of the printed page. Yet it is in no way clear whether the missionaries of literacy will create more happiness in foreign countries than the missionaries of religion. Perhaps each of us, observing in the crowded subway what people read, may sometimes have wondered whether the invention of movable type was not a doubtful blessing.

There is a deep connection between the individualism of the Renaissance and modern nationalism. This individualism was aristocratic in the beginning, but in spreading over wider and wider parts of the population, it changed the feudal collectivism of the Middle Ages and the absolutism of the following period into the modern state of citizens. These citizens refused to remain mere subjects of their sovereign and claimed the right to participate in the affairs of the nation. They identified themselves with it. Its pride became their pride, its defeat their defeat, with all its ensuing hatreds. Thus, the era of total wars emerged, which caused more men to die in battle than in all the centuries before. It was largely nationalism, combined with industrial unemployment, that produced the modern Attila, Hitler.

Modern nationalism, with its imperialistic bent, was one of the causes of colonialism, the recollection of which still burns in the minds of Asia and Africa and kindles the flames of communism. But the European nations would not have imposed their rule on foreign countries without another egotistic distortion of the freedom provided by the liberal movement. This was early industrial capitalism. Actually, in some colonies, the masses were not worse off, perhaps even better, than many of the working people at home. Not only adults were forced to flock into cities as a consequence of the decline of agriculture, where they had nothing to offer and bargain with but their physical strength, but even their children, working ten hours a day, lived in a new form of slavery. Fortunately, this is history. Yet, one of its consequences is still with us. When Marx and Engels observed the misery of the English working class, they wrote the *Communist Manifesto* and *Das Kapital,* and on these works Soviet communism and dialectical materialism claim to be based. With the rapid spread of the new ideology, a sharp cleft has developed in the soul and body of mankind. For both sides, the collectivist and the free world, science is now no longer an instrument for the widening of our intellectual horizon but an instrument of competition. If misapplied by hateful men, it may destroy the fruits of civilization.

A cloud of pessimism has descended on mankind exactly at the time when the path seems free for unheard-of achievements in human welfare. More and more people ask themselves whether there is any struggling and budding good that human selfishness and fanaticism cannot turn into evil.

THE AMBIVALENCE IN MAN

How does it come about that man, so richly endowed by nature and capable of extreme heroism, is at the same time the most destructive, even the most self-destructive, creature on earth? How can we explain that we still live in a divided world although the idea of universality shines through all great products of thought? Indeed, we call really great only that which, so we think, deserves the admiration of cultured people in their totality.

There is no need here for a catalogue of all the disastrous proclivities that have caused man to constantly undo his own doings. We have just as ample a vocabulary for our moral failings as for our moral achievements. All religions speak of sin and self-inflicted suffering, and the mythical Biblical idea of inherited, or original, sin has a meaning perhaps just as realistic as the optimistic picture of man. In fact, the optimistic interpretation of history is relatively new, due to a combination of ideological and material factors that originated during and after the Renaissance. Certainly, when our not-so-distant forbears saw so many children dying and whole regions helpless against plagues and famines, the world appeared to them far more as "the valley of the shadow of death" than as a summer resort place. Millions in many parts of the world are still in the same situation.

Read the history of any of the old European and Asiatic cities, and you will find its inhabitants constantly exposed to armies that threatened before, and to treason that threatened within, the walls. Side by side there lived the saints and scoundrels, the builders and the wreckers, the broad-minded and the fanatics. Even in men of shining genius, pride and lust for power destroyed the work for which they were admired. The fields of history swarm with little Alexanders and Napoleons. Thus when the myths of mankind envisioned a supernatural theater of the gods and demons battling each other, they merely projected mankind's most shaking experiences into the realm of the transcendental. As Zoroaster said, "It is the human soul in which the battle rages." And we should not wonder at the seemingly strange fact that modern man looks not only at the unheard-of achievements of our time, but also at its unheard-of cruelties, and thus listens more readily to a new pessimism than to the optimism of the eighteenth century. To be sure, the thinkers of that period also knew about evil. They fought it all the time, but they thought it might be overcome by our efforts, or at least restrained. Also, Rousseau knew of the difference between the opinions and conduct of the many, and the judgment of those concerned with the general interest. But neither he nor his contemporaries would have conceived of an idea basic in the thought of one of the most influential psychiatrists of our time, Carl Gustav Jung. Jung speaks of "archetypal," or primordial, experiences[9] that rise from the dark streams underneath our personal and collective consciousness. The archetypes may be constructive, as in religion, love, and in man's instinctive knowledge of the ultimate identity of the human race. Or they may be destructive, as man's demoniac urge for the abuse and demolition even of things holy, his perversion of eros into lust, his racial hatreds, and his desire to burn witches and to look for scapegoats.

When applying the psychoanalyst's hypotheses to the problems of peace and internationality, we may conclude that in the course of the history of nations, something like archetypal experiences may have been working for man's good, but also for mankind's evil. In one or the other period of its history, every nation has behaved like a neurasthenic or paranoic person unwilling to accept rational explanations, blindly speaking of honor and glory and revenge when it could have profited from decent co-operation, and prosecuting the few who dared think. Political intolerance now takes the place of religious intolerance, and even surpasses it in magnitude and cruelty. Endless still are the disputes about frontiers and minorities. No one would have expected the extremes of violence that ensued be-

9. C. G. Jung, *Collected Works*, Vol. 9, *The Archetypes and the Collective Unconscious* (New York: Pantheon Books, 1959), Pt. 1, pp. 3 ff., especially pp. 16, 23. Other writings by Jung on problems of education can be found in Volume 17 of the *Collected Works*.

tween India and Pakistan after their long battle for liberation. Tribal warfare rages within the new African nations, and the race hatred between the white and colored assumes new dimensions. We are divided even among ourselves. On the one hand, most of us become irritated when we listen to criticism of our own nation, our ethnic group, and the customs and beliefs of our childhood, even if we no longer share them. On the other hand, our literature and conversations are replete with irrational forms of self-criticism and self-hatred. Thus the good that is in honest self-examination may turn into self-defeat.

Perhaps the whole tragedy of humanity can be expressed still more simply. *Life* of August 25, 1961, contains an article by Ernest Haveman on Judge Learned Hand. There the author reports that the Judge had been reading William Shirer's *The Rise and Fall of the Third Reich,* and that it affected him deeply:

His voice shook with passion. Then he shrugged and stared into space with the patient wisdom of age. "The trouble," he said, "is that it isn't just the Nazis. It isn't just the Russians. It's human nature, through the centuries. We all have totally unreasonable and cruel ambitions, and then . . . we all festoon our lusts with pretty phrases, to justify them."

Unfortunately, the irrational behavior of man is caused not only by his psychological limitations; it has its cause also in our intellect itself. For purposes of clarity, the intellect has to isolate the object of its attention from the whole within which it stands. Even when we try to extend the span of our interest as far as possible, the whole is beyond our grasp; it exists only in our vision, or intuition. Yet, without a picture of the whole we cannot even comprehend the single. Behind and within every leaf we see is whole nature, and it is the same with every person. And behind every person is also his society, his nation, and its history, mankind, and finally the universe. It is good to remind ourselves from time to time of all this infinity in order to acquire this healthy relativism, which should prevent us from idolizing ourselves and our nation, our creeds, our truths, and our little knowledge.

In view of all the forces of separation that work in man, it is utopian to believe that he will ever achieve the millennium here on earth. The chaotic will always break into the painfully constructed human order. And however eagerly we collect the wisdom of earlier ages, it remains an antiquarian enterprise, because we have lost the inner grasp of the symbols that interpreted life and the world to our ancestors. The more we invent, the more we become the slaves of our inventions. "The whole world," so Jung says, "wants peace and the whole world prepares for war. . . . Mankind is powerless against mankind."[10]

On the other hand, civilization has become possible only because man has refused to accept his environment passively, to surround with the supernatural halo of immutable destiny that which he meets in the world. He is a creature of action and hopes he may change the existing, including himself. Metaphysically he may believe that the constructive and the destructive, or the good as well as the evil, are indissolubly inherent in the nature of being. Yet no one, not even the pessimistic Schopenhauer, would deny that this belief contains the challenge to man to direct his aggressiveness (which is a part of his freedom) toward the better, instead of wavering desperately between the positive and the negative poles. To refuse this chal-

10. *Ibid.*, p. 23.

lenge would mean to admit defeat before the battle has begun. However, the battle cannot begin seriously unless we examine ourselves in order to discover the causes of our defects.

One reason, of course, is fear. Although the sources of thousands of superstitions, it is not itself superstition. Man has many reasons for being fearful. Without the warnings of fear he would not have survived. In earlier times nature threatened him from day to day, denying him food, destroying his shelter, sending wild animals into his houses and herds, and forcing him into hostile regions from which there was no escape. Even with all our modern inventions—let us not deceive ourselves—fear is still with us; not only the fear of sickness and death, but the fear of unemployment, competition, and loneliness even in the midst of boisterous crowds. Beneath the veneer of modern technology there still looms anxiety. "Anxiety" has become a modern catchword, as has "affluence." And exactly now, when we should have learned enough from the disasters of history to replace fear with co-operation, we live in a situation of dread and tension. Lack of fear and an unrealistic internationalism might be suicidal. No nation is yet ready for the heroic leap from armament to disarmament. Furthermore, the haves fear the have-nots, and vice versa. And both have good reasons.

Fear is one of the causes of another element in human relations that can be both good and evil—the desire for identification. Advanced minds may welcome the foreign and the foreigner as a source of enrichment, but in the average person, superficial curiosity is mixed with uneasiness. The narrower the mind, the stronger is the urge for undisturbed security and for identification with the close and immediate. This urge persists even when a little wisdom could tell the suspicious that they cannot even save the immediate unless they see it in its wider relations, be it the clan, the business, the creed, the community, or the nation. Thus we had family feuds in earlier times and have them still today. In some countries pluralism, either religious or racial, is still abhorred. Only one creed or one race is nationally sanctioned, and others are just "tolerated," or not even that. Finally, the modern perversion of patriotism into chauvinism has led more men into battlefields and death than all previous wars of history together. And now we construct atom bombs and atom-bomb shelters.

Under these circumstances it would be utopian to expect education to provide the panacea for the future of mankind, or, to use Tagore's words, to produce "the universal man" by a new "science of life."

The history of education proves that, while teaching the gospel of Christ, it followed the various denominations along their evil as well as their good paths; while teaching history and other fields of the humanities, it often buried the free judgment of the pupil under heaps of distorted learning; while teaching loyalty to the nation—as it should—it has often taught the worst of chauvinism.

It adds to the difficulty that education, especially in its lower stages, consists inevitably in the formation of habits that are taken over from the adult society. Parents will not tolerate teachers who in a sheltered classroom filled with uncritical children arrogate to themselves the role of social and political critics. However we interpret the term "indoctrination"—either positively as a transmission of values, or negatively as a violation of the child's right of personal development—something of both is inevitably connected with public schooling.

Yet pessimism is the easiest attitude to adopt. There is no risk in it because something is always wrong. But it is just as perilous as the kind of optimism that shuts man's eyes before the pitfalls of reality. Even in full realization of the dangers with which we have surrounded ourselves, by means of education and other civilizing agencies, we have widened the frontiers of knowledge and developed a sense of respect for honest human endeavor, so that the variety of differences is for many of us no longer a cause of chagrin but a source of enrichment. While some followers of religious creeds stiffen in view of the supposed dangers of comparison, others help in the process of transmutation from religions toward the universally religious—let us hope without destroying the individual languages by which men have established their dialogues with the eternal. Our inquiry into the conscious will perhaps provide better means by which to direct its positive, and sublimate or redirect its destructive, qualities. We all recognize an educated man, not merely by his knowledge, but also by the discipline of his inner and emotional life.

Of course, the days of cosmopolitan illusions are gone. We know that all we have gained may be destroyed by overpopulation, by new torrents of political hatred, and by nuclear war. Only a doggedly persistent and step-by-step effort can lead us forward. Only a dialectical form of thinking that sees the ambivalence and polarity in even the most virtuous proclamations can help us to act wisely. Only vigilance and sacrifice can save freedom.

There are three closely interconnected human characteristics that we must oppose to the eternal frowning of the pessimist. The first is the quality of faith, the second the quality of self-transcendence, and the third the quality of vision—all three disciplined and purified by reason and self-criticism.

Irrespective of whether we explain faith in a religious or in a secular fashion, without it man would not have survived as man. Faith is the inner power that drives him to believe in that which he cannot see but which is, nevertheless, real to him. He has faith in the perfection that he never will achieve, which, however, leads him as the star leads the sailor, and faith in the future, though there may be an abyss between reality and his expectations.

One could perhaps explain faith as a part of the more comprehensive quality of self-transcendence.[11] Existing already in animals, it has evolved most strongly in the human being. It should not be mistaken for the concept of "transcendental"— neither in the technical sense of Kant's "transcendental apperception," nor in the idealistic or religious sense of "transcendentalism." It simply means that man constantly reaches out beyond his given physical and mental situation toward wider areas of life and mind. He possesses the powers of intuition and imagination, which, through training and self-discipline, he can control and mold into coherent and logical forms of discourse. By dint of the capacity of self-transcendence man is able to see relationships and to order his perceptions of things, not only in space but in time, not only horizontally but vertically. Seen under this aspect, the power of self-transcendence is almost the equivalent of dynamic thinking.

As we already indicated when speaking of the desire for identification, self-transcendence is narrow in some people. These people do not go far beyond the visible—the field they have to cultivate, the probably rather mechanical work they have to do, and the family for which they have to care. Yet even primitive cultures are not satisfied with mere everyday experience. The myth, the fairy tale, the desire to paint, to sing, and to dance, something of that can be found everywhere, even in the child. The more a culture develops, the wider becomes the

11. See Robert Ulich, *The Human Career: A Philosophy of Self-Transcendence* (New York: Harper & Brothers, 1955).

expanse of the transcending power. It creates in us the sense of humanity; it follows not only the flight of the poetic genius, but takes into its scope the ventures of empirical research that open our eyes to hitherto-unknown secrets of the universe.

An essential element of the process of self-transcendence— of such importance that it is worthy of special mention in this essay on mankind—is man's capacity for vision. He is able to hold before his inner eyes images of the desirable, the whole, and the truth, which establish the "ought" over and above that which "is." Without this kind of vision there would be no ethics, no progress, no urge to form concepts that unify and direct our single ideas and actions toward even higher syntheses. Certainly, there are illusions and, perhaps, delusions of grandeur in many of our visions, but all the impelling and propelling ideas of humanity are somewhat of that kind. Every milestone in the history of our civilization, perhaps of all civilizations, had an unfulfilled prophecy as its inscription. Pericles' famous "funeral oration" praised the polis of free and educated men, for which we are still waiting; Jesus spoke of the spiritual unity of mankind; the Renaissance developed the literary style of the utopia; the liberal-humanist movement trusted that man would use his freedom for peace and co-operation; Marx and Engels dreamed of the classless society; and, for the second time in the twentieth century, we now put our trust in a league of nations. None of these hopes has been fully realized. Yet where would we be without them? However important the awareness of the attainable is in politics as well as in education—for without some sense of achievement man runs into frustration and rebellion—we must realize that even the attainable would not be attained if there were not behind it the vision of the ever greater.

EDUCATION AND THE VISION OF MANKIND

From the lower to the upper stages of our schools we are confronted with mankind in a twofold sense—one quantitative, the other qualitative—although the two interact.

There is, first, the immensity of mankind that soon may reach the three-billion mark. These three billions go, though on different levels, through revolutionary changes. The developing nations have to lay the groundwork for independence and a minimum of prosperity, while the industrially advanced nations go through technological upheavals unforeseen even twenty years ago. They also have to go through the process of readjustment to a no-longer-colonial but nationalist organization of Asia and Africa. A new political and ideological force has arisen in the form of communism, embraced by two gigantic nations—Russia and China. Europe will either unite within itself and with the United States, or it will be a historical relic. Latin America imposes completely new problems on the statesmen of the world. Everywhere, hunger has changed from passivity into aggressiveness; the humiliated have become militant, and the illiterate begin to reach and to compare.

If a young person today leaves high school and has not yet grasped the significance of this development, the school has failed to prepare him for national and international citizenship. This does not involve more and more teaching about more and more countries, which would mean less and less in terms of understanding. In many schools and colleges our curricula are already filled with subject matter to the degree of overflowing. But young people are excitable. They are eager for vicarious participation in the great events of humanity, hoping that later they will really participate. More so than with so many spiritually worn-out adults, the compassion of youth can be aroused by a few great examples that reach into the heart of humanity.

There is something else that the educator must realize in our time of community pressure and national anxieties. We are inclined to underestimate the scope of freedom that the school possesses and which, as recent history proves, even ruthless governments cannot entirely eliminate. In brief, while the school is dependent on its environment and its restricting influence, it need not be the slave of the society it serves.

Every advanced nation wants its youth to learn how to live according to standards and truths assumed to be not merely regional. However relative our thinking may be in the eyes of eternity, and however much it may be driven by subconscious impulses, certain truths work so well that no one, except a few theoreticians, desires to change them. They begin with the proposition that two and two equals four and extend far into the realm of the ideal and the empirical. They are as valid in communist Russia as in democratic America. If we do not believe in them, why do we teach?

There also exist commonly accepted standards of decency. When they are silenced in one part of the world, the other part begins to speak. And the more man leans toward evil, the more he knows about the good. As our period shows, the more we offend mankind, the more we talk about it; the farther away we are from it, the more it looks through our windows; the more it threatens to break asunder, the more desperately we try to hold it together.

With these considerations we have defined the dual task of education. On the one hand, its cultural and physical environment clings to it like the bark of a healthy tree. The school must not intentionally split the minds of the young from those of the old. It must not talk about topics beyond the comprehension of the pupils. It must adjust the goals and methods of teaching to the mental capacity of the learner. On the other hand, the school fails unless it sets the perennial against the contingent. It teaches science and literature, and through them about the world of nature and of humanity. Even in the lower grades our schools deal with great ideas. It is often exactly in the rudiments where the universal lies. When these first ideas and ideals, which form the rock bottom of civilization, are mutilated and distorted, we have a feeling of revulsion. Mankind, so we feel, should not already be offended in the child.

And here we should go one step deeper. We should see the causes of unity and disunity in the individual as well as in total society, in very simple and elemental relations that mold our mentality long before we are able to express in words what works on, and within, us. The deepest influences on the human character spring not from systems of thought, religious or otherwise. Rather these systems are themselves expressions of basic aspirations formed in the individual by the social and moral atmosphere he should inhale when he grows up as an infant and child. These atmospheric conditions give him the chance to move naturally through those stages of development that the great Swiss thinker and educator Pestalozzi already foresaw two hundred years ago in his essay *The Evening Hour of a Hermit (Die Abendstunde eines Einsiedlers)*.[12] Modern psychology confirmed his intuitions. Like Pestalozzi, it also considers essential the love and warmth of the mother and the directing authority and unity of the family, for within this framework the child can express his first desires for self-gratification in order to transfer them later into healthy self-esteem and constructive behavior. His process of maturing begins through contact with those who are near to him, by whom he feels protected even

12. Partly translated by Robert Ulich in *Three Thousand Years of Educational Wisdom* (Cambridge: Harvard University Press, 1939), pp. 480 ff.

when he is corrected, and whom he can trust even when, in certain unwelcome situations, he thinks he hates them.

On the other hand, if these fundamental processes of inhaling and exhaling, so essential to all life, are disturbed by discord and rancor at home, a child will have great difficulty in finding the strength to develop a feeling of enduring sympathy for his fellow men and of loyalty to humanity. In all likelihood he will be untrained to meet the disappointments and disillusions of life, inevitably more acerbating than those through which he has to go under normal conditions of childhood.

These considerations should by no means diminish the importance of the great movements of thought such as religion and humanism. If they are, as we said, conceptual expressions based on elemental human experiences, they will also work back on them, since there exists in all fields of life a reciprocal fertilization between that which we formulate in words and that which we feel and are. One supports the other. But whether for the religious person the end and wisdom of life may be salvation, and for the humanist humaneness, man can realize both only within a good life prepared largely by the experience of his childhood, together with self-discipline and constructive thinking. Serious effort may be strong enough to balance the dangers of unhappy early years. Nevertheless, it will be a hard life.

If the groundwork is not laid when a human being is most open to the good and most helpless to the bad—which is in him and in all humanity—then humanity is likely to have lost a member. And societies in which parents, either by neglect or by false ambitions, violate the sacredness of childhood must expect the continual eruption of chaotic forces, however lofty and self-convinced the ideological pattern.

Good education, as we have already indicated, is not only a

process of information. It is also an endeavor to help a person respect honest differences of opinion and discover his capacity for continuous growth through enriching experiences. However much comes from outside, it cannot bring out of a person more than he has already waiting within himself. To develop that which is waiting is the art of education. More than ever we need teachers who have both width of knowledge and the inner spark that makes knowledge inspiring. We no longer live in isolated dwellings. Our neighbor is no longer the next farmer or—perhaps least of all—the man next to us in a big apartment house; the whole world is now our neighbor. Certainly, the "next" should also be part of our knowledge and loyalty. Strangers at home cannot be at home in the world. Those who cannot lay a brick cannot build a house. And I even suspect that those who cannot love a dog cannot love mankind. Least of all should we see a contrast between our liberal individualistic tradition and the desire for the unity of mankind.

The contrast appears only when individualism is but a better word for egotism and when unity mistakes itself for mechanical collectiveness. Everyone who works on himself opens the door to humanity, and whoever cares for humanity enters deeper into self, and thus helps to balance the ambivalence that has been part of man through the centuries.

2.

JOHN R. SEELEY

Mankind as Fact by Faith

MANKIND, it goes without saying, does not exist. It is a word on the lips of men, a fiction, a figment, a hope, a means by which we castigate others for their narrowness or praise ourselves for our breadth. It is *not* some that that is; it may be some this that might be.

I have said that the contention that mankind does not exist goes without saying, but were the statement really so trite, I suppose I should not have troubled to assert it. Rather the contrary; it is just because the logical status of such terms as "mankind" is widely misapprehended, and because the action directed toward what they stand for is so generally misdirected, that I feel driven to write at all.

Mankind is not by itself in its nonexistence. Love does not exist; law does not exist; this nation does not exist; the church does not exist; you do not exist and I do not exist—except in so far as we and they are created, constituted, inspirited, cherished, and maintained wholly and solely, in the beginning and continuously, altogether and entirely, by the knowledge, faith, and love of men.

I am never sure how obvious these things are, nor therefore certain as to how explicit I must be in asserting what many may think no one has controverted. Let me cover myself by saying that I speak only to the unconverted, and that I believe these to be negligible neither in number nor importance. I speak thus both to those who think that these things somehow exist anyway, and to those who think them merely altered in logical status by the fact of our "recognition."

It was the late John Dewey who wisely said that "the community exists in communication," and it was his great contemporary W. I. Thomas who pointed to the fact that a social situation is what it is by virtue of our "definition of the situation." I go beyond these perhaps to say not merely that it is *what* it is because of our definition (which suggests if it were not *that*, it *must* be something else), but that it *is*—i.e., exists—because of us; not by our definition, I would have to add, in any *intellective* or *cognitive* sense, but in virtue of faith, love, and, perhaps, hope, as St. Paul asserted.

I suppose if I am to be so blatant, not to say brutal, in assertion, I must dispose of the contentions that *some* something else is either a sufficient or a necessary condition for the existence of the category of "things" under discussion. The illusion persists that some something is the substance, the sub-stance, the under-standing matter to which the faith, the love, the hope relate.

It is relatively easy to dispose of the argument that the existence of such a sub-stance is a sufficient condition for the emergence of the super-stantial existences to which I refer. At my left hand as I write, seated before the television set, wrapped up in the play of light and shadow on the screen, is a little male animal. Super-stantially he is my son. Nothing he is or does can make it so; he is so as I (and/or others) endow him with that "definition," and he is capable of that participation only in so far as he participates in the definition (by behaving like a son and so recalling and augmenting the endowment). As a little male animal, as a protoplasmic blob, he may be begotten, not created; as a son he was created—and is continuously re-created —and not begotten. For son-ship he is clearly an insufficient condition.

To say that he, in his substantiality, is not a necessary condition for my having him as a son will seem to many to be going too far. I think, however, that such is the case. If he is far away, he is still my son—if I so will. If he is dead—likewise. If he had never been—if only faith could go so far—I could surely evoke him as men have timelessly evoked gods without material foundations, and the only problem I should have would be the problem of consent, as they have had, and their gods and other credenda with them.

Perhaps my son is too close, too familiar, to make my point. But surely this *nation* is not. It exists surely—lives and dies— in and out of our belief in it, and nothing else constitutes it. It is not there because we are Americans; we are Americans because we believe in it, and in so far only. In that sense we, as well as the nation, are constituted by that which we believe in; created by our creation. Only the word "believe" is too feeble, unless it is taken in the extended meaning in which we believe in ourselves and one another; not a mere crediting but an accreditation, a belief *and* an endorsement, a thinking and loving into being.

To say that the nation "exists" independently of the belief in it of any particular American is to point up rather than contradict the point. As long as there is any American who so believes, the nation endures in one effect, and so long as a small sufficiency endures, it endures in all.

Not only the fact of the nation, but its character—its characteristics and their organization—is a fidefact, something made by faith and existing in faith. Once brought into being so and sustained, "the nation" is also a fidefacient, or a generator by virtue of faith, justifying its children of their wisdom and substantiating the faith in them, which is its own womb, placenta, and nutrient.

If the institutions of man, then, issue upon the fiat of faith rather than the fall of fate, so also, since man is the creature of his institutions, is he the creature of his creations. This feeding upon what he himself generates is his history—the history of man. Not so, or not precisely so, for the individual.

The ontology of the person is analogical, not identical. He is called into being biologically when he is conceived in the biological sense, inseminated; he is called into being as a human being when he is conceived as such, psychologically, inspirited. It is well said that he is not born human, that he becomes human, and that this his existence precedes his essence, but it has been left to social psychologists to flesh out these statements.

The tale they tell, the tale of *homo hominis creator*, is the tale of that which simultaneously makes and justifies the "dignity of man." It is the tale of calling order out of chaos by preexisting order; the education of a human out of an animal by treating it as if human; the freeing of some something from the kingdom of necessity by the treatment of it as if it were free; the constellation of a role player by the playing of a role toward it and its implication in an ongoing play; the installation of an autonomous self that can regard itself as another self in virtue of its having been so regarded by others.

Even here the rule of reciprocal creation runs. The process that creates that mother's daughter creates by necessity that daughter's mother; they are co-emergents or they are not at all;

they co-constitute each other; they are implicit in each other; they are inconceivable and nonexistible apart. In so far, they analogize the institution-man relation in general. Only in some asymmetry that in a lifetime shifts a balance from differential receiving to differential giving, from dominant dependency to a balance of being depended upon, does the analogy fail fully to serve.

So if mankind is to be, it must be brought into being; and once thought, loved, and cherished into existence, it will make of its creators something other than they are, something they can only faintly imagine, for the joys and pains of union, though in some sense foreseen, are eternally falsely forecast or foretold.

But if men are but as they are, and if mankind is but a wraith, seeking body, wandering upon the wind of discourse, how may they be brought to the act of creation—or, for themselves, re-creation? It passes current that this is the "task of education"—as, indeed, today, what is not? What, then, is education?

It is part of the current intellectual fashion not merely to recognize, but forcibly to assert, that we may define terms as we please. So we may, indeed, but not without risks, at least not in general and public communication. And, whatever specialists may hope, all communication in a day of cheap print, rapid electronics, and awakened curiosity becomes public communication. So, while it is open to us to define "exceptional children" —by the fiat of experts—to mean the intellectually incompetent, the result is in the long run socially catastrophic; counsel is confused, language inflated, and faith in the power of words to compass cases needlessly undetermined.

Unfortunately, such has been the fate of "education," together with so many fine terms of educated discourse: "freedom," "liberal," "humane," "excellent." We cannot appeal to the generality of writing about education to define the sense of it, for it has come to mean, almost without common core, all the various things that commencement speakers, college presidents, "educators," and peddlers of this and that scheme of word-magic wish to claim for it.

We are certainly not helped in coming to terms with our term by "going anthropological"—as another intellectual fashion would have us. I do not think we can satisfactorily define education *for our purpose* (of relating education to mankind) by inducing a meaning from observation or analysis of other or all societies. It is true that looking at simpler societies is simpler, and often throws into high and clear relief what is only adumbratively visible in our own. But we *are not* another society, let alone all societies, and what education is (means) in *this* society is both what makes the society different and evidences its difference. So that a proper appreciation of *this* society in its essential nature is indispensable to a proper appreciation of what education should mean in reference to it.

Now, a proper appreciation of what this society is, is even harder come by than an appropriate definition of education. And again in this the sociological imagination, or want of it, has served us ill, and continues to do so. A sociology conceived as a science of society must, it seems, pride itself on its "realism" unless it is to give up its scientific pretensions. The realism involved turns out—as with novelists and painters—to be a romanticism of the existent, and more particularly of that in the existent that is least evocative of the aesthetic joys. It is a romanticism because it evolves and perpetuates a romantic fiction: that the fossil of what is, is the only reality, or in any case more real than the forming flesh of the not-yet-realized. No more violent distortion of reality can be well imagined, and yet it is, or seems to be, the indispensable prologue for a "science of society." And that indispensable prologue neatly disposes, before it is well begun, with the heart and meaning of the human drama, which, whatever else it is, is a *becoming*. It is a becoming, moreover, in which it is of the very essence of its essence that what it will be is *not* fully in any intelligible sense *implicit* in what it is, so that, Marx to the contrary, the new society is *never* visible in the womb of the old. It is not visible in the womb of the old, in a society such as ours, because it is not there. It is not there to be seen because the new society is conceived *by* the old and not *in* it; and it is conceived in that large sense of conception which is the measure by which psychology exceeds biology and imagination outruns the possibilities of protoplasm.

Indeed, it is precisely this that the sociologist normally excludes out of necessity that is the differentiating characteristic, the essence, of the society about which he purports to speak: its *becomingness*. And, at that, a becomingness of a most peculiar sort.

Failing that recognition, it is, I think, idle to write of "education in," or "for," or "and a free society," or "education for responsibility," or "citizenship" or "creativeness" or whatever the current preoccupations are. For what these key terms mean turns on the society to which they are apposite.

Hence the society is defined by the education that would be properly thought appropriate to it, or, indifferently, the appropriate education would be defined in any adequate definition of the society. This co-definition in theory, or consubstantiality of practice, should offer no more mystery than the commonplace of co-definition in the father-son relation: what a father is in reference to a son is wholly defined in what a son is in reference to a father, and vice versa. On the view taken here, education *is* the society in its ideally constituent activity; the society *is* the education in its phase as product.

It is striking that the society is most often characterized as "open" or "free," and certainly this is a starting point a lot more hopeful and productive than a definition that fails to take these striking, and differentiating, characteristics into account. But this is a curious selection of terms, a secular analogue to the definition of the deity by negative theology: immutable, infinite, incomprehensible, unlimited, unconditioned. For, after all, "open" and "free" say nothing more than unbounded and unconstrained, and these might well be thought virtues under two sets of conditions: where it is an open question what is good, or where constraint or bond stand between present position and known good.

There is a vital sense in which it *is* an open question as to what is good, but it is not the obvious sense, and I do not want to enter on that discussion now. I want to argue that the high, and sometimes uncritical, value put upon openness and freedom actually rests upon the second fact: that bond and constraint stand in the way of a known good. And that known good is the becomingness, the peculiar becomingness, of the society itself.

If becoming is to be valued over being or having been, it can only be for its own sake, or because what is to be is (or is held to be) better than what is.

It cannot be denied, I think, that there does exist a mere preference for becoming over being, as such. But I think it is a degenerate preference, if it rests upon nothing else, comparable to the preferences that also exist for motion over station, change over endurance, novelty for the sake of novelty. Such a preference cannot be much more than an expression, and, incidentally, a cause, of nervous irritability, an analogue to the desperate attempts at self-relief exhibited in states of sensory deprivation. Unless a present state is unendurable or, rather, not *to be* endured, mere preference for change at random is a posture of desperate poverty.

No, the primary preference for becoming in our culture rests upon a far more far-reaching assumption, or rational hope, or faith, or determination: that the becoming is of such a peculiar nature that the $(n + 1)^{th}$ state of being exceeds the nth in the measure of the good that it incorporates, or at least that it may do so. The society that burst the bonds of stasis and tradition to become dynamic did so because, and only could do so because, it believed itself, in the first sense of that term, eugenic: generative of good in its very transition.

It is easy now to make fun of the idea of progress—and that particular variant of it associated with the word "inevitable"— and the peculiar heresy that mistook the material for the significant and the satisfying. But without the notion itself, the still-operative institutions of the society make no sense and, particularly the more modern of them, have no foundation. The market, such as it is, the political forum, the free expression and interchange of ideas, the institutions of self-government are to be valued in so far, one presumes, as they facilitate the realization of a *volonté générale,* which mediates between mere sums of private preferences and dimly sensed but dearly served ideals. The centrality in our society of the school as the preferred institution and of the child as the preferred socius is, at best, testimony to our indefeasible hope that things may be better if we really will it so, and, at worst, tribute to our determination that they shall be no worse.

I am not so naïve as to think that a generation that witnessed, and participated in, Buchenwald and Hiroshima can continue to believe that a great deal of progress has been made, nor that such as has been made is other than precarious. But evidently the sense of man is too sound, or the faith too strong, or the tradition too abiding, for men to have learned only the too-obvious lesson—despair. Indeed, the horror before these and our other characteristically twentieth-century atrocities is due less to their magnitude, or to the degree of brutality and insanity exhibited, but more to the fact that they inferentially force us by their wickedness to the *impietas impietatis:* to doubt in the fact or possibility of progressive incorporation of the good in man and society, in history, at all. Or, if this is not the first shock, it is certainly the second and profounder—so profound, indeed, as to threaten the very survival of the society that survived. (Incidentally, the atrocities themselves were founded on, post-cedent rather than antecedent to, doubts on the same score, doubts growing out of the first great war and the Depression of the thirties. The Depression, in turn, was a result of—not a doubt about, but a denial of perversion of—the faith in the form of idolization of the gold standard.) The lesson learned— even *Nineteen Eighty-Four* is an object lesson, a sermon against, rather than a prefiguring of, an alternative—is that the struggle for progressive incorporation of more and ever-higher good must be redoubled, for the alternative is not stasis in such goods as we have, but a collapse into evils more primitive than any our more primitive ancestors or contemporaries practiced or even contemplated or conceived. What we learned, I think, was that good and evil in matched magnitudes are ever and equally imminent, and that shaken faith or failed devotion may at any instant tip a balance, perhaps irretrievably, in the direction of the latter.

It is in this context—in one sense, for this reason—that education is properly looked to as the hope of mankind; not the existent hope of an existent mankind, but the end that education, if it has any meaning worthy of "its" society and its society's principle of being, wittingly or unwittingly, seeks. Education is that process whereby mankind may come into being; just as a society that seeks, however falteringly, the progressive embodiment of a catholic good is potentially mankind in process of realization.

But, if so, if education is legitimately to hold out such a high and holy hope, it must become something altogether different, different in conception and different in practice, from what it has in our era *deemed*—and thereby doomed—itself to be. It cannot continue to go wandering upon the wind, pursuing all aims or none or any accidental assemblage of them that fashion dictates or the passing vagaries of "science" approve.

More particularly, three common and convincing fallacies must first be abandoned: that education is to be tested by the fraction of a body of "facts" mediated to the students; that it is to be tested by a test of acquired analytic skills; that it is, in any ordinary sense, to put the student "into possession of his culture." Perhaps another also: that education consists in imparting a set of invariably dubious or trivial "right" attitudes.

This is not the place, I trust, to demolish the altars of these gone gods; they carry their death warrants writ upon their foreheads. The facts that are relevant, and hence facts, are in any case relative to the task in hand and cannot serve for its definition. The analytic skills are mere instrumentalities, and idle, failing an enterprise of sufficient strength and worth to withstand and utilize their employ. The culture is precisely that which is not to be possessed but made over, the cocoon to be fragmented and escaped. And what attitudes are "right" is a function of the present situation in relation to the situation that is to be brought into being. "Co-operativeness," a presently much-touted attitude, is a positive ill unless the ends sought in common are themselves good: Eichmann was co-operative.

What is required of education, if it is to be true to its social trust—to the trust it cannot escape, laid upon it by the very nature of the society, regardless of the mandates of officials or the sayings of psychologists—is that it induct the children of men into a company. The company is a company unbounded by time, stretching backward indefinitely and forward to virtual infinity, a company that stretches *through* them, the children, and that will be what it will be only because of them, the students, and it, the process. *It is the company of those who have striven and those who do not and will not strive for that progressive realization and unending transformation of men into Man, of the kinds of men into Mankind.* The real, and those, the imagined, who are more real than reality, are in that company, and it is to it that the children of men are called, and the privilege and prerogative of the educator is to call them to it, or, rather, out into it.

For some time now, professional educators have seemed to hesitate, or oscillate, between two views of education in relation to values: a value-free position and a value-parochial one. The first represented an attempt—unsuccessful, I think—to sterilize schooling; a sterilization that, intended to be prophylactic, succeeded only in being castrative. To change the analogy, value the heart of education, and a cardiectomy is an odd operation. The second represented the attempt to indoctrinate for less than catholic values: for Protestantism (or "religion"), or the "free market," or against communism, or for "brotherhood" (in some constricted sense), or "citizenship" in some particular interpretation.

These positions are, I think, simply not defensible, simply

not tenable, unless the society is to deny its very genius. For, halting, tentative, now in major, now in minor, error, the society is committed to the discovery and realization of ideals catholic in their range and all-embracing in their matter. And again, it is into the company of those seekers after that that education is to enlist and induct the child.

Such induction has only oblique reference to facts, for the central fact is that the central facts are *constituted* by faith: the very existence of "the one" and "the other," the self and the nonself, is a *Darstellung* in which the emplacement is the act of an illuminated and loving will. Such induction has little to do with training, except perhaps as a condition, and much to do with being "caught up" into an enterprise. This enterprise is the emergence of mankind into an existence now only faintly foreshadowed. The vehicle of education is not communication, in the merely horizontal sense, nor, particularly, in the strange modern sense of the communication engineers with their "bits" of information, but trans-portation—that which results in "transport," with all its overtones of danger, of being carried away, of being enslaved by that which imposes no bonds but demands a total devotion. Nothing can command such devotion, or should, short of the whole human enterprise in its ideal, becoming aspect.

In the society, then, the school that is instituted by the society is not to represent the society as it is, but to recall it to that which it would wish to be, what it is only in hope and becoming. The school is rather to represent, as over against the society, that to which it is hoped the society tends. And for that tendency, if any one word will serve to cover or discover it, the word "mankind" will serve, if we would but serve it.

For, by mankind we mean, must mean, not men in their mathematical summation at a given moment, in all their contingent, temporal, and spatial givenness, but men in their unity, or rather that unity itself, a unity as yet only latent or potential, but clearly that. That unity is not merely something to hymn now or praise, but something that is to be wrought as we make ourselves over in the hope and image of it.

How that is to be done is no more to be declared in advance than the detailed course of a specific love affair, of which it is, of course, a unique example. We cannot foresee, except in crudest terms, what existing loyalties and comforting habits must be renounced. We cannot foretell what intellectual reconstructions must be made before we can think intelligibly and securely in such terms. We cannot now tell what new passions must be let loose and what new bonds of loyalty to what particulars forged. We cannot say what novel institutions must be instituted to order such passions and make such loyalties effective. What we do know is that commitment has a way of bringing with it the light that is needed both to clarify at each next step whatever further commitment and following act is needed, and to revise and reconstitute the whole. Like science itself, the process is self-corrective under the same conditions of devotion and sensitivity.

What is called for, then, if mankind is to be called into being—and heaven knows what catastrophe awaits us if it is not—is a far-reaching reconstruction of persons, *ourselves*, of thought ways, of institutions, *our* way of behaving together, of imagination, sympathy, and faith. That reconstruction begins in desire, in hope, even when, or because, the details of what we desire become clear only in its devoted pursuit. But the first thing is to know, not in the narrow cognitive but in the full sense of that term, what it is that we desire, in spite of our not knowing the details. What we desire—as we always have, except that now it trembles on the border of potential achievement—is our *unity,* the unity of our kind. It is the want of that unity that makes so difficult and precarious the search for personal, "psychological" unity with which Western man is so preoccupied ("Peace of mind") in the twentieth century; it is the want of that unity that makes so arduous and risky the search for some sort of political order ("Peace in our time!").

And yet the unity is all but there. The hope of it is widespread, well-nigh universal. The supporting means are at hand. A breath upon a spark here or there:

> I am in thee to save thee,
> As my soul in thee saith,
> Give thou as I gave thee,
> Thy life-blood and breath.
>
> —SWINBURNE

What other commitment is consonant with the spirit of the Western world, implicit in its cultural roots, explicit in the visions of all its high and flowering moments? What else unifies and gives substance—sub-stance, under-standing—to educational policy? The community of man, mankind, waits only upon that title of faith, love and labor sufficient to animate it so that, like any chain reaction, it becomes self-sustaining; sustaining and rescuing, in the process, the very men who first cherish and sustain it.

"What is to be done?" asked Lenin. The answer, not his, seems clear enough.

3.

GEORGE N. SHUSTER

UNESCO and Cultural Commerce

THE MILLIONS whom the chorus of the Ninth Symphony bids partake in a universal embrace were never far from the minds of the idealists who, in the Europe of a century and a half ago, realized that hardly had the horrors of the Thirty Years' War been forgotten than the blood was running fast again during the French Revolution and the Napoleonic wars. In the company of Schiller, who had written the ode, and of Beethoven, who had set it to music, was the great poet Goethe, who ended his career reflecting on the "universally human," which, it seemed to him, had long since been the central theme of literature and art and must therefore become the topic of history as a whole. But there were others, and their number would increase, who held that the nation was the basic, abiding social reality. For them history was always destined to be determined by the grim verdict as to which nation would prove the fittest to survive. The debate thus outlined had its ghastly epilogue in World War I and II, which were probably only one, with an armistice in between. This epilogue took about all the starch out of idealism that was in it. When afterward the phrase "the moral solidarity of mankind" was fashioned, most of us were wondering whether any such thing as morality was to be expected of the two-legged beast and angel who had killed and been made to die in Dachau.

Some idealists can still be ferreted out, if one looks hard enough, but our present popular conception of "mankind" stems from quite different roots. We believe that it is slowly becoming a reality because it *has* to become one. The drive of the determinism that is engendered by economic, political, and social forces is pushing us that way fast. We can no longer fight anything bigger than a brush-fire war, because a few hours after we tried the real thing, most of us would be dead and the lucky ones would soon find out that they had the worst of the bargain. European colonialism has ended—or virtually so—and new nations have sprouted by the dozen. Urbanization and industrialization are the waves of the future. Jet travel has made it impossible for the provincial not to turn into a cosmopolite. Experience with the United Nations and its subsidiary organizations, one of which will be the theme of this chapter, indicates not merely that world government is as certain to come as cricket noise will when fall sets in, but must be here any day now.

So one hears, only to wonder whether the "realists" of the present are any more reliable than the "idealists" of the past. Certainly the critic, if he be so minded, can challenge their conclusions even as did the nationalist of Fichte's persuasion in Schiller's time when idealistic assumptions were discussed. It is true that, since some kind of warning to the Chinese was in order—so the critic will say—Khrushchev entered into an anti-test pact that means nothing in military terms but may or may not add up to something as a gesture. One may agree that, tests or no tests, wars between major powers will henceforth be unprofitable. But if a series of conflicts necessarily fought out with conventional arms break out in densely populated continents like Asia and Africa, they may consume more resources and cost more lives proportionately than did the war that ended with the Treaty of Westphalia—no small scrimmage, by the way, and no model treaty. The critic may likewise argue, and not infrequently does, that except for Franco-German understanding, which is a great boon and for which we are indebted to Adenauer and De Gaulle, in every other way the European Common Market has accomplished little that Europe had not already achieved before 1914. In a more general, world-wide sense, he will say and will be difficult to worst if argument ensues, that the mercantilist arrangements that came into being under the Pax Britannica were superior to anything we of the present hour have accomplished—except the somewhat dubious methodology of the outright grant to a needy country from a prosperous one.

No attempt will be made to reach a conclusion here, except the quite modest statement that surely we have need of both the idealism of the past and the realism of the present. If we hope to make the concept of man a practical reality—it is extremely difficult to see why we should not—we are hardly privileged to forget that great men have believed that if stress were placed on humanity as a whole rather than on some part of it, such as the nation, we should have a better time on earth and doubtless an equally satisfactory one in the life to come. On the other hand, how can we ignore the incontrovertible facts with which the realist lives? He may attach too much importance to this or that aspect of the situation, but on the whole it certainly looks as if he knows what is happening.

Accordingly, one may perhaps suggest that ours is an era of intensive experimentation in the ways and means of international thinking. Americans are often accused, sometimes probably with good reason, of being too pragmatic. But there can in all candor be no question about their being the people, more than any other people, that continues to believe in the values of idealism. That is why UNESCO would seem to be pertinent now.

The story of UNESCO—the United Nations Educational, Scientific, and Cultural Organization—is that of an effort made by the nations of the world to share their educational and scholarly resources for the mutual benefit. It is, of course, not the first attempt to do so. The network of medieval universities adds up to something of the sort, and, indeed, in European classical antiquity Greek culture was what was or could be fostered jointly by the peoples under Roman rule. The era of modern international organizations dawned with the formation of the League of Nations; attached to it was the International Institute of Intellectual Cooperation, which tried hard to supply the informational and statistical services that scholars needed the world around. But UNESCO, established in 1945, was to become something very different. For the first time in history an international educational agency was to possess the housing, the staff, and, to a certain modest extent, the financial resources that form the bare bones of a viable cultural enterprise.

Since the endeavor was quite novel, and since the year 1945 was characterized by moods and hopes growing out of the most widespread, savage, and sanguinary war in the annals of mankind, no one quite knew what the organization was to be or accomplish. The authorization given in the charter of the UN was terse and vague. Perhaps it reflected some awareness of the deliberations of the Conference of Allied Ministers of Education, which had been formed in London during the war primarily to consider what could be done to get the schools going once again when the conflict was over. The government of the United States had been informally associated with this. The Department of State had also given some attention to the general problem, and there existed a private organization of American citizens who hoped that a democratic reorganization of education throughout the world would help to make such a terrible revolt against decency as had been witnessed impossible in the future.

The international conference, which at the behest of the UN convened during November 1945, was charged with preparing a tentative draft of a constitution in accordance with which the new agency could come into being. Though a number of conflicting points of view were in evidence, the United Nations Educational, Scientific, and Cultural Organization was successfully created, needing only formal ratification by the first official conference, scheduled to be held in Paris during the following year. The Constitution and the name reflected a spirit of compromise. First, ample recognition was given to the universal desire that education should henceforth do its utmost to foster the love of peace, mutual understanding among the peoples, and, indeed, the "moral solidarity" of mankind. Since scientists believed, with some reason, that for contemporary men their culture was supplanting the old humanistic and basically still-Greek culture—passed through a Christian alembic though it was—they demanded that the word "science" be stressed. Above all, they had no doubt that since the language of science is universal, a dialogue with the Russians would be possible, despite the unwillingness these manifested to share in the London deliberations.

On the other hand, the concerns of the Allied Ministers of Education were not embodied in the structure of the new organization. They had to be relegated to the background because the United States delegation had been instructed to oppose any identification of the UNESCO-to-be with financial or other forms of assistance to the world's schools. This was due in part to the cherished doctrine that education was entrusted to the several states and not to the federal government, and in part to the opposition of influential members of the Congress to undergo a drastic change as the Cold War was intensified and a new social dynamism was made evident throughout the world. But, for the time being, UNESCO could not envisage the immediate practical tasks and was constrained on the one hand to accept the legacy of its predecessor, the International Institute of Intellectual Cooperation, and on the other to conceive of education as a barrier against war.

These decisions were reflected in the deliberation of the Paris Conference of 1946, which was in many ways the most brilliant convocation of the artists, writers, and intellectuals of the world ever to assemble, though many great cultures and traditions were not represented. The Russians did not come, despite earnest efforts to win their co-operation; and, of course, the defeated powers and Spain, alleged to be their ally, were still kept beyond the pale. But leading scientists, famous writers, scholars of distinction, educational leaders, statesmen of eminence packed the rooms of the Hotel Majestic, the splendor of which had grown somewhat dim and tawdry during the war. The experience was one no person in attendance would ever forget. That, as the UNESCO Constitution declared, wars begin in men's minds and therefore the defenses of the peace must be erected in them, everyone at least hoped.

But when everything had been said and done, the two parts of human society had not come together any more closely than they had at Yalta or Potsdam. And UNESCO was an agency flimsily organized and haphazardly staffed, with a program consisting of a potpourri of items, some miniscule and others grandiose, which had been wadded together during the debate. Every one bore the stamp of a product approved as serving the cause of peace. Many were the results of imaginative thinking, but dangled precariously in the morning air because there was no visible means of putting them to practical use. Yet little of this was apparent at the time. The principal concern soon was with the cogs and the wheels the wagon needed if it was to proceed down the road to glory.

The administrative structure, and, indeed, the organization itself, was as complex as battle logistics and quite as difficult to handle efficiently. There was, certainly, to be a Director-General and a staff. But he was hemmed in by the spirit of democracy given free rein, and by what had been written in rule books about administration. The will of the peoples was provided for by placing the sovereign authority in a General Conference, to meet biennially. Initially, it was believed member nations would send eminent scholars, intellectuals, and statesmen, who would gather in a friendly fashion to shape the future of the spirit of man. But as time passed, though very able men and women were included in the delegations, the main stress was laid on appointing representatives as government ministries or agencies, because only these could safeguard the various national interests.

It was not in the early years, before the Russians accepted membership, primarily a question of conflicting ideologies, though to be sure these were upon occasion manifest. It was rather a dichotomy between those who could give and those interested in receiving, which no doubt made what soon amounted to a kind of diplomatic representation inevitable. As the roster of members grew longer, the number of potential donor countries was reduced proportionately. Though all states were assessed according to the scale established by the UN, there were times when UNESCO tended, from the point of view in our country, to resemble a benevolent slot machine into which a needy nation put a dollar and inevitably got ten in return. Of course, the educational needs of the world were also tragically real; and so the biennial conferences were forums in which the United States and its friends learned to know the human educational situation as it is.

Inside the member states, or at least in some of them, a brimming measure of democracy had also been provided by the establishment of the National Commissions. The idea was good. In order to forestall bureaucratic control, primarily by the Department of State, there was established through legislation a U.S. National Commission of a hundred members, only a few of whom could be appointed. The others were to represent organizations chosen by the body. Since some of these organizations, like the National Education Association, were powerful forces for determining policy in the realm of the schools, they have enjoyed virtually permanent membership, while others have flitted in and out. Therefore, in practice the Commission has been unwieldy, though, to be sure, because of its knowledge of and support for UNESCO, it is probably more widespread than it would otherwise be. Few countries have followed the American pattern. In Great Britain, for example, the National Commission is to all intents and purposes created by the Ministry of Education.

Yet no sooner had the rights of democracy been fully recognized than the book of rules about the administration made its impact. There was created in Paris an Executive Board, to which representatives of an indicated number of states were to be elected, and which would act as does the board of trustees of a university. It has very considerable powers; and since each member is a diplomatic representative of his government (some, indeed, have ambassadorial rank and are stationed permanently in Paris), it is at meetings of the Board that the positions of the various states are first presented for discussion, support, and modification. Were it not for the character of the Board, and also for the fact that a Director-General is very difficult to elect, he might well have an impossible assignment. But, for the most part, the Board tends to be a courteous body, which is in the tradition of diplomacy in many countries.

The entry of the Soviet Union into the organization has not made for tranquillity, as was to be anticipated. Soviet delegates to the General Conferences and Soviet appointees to the Executive Board are instructed to speak on the same issues that plague the UN. A whole morning may pass while the Board listens to a long speech, doubtless prepared in Moscow, that argues the Russian position on nuclear disarmament, excoriates the West German Federal Republic, or advertises the glories of the Soviet Union. But the core of the Russian drive is concerned with power. It seeks by every means possible to reduce the strength of the West in the Secretariat and to prevent the formation of an International Civil Service, which would mean a solid group of civil servants instead of constantly shifting personnel. For it is part of the Soviet method not to appoint Russian citizens to posts where they are to remain indefinitely, if that can be avoided. Everyone is carefully observed and meticulously instructed, so as to make impossible the formation of a mentality which would assure the truly international outlook that characterized Dag Hammarskjöld. Despite all this, some Russians appointed to the Secretariat have been able, conscientious, and co-operative.

The opposite situation exists in so far as the United States is concerned. Very probably, a number of competent persons would choose the International Civil Service as a career, inside the framework of UNESCO, if such a service existed and if the prospects for advancement were reasonably good. As things are now, American citizens with a genuine interest in international educational advancement accept assignments only on a temporary basis. Educators, scientists, and others look upon appointment to the Secretariat as just another variant of a Fulbright grant or a Ford Foundation assignment. After a couple of years in Paris, they return home, so that there is no continuity of American leadership. Mobility has, of course, become a characteristic of our academic, as it is of our business, life, but the core of the faculty of any distinguished university or college campus remains sufficiently stable to insure cohesion. This is hardly true at UNESCO.

It is not possible for the developing countries to release their ablest men and women for service with UNESCO. The posts themselves are attractive from a financial as well as a status point of view, but since candidates must be nominated by governments, they can seldom secure a release from obligations at home on such a basis that when they return their future is more or less assured. And yet nearly every country desires representation; and accordingly the principle of "geographical distribution" plays a great role. The Russians would like to replace this with a "troika" system, which would exchange bloc for national alignments. So far, however, they have obtained little support for the idea.

Perhaps the most widely criticized and disputed of the positions taken by the United States is its opposition to the admission of Red China. This issue is, to be sure, not decided in UNESCO, where the lead given by the UN in the matter is followed. But, although friendly powers vote with us when the problem is debated, they do so with mounting reluctance and for a variety of reasons. Some feel that so numerous and powerful a people as the Chinese ought not to be excluded from counsels having to do with education and culture on a world-wide scale. Others, in a sense more pragmatic, are persuaded that the rift between China and the Soviet Union would be intensified if co-operation with the West were made possible. There are very, very few who gloss over the brutalities of the Chinese regime or who do not wish that this could somehow be overthrown. Nevertheless, many are convinced that the policy of exclusion must in the long run prove ineffectual.

What has been said will serve to indicate how difficult it is to establish an organization that is international in membership and scope, particularly when the problems dealt with involve men's convictions and emotions as strongly as do education, science, and culture. And so it is perhaps not to be wondered at that in the United States, criticism of UNESCO, especially by groups of an ultra-conservative complexion, was for a time quite bitter and unrestrained. Some of it stemmed from those who opposed the humanistic philosophy that Julian Huxley, the first Director-General, very indiscreetly proclaimed to be UNESCO doctrine. But, for the most part, it was rooted in the unbridled imagination of citizens who proclaimed, without a shred of evidence to support their contention, that the school system of the United States was to be taken over by foreigners, that its children would be turned into pacifists, and that subversive activities would be a sort of horrendous dividend paid in addition.

But in spite of these and other handicaps, a program did begin to emerge, and in many respects, it was a rather impressive one, which may be said to have congealed around two or three main concerns. First, UNESCO was to be a service organization to various cultural activities that needed an international agency. Thus it compiled and made available to education a variety of statistical data, provided through good publications, as well as information about libraries and museums the world round, and

issued surveys of progress in the social sciences. Some of its bib-
liographical services, notably the voluminous *Index Transla-
tionum,* were legacies from the past; others were novel. Second,
it was to provide a common platform either of action or of planning for member states and private groups, in a great variety of
ways. Upon occasion it was very successful. Thus, it brought into
being the Berne Copyright Convention, which not all the nations
have signed but which has meant a great step forward in the protection of the rights of authors, laid the groundwork for the International Geophysical Year, and fostered an impressive variety
of international cultural organizations more or less closely affil-
iated with it. Third, it embarked, though with varied degrees of
success, a publishing program of its own, which with the passing
of time became more complex. Directly or through organizations it supported, it issued magazines, books—notably, on the
race question, *The Cultural and Scientific History of Mankind*
—and a considerable number of symposia. All this work was
done by men for the most part relatively unknown, to whom
the educational and scholarly community now owe a great deal.

Finally, at a conference of some historic importance, held
in Montevideo, the whole program was reorganized by enunciat-
ing the principle that henceforth, though many of the services
previously alluded to would be continued, UNESCO would concentrate its main effort on a few "major projects," one of which
would be aiding the development of primary education in Latin
America. This was then begun with some fanfare, but it never
actually accomplished what was hoped for, owing primarily to
the vastness of the enterprise and to a dearth of money to carry
it out. Meanwhile, the scientists, particularly those of the United
States and Great Britain, had discerned the value of an international organization that could serve as a kind of diplomatic instrument for securing the co-operation of countries that might

otherwise not support a common effort. Research in arid lands was the first of these, to be followed later by a great effort to increase human knowledge of oceanography. Similar inquiries were undertaken—for instance, in seismology—though on a more limited scale. In all these UNESCO has not acted as an agency that created a scientific body of its own, but rather as a participant whose presence helped greatly to make co-ordination possible.

Nor were the arts and the humanities ignored. UNESCO has gained a measure of renown for its publications in the field of the arts, notably a series of large and profusely illustrated volumes that made known art treasures in India, Iran, Yugoslavia, and elsewhere of which even the normally well-educated public had not been aware. There were also catalogues of art reproductions, greatly appreciated, which have assisted people everywhere to collect prints of great paintings. This was in part preparation for a major project in East-West cultural understanding. Here again was a vast theme, probably much too broad in scope to insure success. But under able leadership the effort became one of trying to establish for the future soundly planned centers of exchange.

Then, with all but astounding suddenness, the climate of world opinion changed. The emancipation of peoples in Asia and Africa from colonial rule, revolutionary trends of a new order of magnitude in Latin America and the Near East, the awakening of Islam, and, above all, the conviction that before technological improvement could raise the standard of living education must be firmly established created a demand for the service of UNESCO that no one could have foreseen. It was true enough that the United States as well as the former colonial powers of Western Europe had been giving a very great deal of assistance to education in the emerging countries. But the task was far too great for any of them to manage, and the obstacles they confronted in pooling their resources outside the framework of an international organization were embedded both in history and in present-day educational philosophy and method. For all of these reasons, as well as for others, which were products of the Cold War, more and more responsibility was shifted to the UN and its specialized agencies.

Writing in the *Saturday Review,* I tried to characterize the work of these agencies, and so shall quote from what was said there:

Nearly all of them engage in education. ILO fosters vocational training, UNICEF is concerned with the teaching of nutrition, WHO prepares leaders in health education. But by far the greatest share of the burden is carried by UNESCO, at all levels from elementary and adult education to the secondary school and the university. It also conducts or shares in research activities. Startling as developments during the past decade have been, those of the next ten years may greatly outdistance them.

Therewith UNESCO has entered a new period in its development. For the first time in history an international educational counseling agency has come upon the scene.

One can perhaps best understand what this means by beginning with an episode, slight in comparison with other school problems the world round, but dramatic and therefore arresting. Following the precipitous and to a great extent still-inexplicable decision by Belgium to confer independence on the Congo, without adequate preliminary preparation, it was to be feared that the educational system there, relatively advanced in terms of Africa as a whole, would break down unless non-Belgian teachers were provided in some number. The task of recruiting them was entrusted to UNESCO, which succeeded even though, it may be remarked incidentally, the supply of French-speaking teachers in the United States was found to be infinitesimal. This brought UNESCO to the center of the world stage.

There it is now, in the midst of a rising plea and clamor for schooling, which must either be sated during the half century that lies ahead or be written off amidst the collapse of culture in many parts of the world. For UNESCO the task is a threefold one. First, it must act as a counseling or even as an administrative agency for the great task forces that the UN has created— the Technical Assistance Program, the Special Fund, and the International Development Bank. Each of these has a special function to perform: Technical Assistance is concerned, as its name indicates, with all the manifold tasks that must be accomplished if even elementary progress is to be made in applying the resources of technology to regions in which primitive agriculture has hitherto been the dominant economic activity. The Special Fund, entrusted with preparing a given human landscape so that planting capital resources in it will prove a rewarding enterprise, has saddled UNESCO with heavy responsibilities for educational administration. The International Development Bank must likewise reckon constantly with education as an indispensable prerequisite and so counsel with UNESCO.

Second, it is obvious that if UNESCO is to make a serious contribution to education, it must stimulate planning. The days are gone when any administrator, however able, could come to a country and lay down rules for education. It is now a co-operative venture, because the world in which we live is one in which every people will naturally be on guard against indoctrination, whether by us, the enemy, or someone else. And so, naturally, the vast planning conferences that have dealt with education on a regional basis are primarily explorations, undertaken with the help of UNESCO experts recruited as effectively as possible from around the world. At Karachi in 1959 a vision was conjured up of what would have to be done in Southeast Asia to bring about the desired improvement in education. The report was staggering, alike in terms of the financial resources that would be necessary and in its projections both of the numbers to be served and the desirable size of the teaching force. The 1961 Conference at Addis Ababa dealt in a comparable way with the problems that Africa as a whole necessarily confronts. Here, too, the bill presented was enormous in the human as well as the financial sense, though the problems to be faced are in some respects less formidable than are those of Asia. Density of population is less marked, and the rate of increase therefore less fearsome. And, finally, the Conference at Santiago, which convened early in 1962 to consider with some care educational progress of Latin America—though this was primarily an affair of the Alliance for Progress and not a direct UNESCO responsibility—likewise conjured up tasks of quite bewildering complexity and magnitude.

But after one has seen the pattern in broad outline, it becomes necessary to plan for each country, region, city. Each will have problems quite its own, resources will vary, and the personnel needed cannot be supplied from a standardized catalogue. Pakistan, for example, may require a laboratory technician almost more than it does any other part of the educational force. Many areas in Latin America can probably be served effectively, in so far as the lower schools are concerned, only if audio-visual aids are expertly designed and quite as expertly serviced. As every educator knows, more money can be squandered on poor or unsuitable schooling than on almost any other enterprise. The responsibility that rests on UNESCO experts, who are to assist governments, regions, and communities, is therefore very great. They must also strive to bring about the largest possible measure of co-ordination with what is being done through bilateral programs or with the assistance of private groups and foundations. Therefore, in the long run UNESCO's success or failure will depend more on the quality of those who represent it in the field than on any other single factor. They must be educated men and diplomats at the same time.

Third, provision must be made for careful research, especially in the thorny questions that multilateral assistance raises. Perhaps the lack of adequate provision for this was the cause of a major UNESCO weakness. Too much reliance was placed on conferences or colloquia of experts, which are of course valuable and sometimes almost invaluable, but which cannot substitute for patient and continuing inquiry. Recently an effort has been made to bring about improvement. The Hamburg Institute, which opened its doors early in the fifties primarily in order to assist school reform in Germany, has taken at least the first steps toward becoming a center for research in comparative education.

But perhaps the most important and yet also the most problematical thing to say about UNESCO at the present time is that it has become a symbol of hope—hope, on the one hand, for developed societies like our own, that the conquest of poverty, ignorance, and disease in the crowded, striving areas of the globe, which were not so long ago considered culturally stagnant or primitive, can be managed without revolutionary upheavals that could set back improvement for many decades; and hope, on the other hand, for the needy peoples, that words about assistance will be followed by deeds. Then there is also another kind of effort and aspiration. This is for and toward the sharing of cultural goods. It is comparatively easy to flood the world with literature and, above all, propaganda, which reflect the cultures of the United States, Russia, and Western Europe. The Kremlin can blanket Asia with copies of the writings of Lenin and the speeches of Khrushchev. We can counter with Jefferson, Lincoln, and *Profiles in Courage*. It is another thing entirely to provide for a free flow of information between, say, the Russians and ourselves, or to give the cultures of Brazil, the Philippines, and Japan their share of the world's cultural commerce. But until this is accomplished, the peoples who are not brought into the main stream must grow progressively more stagnant, while those who command the current and the tides will become constantly more aggressive.

The only reason for believing that the stubbornly one-sided drive of Russian propaganda can be halted is based on the quite reasonable assumption that cultural exchange, if once established, will make its lack of objectivity and universality apparent, not merely to the rest of the world but to the Russians themselves. We are very far from having attained that goal. But the UNESCO program is at least a continuing effort. Its successes to date are modest ones, but they are an exciting part of a program that may eventually prove its worth. If one notes as a simple instance that the UNESCO Catalogues of Art Reproductions are circulated in the Soviet Union, one cannot help feeling that over the years many Russians will know the language of universal art and desire to share in its use. That may be a feeble reed on which to hang the future of mankind. But one cannot easily find another, unless it be the grim and fundamental fact that the world's power to destroy itself is so evenly distributed that it cannot be used. This last is one form of the language of science that gets spoken around the earth. One cannot, however, ignore the constant danger there.

UNESCO, despite its weaknesses and its bureaucratic organization, its problems of recruitment and its constant struggle to balance the weak and the strong, is about the only instrumentality of free cultural exchange now discernible. There are, of course, other potential sources from which cultural co-operation could spring. We might as Americans, for example, develop a more fruitful pattern of fellowship with the other countries of the West. But it seems to me, writing after sixteen years of participation, often enough of necessity critical, that UNESCO is now potentially the cultural force that might conceivably grow strong enough to make freedom rise again over the horizon as a light for all mankind.

I shall close with some observations on the strength that the organization might acquire were it to have the full confidence of universities and other educational establishments, including foundations, in all parts of the world. There is, to be sure, no dearth of interest or concern among scholars. One part of the UNESCO program that has been especially fruitful in this respect is that which fosters consultative arrangements with non-governmental organizations. The list is now a lengthy one and includes a considerable number that all but owe their existence to UNESCO because of financial or other kinds of assistance. There is, for example, the International Council for Philosophy and Humanistic Studies, which owes such progress as it has made primarily to M. Jean Thomas, an able French scholar who was until recently Assistant Director-General of UNESCO. The efforts of this and other organizations to bring together scholars or experts from all countries reinforces what has been said about UNESCO as a symbol of hope. But as yet the ties with the universities in particular are not firm. Oxford, Harvard, the Sorbonne, and Göttingen do not hold out a welcoming hand to UNESCO. One of the other of our foundations have begun to utilize the good agencies of the organization for tasks in which they are interested, but as yet the relationships are casual and sporadic. Naturally, some of this aloofness can be attributed to the reluctance of the universities in particular to concern themselves with pedagogical problems, often relegated to departments that the more academically minded consider poor relations. This is not the place to argue the point. Assuredly, the basic program of UNESCO would be greatly strengthened and enriched if it had university assistance or sanction. One hopes that the time will come when the president of Yale or the University of California will think that attending a UNESCO meeting or welcoming UNESCO representatives to his campus is a normal part of his occupation. I think that if it does come, the fruit of the tree planted in London in 1945 will be reasonably ripe.

PART TWO

The Understanding of the Idea of Mankind at Different Stages of Schooling

4.

Preschool Education

EDUCATION, at all age levels, has short- and long-range goals and purposes. The teacher who welcomes back the four-year-old, exuberantly returning from his first venture on an errand that required finding his way down a flight of stairs and through a winding hallway, responds directly to the child's pleasure in his new-found powers. Her own pleasure is more complex. One of her goals in teaching four-year-olds, whose impulse to explore beyond established boundaries is strong, is to help them become oriented in their own extending spatial world. This she has already done by leading them to wonder—which children are in the room above, which below; by accenting for them the decisions that she, as an adult, would make automatically—which turns to take on the way to the play yard; or by engaging them in a collective recounting of the turns and crossings each one must perform to cover his route from home to school.

In these ways she works toward a short-range goal: to help the children map their immediate spatial universe and, in gaining orientation, to be more knowing of the world around. Something has been accomplished that the teacher feels is important for these four-year-old children to know in order for them to function more effectively. Four-year-old effective functioning, however, is not the outer limit of her purposes. In this small incident she sees another meaning, related to how this child will function at fourteen or at forty, in life experiences infinitely more intricate than the path between hall and stairway. Her hope, her long-range goal, is that through this, and myriad other experiences, the child will be learning that it is not necessarily dangerous to venture from the known to the unknown, that the "scary" feeling does not have to turn one back, and that the pleasure of conquest is warmly shared by the very one who at other times seems so unreasonably to have clipped one's wings.

Similarly, the teacher of science at the college level enjoys his students' mastery of the exercise in the laboratory manual; but he has a goal far more grand in view: to guide his students toward understanding under what conditions and to what extent the canons of the scientific method provide a tool for probing the unknown, and, still more ambitiously, he wishes to enlist their drives and energies in the search for truth as scientists, far beyond the immediate goal of developing their competence in the laboratory.

It can easily be argued, and agreed upon, that these attitudes are unusual, that on the whole, teachers are content with their own and their students' competent performance in the daily round of tasks, lessons, and examinations, functioning as practitioners, with little awareness of the fundamental social processes of which they are part. Long-range goals, however, are necessarily part of the fabric of education as a force through which the future of the culture is forged. Moreover, the long-range goals of education, whether consciously pursued or passively accepted, represent the dominant value system of a culture.

The contemporary hue and cry criticizing education for not doing a good enough job in developing students who can conceptualize and engage in systematic thinking illustrates this point. In a culture where independence of thought and judgment is an ideal, education is expected to find ways and means to fulfill this long-range goal. Directly and indirectly, by percept and identification, in books and through relationships, children learn to live by values such as these while they are in school and to incorporate them into a way of life for the future. This encompasses codes of behavior with people, ego ideals to strive for, decisions involving adaptation or compromise, idea systems for taking attitudes and focusing opinions. The drift of these values in response to social, economic, and political changes in a democratic society is of broad social significance, although we are likely, more often than not, to be preoccupied with the more personal perplexities implicit in the increased gap between generations created in eras of rapid change.

The intrinsic worth of the individual, a value recognized as the foundation of democracy, may be considered in two ways, both of which are relevant to the place of preschool education in a democratic society. For the individual, on the one hand, the primacy of this value in his society is a protection and a privilege. There is a constant upward movement, despite the social faults that act as obstacles, in providing equal, universal opportunity. How opportunity is perceived, on the other hand, varies from era to era and generation to generation. Multiple meanings accrue to the concept. Historically, these meanings have included opportunity to move across social classes, to be educated at public cost, to make independent vocational choices. Part of the guardianship of democratic functioning also rests in the freedom of the individual to call out against its shortcomings in formal or informal protest, through such diverse social instruments as the law and literature. Admittedly, these are ideals against which the reality falls far short; a serious contemporary problem, for example, is the younger generation's feeling that they have no means of influencing the course of social change.

In recent decades a new ideal of opportunity for the individual has come to the fore as a result of the revolutionary progress made in understanding the psychology of human behavior and development. Man has been held back from within himself; if the processes of emotional maturing, the integration of unconscious forces with conscious powers, can be "well educated," it is felt that each individual can function more intelligently, effectively, and creatively.[1]

In addition, then, to the opportunities and rights embedded in legal and social institutions and bound up with them, opportunity has also come to mean freedom from neurotically generated miseries, and maximum fulfillment of potential capacities. This opportunity is not one to be reached for in the manner of the "rugged individualist" of the early twentieth century, when those lacking in a defined series of explicitly virtuous ways of dealing with the environment were left behind to lesser individual fulfillment, with little accompanying social concern. The opportunity for resolution of debilitating conflict and self-realization of the individual has become a public trust.

Evidence of this change in the social climate is beginning to make itself felt institutionally in various ways: in the pressure to provide all groups of the population with financial support for higher education, the increasing spread of guidance services in the public schools, the concern for psychological problems in social casework, the emphasis on promoting positive health as an essential addition to cure of disease in the mental-health field,

1. Lawrence S. Kubie, *Neurotic Distortion of the Creative Process* (Lawrence: University of Kansas Press, 1958).

the changing emphasis toward psychologically oriented child-rearing practices as mirrored in government publications.[2] Disturbing as it may be to some people, the fact is that we are moving toward becoming not simply a welfare state but a psychological welfare state.

That a democratic society should undertake to provide this extended opportunity for the sound fulfillment of individuality makes the only possible good social sense, since the culture survives, moves, and takes its directions through the imaginative adventuring and practical decision making of collective individuality.[3] This expansion of opportunity, circumstantial and psychological, for fulfillment of individuality cannot remain a privilege or a right granted from society to the individual if it is to be a basic source of strength for the social fabric of a democracy. Ways must be found for a reciprocal process between individual fulfillment and social commitment and responsibility.

These considerations return us to the question of how these values relate to education. Fulfillment of the individual alone, even by the ambitious criteria of psychological health and realization of potential, does not constitute a system of values. The Nazi ideal, which exemplified the grotesquerie of effective functioning and was pathologically fulfilling to so many individuals, stands out as the epitome of violation of all that we regard as the basic code of human functioning. *The worth of the individual becomes the cornerstone of a value system only when fulfillment of the individual, abstracted from personal right and privilege, culminates in a universal concern for everyone else's individuality.*

Some people have incorporated this goal into a concept of

2. M. Wolfenstein, "Trends in Infant Care," *American Journal of Orthopsychiatrics,* Vol. 23, No. 1 (1953), pp. 120-30.
3. Norman Cousins, "The Human Commonwealth," in Eli Ginzberg, ed., *The Nation's Children* (New York: Columbia University Press, 1960), Vol. III.

emotional maturity[4]; others have integrated it into a philosophical scheme of things.[5] For education it is the central concept around which to build long-range goals.

The evolution of the socializing process of the individual can be seen as a sequence of breaking the boundaries of the self; it means extending the sphere of kinship from parents and family, to school, to teachers, to sex, to neighborhood; to those who share one's skills, one's interests, one's religion, one's viewpoint; to profession, community, region; to ethnic group, to a nation, and now to mankind. This development, optimally, consists of a cumulative extension of self, not a bartering of one identification for another. In the process of growing up, therefore, the primordial self of the infant gradually becomes a multiplicity of selves acting in complementary ways in the integrated individual.

Some of the child's struggles in the preschool years are closely related to this complex aspect of human functioning. When the father is being the husband, for example, can he still be felt to be the father? In the spontaneous play about family life among three-year-olds, it often takes two children to deal with this, one being the father, the other the husband. This innocent separation of functions makes it possible for the young child to discipline cognitive complexity. One also may read into this characteristic play form the expression of the child's unconscious wish that the father should have no identity with the husband. A year or two later the child may have mastered, abstractly, the concept of multiple selves; nevertheless, he is considerably surprised when, in the second grade, he is confronted by the thought of his teacher putting her baby to sleep. His surprise is

4. Erik H. Erikson, *Childhood and Society* (New York: W. W. Norton & Co., Inc., 1950).

5. Robert Ulich, *The Human Career. A Philosophy of Self-Transcendence* (New York: Harper & Brothers, 1955).

not unlike that of the college freshman who learns that the lady professor of Greek can turn out the best cable-stitch sweater on the campus. It seems as hard to accept a basic constancy of self that is sustained through a variety of roles and functions as it is to achieve a continuity of self through the successive periods of a total life span.[6] Pulling away from attaining such constancy and continuity of self is a tendency toward a negative polarization, as though what one is, at any stage or in any context, is definable, realizable, experienced, in terms of what one is not. This is often clearly projected in the club formations of children. The club derives its meaning more from the definition of who cannot be in it than from common interests and activities. In one very young club idea, at about the first-grade level, the criterion was an intellectual one: "Anyone who thinks that steel floats, can't be in."

Where this tendency toward negative polarization of self identities is dominant, one often finds a parent who cannot empathize with the child because his feeling that he is a parent rests on feeling himself *not*-a-child, like the man of wealth who represses the memory of his childhood poverty and like the white man whose feeling of whiteness rests on being the opposite of, and therefore maintaining the greatest distance from, the black man.

There is another kind of internal war having to do with the extension of the self that is easily recognized as a product of a particular form of the socializing process. It springs from the morality of sacrifice and assumes a dichotomy between fulfillment of the self and extension beyond the self, as though to care, to live, to love beyond the bounds of the personal is glory, a kind of godliness that calls for sacrifice and the loss of a smaller

6. G. W. Allport, *Pattern of Growth in Personality* (New York: Holt, Rinehart & Winston, Inc., 1961).

self, intrinsically of lesser worth. Yet neither the centuries of exhortation from parents and pulpit not to be selfish, nor the knowledge that there have been people who have achieved great heights of selflessness, has produced an ethically superior kind of man, endowed with a capacity to consider all men as part of his own existence and feel his identity as part of all mankind.

It appears that a concept of individuality in which self-realization comes to fruition, not through a survival by competition of multiple selves, nor through moral repudiation of baser selves, but through an integrated progression from a personal to an extended self, is essential in order to give reality to any expectation that concern for mankind can become a potent social force. This concern, expressed verbally, albeit with sincerity and even passion, is not an ideological creation of our generation or century. Many of us, if we recall anything at all of what we learned in our study of the classics, are likely to echo the phrase: *nihil humani a me alienum puto.* The problem of our times, the challenge to education, consists in transmuting this value from an exalted position in an ideological system—where, admittedly, it has the power of any great idea or ideal[7]—into a more earthy existence, where it can govern the functions and feelings, the dreams and decisions, of the hours and days that are filled with ordinary living.

The hope of our era, if there is time, lies in our new-found knowledge of the deep-lying motives of human behavior, in our ability to bring this knowledge to bear on this ideal for mankind through the social institutions of the family and the school. Progress in this direction will condition how far the nature of man can be cultivated so that his ways of feeling, thinking, and being support the ideals he professes. The goals of education are thus

7. L. K. Frank, *Society as the Patient* (New Brunswick, N.J.: Rutgers University Press, 1948).

clearly bound up with available knowledge of inner processes, with the transmission of values through experience rather than verbal precept, with consciousness that the educative process has a vital impact on a manner of man as well as of mind.

During the last few decades a philosophy of education, consonant with humanistic ideals, has emerged in which the concept of extended individuality is a primary value. In this philosophy, the principles and methods through which teaching and learning are enacted utilize psychodynamic theory concerning the nature of experiences and relationships presumed to be conducive to developing ego strength. The maturity of an extended self, by this theory, depends on the development of psychic strength at every stage of growth, incorporating basic affirmative attitudes, the capacity to resolve conflicts noncorrosively, and conduct adaptive and creative interactions with people, work, and ideas. This philosophy and method in education is young and difficult to enact. It has been an imaginative forefront in American education and has suffered from distortion and misinterpretation; it takes hold slowly because it demands fundamental departures from traditional concepts of education, as well as the development of a new kind of teacher. Its foothold is firmest in preschool education because there is less tradition to be put aside and because the interaction between the child's inner processes and his mode of relating to his life environment is more open to observation and understanding.

It is possible to find illustrations of the links between (a) a theory of the developmental processes in children from three to six, (b) a method for guiding the educative process, (c) the goals for positive growth as a child during this period, and (d) a rationale for the presumed relation between this positive growth and commitment to humanistic values in maturity.

To understand and educate the preschool child it is necessary to take cognizance of certain elemental processes that inevitably involve conflict. The way in which these conflicts are resolved furnishes basic attitudinal material for the personality in formation.

The younger the child, the more dependent is his perception of reality on the particular configuration of each separate experience. Recognizing the lines of connection and constancy between experiences separated in time or differing in constellation is part of gradual maturing from infancy on. The faith that the mother, when gone, is not lost forever is part of learning; the absence of this faith easily becomes a generalized separation anxiety. For the preschool child the ultimately reassuring rhythm of separation and reunity has usually taken place within the familiarity and constancy of the home. When he enters school, he relives this experience in a new, unknown setting. Awareness and acceptance of the child's possible anxieties by school people becomes educationally fruitful when they supply for him the bridge between what is being left behind and what is being entered, by acts relevant to the child's emotionality: no stricture against crying or regressive behavior, bringing home-toys to school, having parents stay in school during early phases, offering food and supporting physical contact.

Yet, support for anxieties associated with the child's loss of familiarity of setting and separation from the closest figures in his life is only part of the educator's task; it is primarily her task also to offer the child a meaningful new phase of life in which to partake, rich in opportunity for finding gratification for the maturing powers of body and mind.[8] Optimally, then, the goal is twofold: first, to reduce the possible trauma of experiencing separation as irretrievable loss, and, second, to make the expe-

8. Heinz Hartmann, *Ego Psychology and the Problem of Adaptation*, trans. by David Rapaport (New York: International Universities Press, Inc., 1958).

rience of entering new orbits of life experience stimulating and satisfying to the forward drives of the individual.

The problem of possession represents another basic process in the emotional life of the preschool child, one that is rooted in the experiences of infancy, and is relived and reshaped during these years. The infant's basic feeling of safety in belonging to the protective mother is inevitably threatened as the child encounters the reality of the mother's other ties—to husband, to siblings, to her own parents and friends. After infancy, the preschool child's deepening ties to the parent of the opposite sex involve him in the resolution of a mighty conflict, in which denial of possession must once more be resolved.

In his school life, looked at superficially, he has a few simple rules of civilized social conduct to learn: to wait his turn, to share the things he plays with and becomes attached to, to accept his place as one of many in the teacher's feelings and thoughts. Certain moral precepts derive from this view: he should not demand too much attention, he should yield things and priorities quickly and smoothly, and above all, he should not be "selfish."

By contrast, the teacher who recognizes that a child who desperately clings to a favorite "thing," or pushes to sit right next to her in the story circle, is involved in living out and working through deep, universal human conflicts of possession and rivalry is faced with more complex goals than the teacher who wheedles or forces children's behavior into pleasing social molds. Arbitrary demands on young children to give up, to give away, without a feeling of loss may exact a terrible price. It may be teaching them to avoid loss by giving up the disposition to care, or to want, deeply, in any way. For the child to whom beloved things may be almost part of his psychic self, the demand may be felt as a deep violation. This does not mean that children do not need to learn to give, to yield, to wait. It does mean that the teacher's feelings, insight, and technique should make it possible for her to guide the child gradually to give up what may be dear to him without feeling decimated as a person, to feel a deep tie to her while knowing she is similarly tied to others, to control his primitive ways of expressing his rivalry with other children without feeling overwhelming guilt for having had such feelings in the first place. In such an educational atmosphere the primitive self does not have to be castigated, thrown off, and replaced by the civilized self. Its vital energies and passions are needed for the ultimate capacity to live deeply and fully: they should be educated, not censored or denied.

Another basic transformation of the preschool years takes place in the sources of pleasure. The self, even after infancy, is in important ways still a body-self, and it is understandable that in a puritanical society such as ours, there is pressure, conscious and unconscious, to wean the child as fast as possible from the natural pleasures he can find in body sensations and in the active exercise of his physical powers. Thus shame, if not threat, and, in either case, the arousal of deep guilt, are the means used to train the child in his habits of elimination and to stop his impulses toward thumb sucking or masturbatory activity. Once more, by these methods, a part of the elemental self is chipped away and lost as a wellspring for full growth toward emotional maturity.

Education during the preschool years has a delicate task to perform in this area of development. It must create an atmosphere in which body functions and impulses are not associated with disgust or shame while at the same time gradually initiating the children into handling these drives in socialized ways. A second task is to provide the opportunity and equipment for finding pleasure in discovering endless possibilities of engaging physically with the world of things and space, of experiencing mastery in the skills of the body. The goal is to help the child gradually outgrow the autistic sources of pleasure, and instead find gratification of the body-self through an outward course into an extended environment. The image of a four-year-old who has not only reached the top of the jungle gym, but who has managed to suspend himself head down and explains excitedly for anyone to hear what an "upside-down world" looks like, can suggest in what way the fulfillment of the powers of the body-self is part of the educational task in the preschool years. This is particularly true when one of its long-range goals is to develop individuals with the capacity for deep involvement in the orbit of the self and, ultimately, extended commitment beyond the self.

A few general principles emerge to serve as guidelines for the education of the young child: elemental impulses are to be accepted and rechanneled, not denied and stamped out; impulsivity in general is an irreplaceable source of vitality and depth, not to be sacrificed by premature socialization or taboo setting; to strengthen the self, education needs to provide appropriate encounter between the child and his world, at every stage.

One of the significant confrontations for the young child is his experience of the strength and authority of the people in his world vis-à-vis his own weakness and social impotence. In the nature of this experience lie alternate possibilities. His natural drives to explore beyond possible bounds, to release aggressive impulses in dangerous ways, or to seek his own strength by resisting adult authority cannot be given free reign if he is to be physically or emotionally safe. If these drives are harshly, arbitrarily, or punitively curbed, the child's resulting good behavior will be accompanied by a sense of inner badness and the kind of repression of primary and retaliatory anger that is most likely to become a dangerous reservoir of latent hostility. There are alternative ways of exercising control over the young child that avoid the stamp of sin, which invite him to enter into the rationality of authoritative acts, and which leave room for expression of negative feeling within limits. This is one of the most studied aspects of preschool education at the present time; it is worth noting that it is also one of the areas in which neophytes in the profession find themselves most troubled by the rearousal of feelings connected with their own childhood relations to and conflicts with authority figures.

It is not the intention of educators to spare the child the inevitable conflicts of growing up; this, if it were true, would be the most egregious error of all, since it is through the meeting and resolution of conflict that the self gains and feels its deepest strength. The goal is to guide the child in his preschool years through the inevitable conflicts associated with the family drama and his induction into socialized living, in such a way that he emerges capable of accepting control but uncowed, capable of love without demanding exclusive right of possession, without a feeling of sin attached to his psychic or physical self, ready to move on to taste the pleasure of knowledge and mastery in an ever-widening world.

One elemental process during these years that can be the very handmaiden to the educative process is the child's ambivalence and the ready accessibility of his opposite feelings. He has not much face to lose if the child he tried to pummel on Monday is his best friend on Tuesday; while he may join enthusiastically in a contagious outburst of stamping feet, he is happy and relieved when the teacher restores the collective calm he also wants; the lingering pleasure to stay young, to depend on adults for support, reassurance, and control live alongside the deep wish to grow up, to strike out for independence and forego the comforts of enveloping protection. The skillful teacher, dedicated to the growing rather than the training processes, can tune her response to the shifting behavior that bespeaks the child's ambivalent feelings. She can believe in his positive drives and wishes even when he is engaged in maneuvers that are destructive to himself and others, and help him bring his positive self into dominance and show him to himself in a warm good light. Perhaps this can be considered the essence of healthy self-knowledge—to know and accept one's self as a source of good and evil, and to trust that the positive self will provide the major dynamisms for living.

At this point, it is time to consider other growth processes that characterize the preschool years and the known possibilities for channeling these processes toward deepened and extended identification of the individual with his environment. If a single term could be at all adequate, the term "extensor" processes might be employed to refer to the burgeoning impulses of the healthy young to make contact with his world, from the earliest days when all he can do is taste and smell it, to the time, four or five years later, when it is an idea world as well as a thing world that he feels challenged to master through understanding. The stubbed toes and dirty knees of the two-year-old determined to explore every unknown corner, to achieve the top of the stairs at the cost of no matter how many bumps, is the forerunner of the wrinkled brow of the five-year-old trying to sort out his scrambled ideas about "olden days," when people had only candles for light, when his father was a little boy, and no airplane, not to speak of a jet, had flown across the sky.

The urge to get at and into the world beyond the self goes through miraculous transformations in the short span of the preschool years: they are characterized by accelerated maturing of the human apparatus in its physical and mental capacities, and the momentum generated by the powerful drives for motility[9] and curiosity.[10] What these transformations shall be are the resultant of native equipment and social impact. Every child enters the sphere of symbolic discourse, which leads eventually to a system of explanatory and interpretive thought, synchronous with the logos of his society; every child creates a pattern of coherence for his perceptual and ideational experience that has attitudinal as well as cognitive elements.

In relation to the issue of education and mankind, there are two intrinsic questions to be raised. What can early education do to lead the young, groping mind toward the kind of intellectual potency that is represented by the capacity to deal analytically and synthetically with the ever-widening world of objective knowledge and personal experience? How can the young child experience the deep, creative involvement in his early encounters with the world of things, problems, and ideas that will insure against superficiality and indifference and lay the groundwork for an attitude of commitment to hopes and ideals for man's progress?

Children themselves, under almost any circumstances, construct an era of discovery out of the span of the preschool years. Education for this period holds the possibility for helping the child build an image of himself as a discoverer of a way of life within which one expects to move from the unknown to the known, from the mystifying to the comprehensible. For such a possibility to be approximated, it is essential that teachers are

9. Bela Mittelmann, "Mobility in Infants, Children and Adults: Patterning and Psychodynamics," *The Psychoanalytic Study of the Child* (New York: International Universities Press, Inc., 1954), Vol. IX.

10. Gardner Murphy, *Human Potentialities* (New York: Basic Books, Inc., 1958).

themselves attuned to the ordinates of early childhood: sensory-perceptual-motor modes of relating to experience, establishment of meaning through self-reference and personal experience, rapidly shifting bases of idea structures from contextual simultaneity to cause-effect paradigms, and, most important of all, the pre-eminence of the subjective life, expressed in the child's satisfaction with phantasy as a mode of bringing coherence into the welter of fact and feeling that constitutes his experience.

It takes an open mind to be aware of the child's ways of "seeing" the world around him; but it takes a disciplined mind to plot the course by which the child can be guided toward increasingly objective mastery of reality without sacrificing the idiom of his own perceptions and transformations.

On the simplest level there is the concrete, physical world, to be known through exploration and discovery. Every home has a chair to creep under and climb over, a dark corner to hide in, things hard to reach for, and in-between spaces to squeeze into, all of them opportunities for knowing the physical world. In school during these years another kind of setting is carefully created for this aspect of experience in "knowing": greatly increased opportunity, through the provision of equipment and space, to engage with the physical world in a varied round of maneuvers, including climbing, swinging, sliding, balancing, heaving, and stacking, and freedom to invent new variations of accomplished patterns of manipulation and co-ordination. In this setting, freer of the restrictions that must be made at home to keep life safe and enjoyable for all those who compose a family, the limits on courage and opportunity to try new feats can be set in terms of the child only: at what point will his drive to explore lead him toward physical injury or psychological damage in the form of excessive frustration? What kind of support can one child have for his bold, courageous adventuring? How can another be weaned from a tendency to hang back from the uncertainties of such new frontiers?

To the outside eye, they are busy, active children enjoying themselves. To the conscious educator, they are learning new skills; they are accruing new knowledge of themselves. Not only a child but a new self-feeling swishes down the slide with outstretched arms after he has climbed to the top of the jungle gym for the first time and, standing alone, has scanned the endless vista of the neighboring roofs. They are gaining direct knowledge of the nature of the physical world, knowledge that, in a few years, will be transformed into abstract concepts of weight and pressure, of wheel and axle, of hoisting and leverage. The adults in this world echo the child's pleasure in the expanding sense of himself as he moves about in his physical world, and see in his playful elaboration of physical feats the evidence of his individuality, making over in his own shape the "world" he has been given.

In an address a few years ago, Dr. Karl W. Deutsch applied his thinking about computer models and communication systems to questions of education and said:

Openness—the ability to increase the sensitivity in the range of our channels of intake, the ability to interact and to receive, to learn more about the universe around us and from the human beings around us—is perhaps one of the most critical and most precious qualities of any system of communication. . . .[11]

Almost the same words have been used by this writer in formulating a first principle in the education of young children as "increasing the range and depth of children's sensitivity to the

11. Karl W. Deutsch, "What Do Our Computers Tell Us About the Way Our Children Grow?," *Child Study*, Summer 1959.

world around them."[12] In application, this principle guides preschool organization at all levels, from decisions on purchasing to criteria for selection of teachers. The "things" of the preschool world offer a wealth of sensory experience: the rough sand in the box, the smooth velvet covers for the doll bed, the red paint jar beside the black one, the hard blocks that cannot be squeezed into a small space, the too-soft clay that cannot be made to hold a shape, the tap on a triangle, and the rush of water in a sink. The "things" alone are not adequate teachers, though, unfortunately, there are many schools even at more advanced levels where there is a false dependence on materials, equipment, and buildings as the carriers of learning. In this young world it is the sensitive teacher who supplies the accents for the child's experience, perhaps by standing quietly with a few children, so quietly that one can try to hear the sounds the fish make when they pass each other in the tank, or still for so long that there is time to see the last bit of the boat pass over the horizon; perhaps by clutching a pan of snow under her arms, after the excited tramp in the snow piles, for the children to watch as it melts inside the warm room and to touch its smooth, icy surface when it is brought in from the window sill the following morning. The teacher's sensitivity can sometimes be measured indirectly; it is almost as if it correlates negatively with the amount of verbalization that accompanies this aspect of her teaching capacity.

The young child's naturally high impressionability, his freedom from the need to act through a structure of systematic purposes and means to ends, the available energy of the extensor processes provide his teachers with limitless possibilities for

12. Barbara Biber, "Integration of Mental Health Principles in the School Setting," in G. Caplan, ed., *Prevention of Mental Disorders in Children* (New York: Basic Books, Inc., 1961).

deepening his powers of perception and response to an accented, differentiated life environment. Through these experiences he becomes an observer; through observation, he is being introduced to one of the basic processes of learning; by deepening his own capacity for observation he is strengthening one form of vital communication between the self and the environment.

When he learns to walk, long before he gets to preschool, the child graduates from the plantlike existence of the infant. When he learns to deal with experience by means of symbolic reference systems, he leaves the animal world behind.

It is during the preschool years that the human mind performs its greatest magic: the child is freed from dependence on sensory-perceptual-motor experience as the sole channel of communication with his environment.[13] The evolution of the capacity to deal with experience symbolically represents the key extensor process of the maturing organism. It manifests itself in every medium of expression known to man, and runs the full course from the simplest gestural representations to advanced levels of abstraction. The string held to the ear is "telephoning" to the child who is nowhere near a three-syllable word in his vocabulary; the spinning five-year-old who drops to the floor in delicious exhaustion is the astronaut in orbit; from the crayon lines of the three-year-old a "face" appears; the clay in the hands of the four-year-old walks like a dog; the left-over strips of lath in the wood box are regenerated, to live again as a helicopter. Symbolizing through gesture, through two-dimensional and three-dimensional representation, are natural child modes of reiterating the more meaningful aspects of experience, thereby strengthening the joining lines between the inner self and the outer world. Equally exciting to the child, and ulti-

13. C. M. Solley and G. Murphy, *Development of the Perceptual World* (New York: Basic Books, Inc., 1960).

mately the keystone of his ability to deal effectively with the complexity of human living, is his gradual mastery of the word and the idea as tools for symbolically organizing experience. The telescoping of this growth process within the preschool years is forever astounding even to the most experienced adults. The very young child, intoxicated with the insight that everything has a name, stumps the adult with his unanswerable question: What is the name of yesterday? A very few years later, the six-year-old's unanswerable questions are of another magnitude: If settling arguments with words instead of fists is a sign of growing up, then why do we send soldiers to fight in wars?

The intermediate steps in this progression toward more complex, conditional, and comprehensive concepts are not random; patterns of increasing differentiation and integration follow a discernible sequence. Elements in experience are seen by the child as belonging together through acts of repetition, through similarities of projected affect as well as object attributes, through classification based on use and function. Differences in degree are added to absolute contrasts; time perceived at first through sequence of familiar events matures into the syntax of seasons, days of the week, hours of the clock. The child's first universe of given things in an eternal state of the "present" gives way to a world of change over time; his fascination with the "how" processes of making, doing, and fixing is close to the generic meaning of "manufacturing"; the span between beginning and end, then and now, expands to a primordial sense of history.

The responsibilities of education for this period of growth become clearer when it is recognized that it is possible for the child, not only to acquire knowledge of what constitutes his world and how it functions, but also to learn an attitude toward himself as one who can gain mastery over ignorance, perplexity, and confusion; not only enlarge his vocabulary and engage in traffic with ideas, but also learn how the process of thinking can be an exciting, gratifying form of exploration and discovery; not only look to adults as the source of information and know-how, but learn how to transform what, in the last analysis, can only be borrowed from others into a self-absorbed and internal-ized understanding of one's own. To fulfill such possibilities requires highly specific attitudes and techniques on the part of teachers; these can only be briefly referred to in the context of this paper.

There is a concrete method for firsthand study of the environment, creatively conceived and skillfully developed by Lucy Sprague Mitchell,[14] which is adapted to the constant revision and revolutionary changes in the child's world of reality. The emergence of television and the space age, for example, requires basic rethinking of what a child's world of ideas is. Techniques of group discussion in school make thinking a socialized experience, in which a wide score of accepted relevance and a minimum of right-wrong orientation invite the child mind to roam fully with the raw materials of thought and allow the teacher the role to guide in accenting connectives, by opening up new and richer fields for wonder and research, by leading thought processes to more advanced organization, as, for example, when children first engage in cause-effect reasoning.

There is a danger, of course, that the teacher may overdo her function as a guide toward mastery of reality in terms of increasingly clear and logical thinking and, in so doing, sacrifice the opportunity to nurture creativity at its source.[15] In the intellectual realm, this problem is analogous to the damage to

14. Lucy Sprague Mitchell, *Our Children and Our Schools* (New York: Simon and Schuster, Inc., 1950).
15. Barbara Biber, "Premature Structuring as a Deterrent to Creativity," *American Journal of Orthopsychiatry*, Vol. XXIV, No. 2 (April 1959).

creativity in the sphere of the emotions inherent in too early or too strict denial of impulse expression, as discussed earlier. There are manifold ways in which the young child's creativity in assimilating and organizing experience can be kept vital and gratifying. One of these is to provide the materials, the setting, the atmosphere, for full and free activity in the nonverbal modes of symbolizing and reorganizing experience, to give psychological space to physiognomic as well as representative symbolizing activity.

Another way is to understand and accept the young child's need to use the self as the nucleus around which meanings and concepts are developed. To develop the mind, the teacher needs to be in close touch with the self. Concepts of time are threaded around the emotions of birthdays. When a five-year-old, watching a group of three-year-olds with his teacher, turns to her and asks, "Do you remember what we looked like then?," he is comprehending growth. The boundless curiosity about all origins, about where things come from, is rooted in the great mystery of one's own birth. The skillful teacher constructs a continuous bridge from the central self to the extended realities of the nonself, thus presumably preventing a system of dichotomous affect between the personal and nonpersonal, between the individual and the outer world. Unless such processes as these are rooted in the early years of personality development, is there much reason to hope that self-transcendance can be psychologically healthy in mature life?

The most significant opportunity for supporting creative processes in young children lies in the way in which their life of pretending is understood, responded to, and provided for. A first principle is to recognize the dynamic aspects of the play life of children and to perceive it as a complex counterpoint of active selection and transformation of experience, in which material from the deepest levels of affect can be merged with recently acquired factual knowledge. There are transformations of self-roles: the child turns himself into a baby, a tiger, an engineer, a cyclone. The interpersonal and mechanical relationships of everyday life are relived and reinstituted; meals are cooked, babies lovingly tended; windows and elevators appear in block buildings; planes crash and cows escape from the pasture. The complex of relations among the children within which the play sequence develops is characterized by its fluidity, but is never random with respect to individual personality. Some children project relatively fixed roles: the baby, the victim, the captain, the pessimist, the idea man. Some move in and out of a variety of roles as varied qualities of interaction take shape: dominating, supporting, joining, aggressing, manipulating, distracting, and so on. There are no mandates for what the things in the real world shall be; a rusty muffin tin is a beautiful cake; a small wooden cube is a traffic light; a sawhorse is a bridge or a tunnel or a mountain; an enclosure is a house or an airport or a jail or a field of wild flowers.

When the educational setting and atmosphere offer guidance without imposing direction on the play life, the children are the masters of selection, sequence, timing; for future development, it is important that the child counteract his feelings of powerlessness by being given the chance to experience autonomy in such creative, constructive activities, not through his natural resistance to an adult-ordered world alone. By reliving the most meaningful aspects of their experience through self-initiated play, children actually master the realities of life experience. Thereby, they intensify their insights and, at the same time, create situations that lead them on to new and deeper levels of wondering and questioning; how great the gain depends on the quality of teaching available to them.

The play of young children, however, serves a far more intricate function than to advance and extend their mastery of reality: it is the child's natural vehicle to bring about a dynamic fusion of mastery of reality with subjective expression. Emotional responses—positive and negative—are projected and relived as actively as cognitive responses. The freedom to symbolize experience through play, away from objective, logical modes, gives the child emotional safety. This, in turn, makes it possible for his play to become a catharsis for living through defeats, frustrations, and pain, and thus has value, in general, for working out inner conflicts in an external field.

For play to serve these multiple functions, it is necessary that teachers be able to read the language of play and be aware of the extent to which coherence can be achieved on a symbolic level, while play roles and relationships may deny the simplest facts of reality. Only then will teachers be able to provide the balance between the child's dual impulse toward phantasy and reality while at the same time respecting the integration of the two, which the child is accomplishing at a deep level, in his own idiom.

In this paper an attempt has been made to illustrate how preschool education is related to the nurturing of individuality, conceived in terms of self-knowledge, self-realization, and self-transcendence. Two major propositions have been developed. First, the socialization of the young child need not, should not, mechanize the impulses associated with the elemental processes of development, lest, in doing so, it sacrifice creativity, spontaneity, and a positive self-image at the source. Second, the intellectual development of the child, identified as the extensor process, can be guided so as to enhance his powers of establishing a pattern of deep, personal involvement with the world around him, by protecting his modes of integrating experience through phantasy as well as reality, by fostering an image of self-strength and an expectation that it is the individual who, through his own potentialities for being impressed and making impact, continually makes and remakes his world, as a child and in maturity.

5.

JOHN I. GOODLAD

Elementary Education

MAN HAS ROCKETED his kind into space. He has brought back into pulsating life a human being already pronounced dead. He has fashioned in his own likeness robots that remember, file, and sort, and then answer in moments problems to tax a hundred men for a thousand days. But men still cheat and steal and kill as they did a thousand years ago and thousands of years before that.

These are not always trapped men or hungry men or threatened men who cheat and steal and kill. Some men pronounced learned cheat because they are vain. Some men pronounced holy steal because they are greedy. Some men pronounced wise kill because they have established no identity with their fellow men. The people who soon may bring down upon themselves a holocaust are or will have been the *most* educated of all time.

The central task of education—and, therefore, for elementary schools—is to develop men of good will who do not cheat, or steal, or kill; universal individuals who value as one both self and all mankind, sensing immortality as the idea of mankind and not the fact of man. What is the nature of such men and what goes into their making?

GOAL

The central aim of education is to develop rational men who do not sin against themselves and their kind. To specify *rational* rather than, simply, *men* is to appear to state a redundancy, for men who neither cheat because of their vanity nor steal because of their greed nor kill because of their malice *are* rational men. Nonetheless, so as not to mistake the intellectual man or the much-schooled man for the rational man, we must specify what rational men do and do not do.

The intellectual man thinks about the problems before him, but he is not necessarily committed to the conclusions to which his intellectuality brings him. And the problems he considers may be of little more than passing whimsey, of little import in the affairs of mankind. The much-schooled man is more likely to come face to face with the drama of mankind's triumphs and tragedies and to be committed to the tentative conclusions of his inquiry. But he does not necessarily act or see the need for acting upon these conclusions. Some "educated" men regard action as beneath them, as unsuited to their learned state.

The rational man not only is committed to the rich fruits of inquiry but also is prepared to act and, indeed, acts upon insight rendered compelling by commitment. He knows as perhaps the most vital ingredient of his rationality that only through action following understanding and commitment does man forge the links in the chains of his own humanity and of mankind's immortality. He senses his place in time and space and his individual responsibility to that place, time, and space.

The intellectual man standing disdainfully uncommitted, the educated man standing impeccably uninvolved—these are the living symbols of imperfection in education and schooling.

For all nations that approach universal elementary and secondary schooling, these—not the stumbling reader, the guessing speller, the by-chance figurer—are the challenge to educational reform. For those nations where adult illiteracy prevails, the challenge is to assure rationality in that large segment of the childhood population fast becoming literate. For both, lethal danger lies in equating literacy with rationality. Literate nations, in seeking to assist preliterate nations, should remind themselves that their own universal schooling has not assured development of the universal individual.

There is no point in redefining the qualities desired in what we are calling here "the rational man." Robert Ulich, in Chapter One, elaborates three closely interconnected human characteristics: The first is the quality of faith, the second the quality of self-transcendence, and the third the quality of vision —all three disciplined and purified by reason and self-criticism. In the words of Phenix:

. . . the rationalist faith is that there is one standpoint—that of disciplined reason—which comprehends all the others, making it possible to escape the relativities of time and culture and the illusions of provincialism. This is the peculiar property of reason, that it enables man to achieve a degree of universality, to rise to some extent above the limitations of circumstance and history. . . . In this power of rational self-transcendence lies the justification for the concept of mankind and for an approach to education formed around that idea.[1]

"To develop the power of self-transcendence" is a compelling, overarching goal for all levels of education. It needs no restatement for each step in the vertical structure of schooling.

1. Philip H. Phenix, "Education and the Concept of Man," *Views and Ideas on Mankind* (Chicago: Council for the Study of Mankind, 1961), Bulletin No. 9, p. 10. See also Robert Ulich, *The Human Career, A Philosophy of Self-Transcendence* (New York: Harper & Brothers, 1955).

But "rational self-transcendence" is a condition neither found full-blown nor produced by magic formula. Nor is it assured in the much-schooled and necessarily absent in the near-illiterate. Schooling, we think, contributes to its attainment and would contribute more if disciplined by a unifying concept of mankind.

Stirrings representing a growing awareness of self and others are visible in the very young. They come into sharp focus as the infant seeks to establish and comprehend a relationship with the adults, usually parents, close to him. Quickly, these stirrings crystallize into surprisingly persistent and consistent behavior patterns as the young child moves out into a world of other children and adults. By the time he comes to school, at the age of five or six or seven, he has established characteristic ways of acting and acquired various labels—sweet, bright, happy, aggressive, dull, bully—that both reflect the reactions of others to him and hide or distort a conflict of traits in the developing self.

What should and can the school do to modify these traits? Philosophers and psychologists have long pondered the two questions implied. Their answers, at best, have provided an illuminating picture of part of an elusive whole: schools must teach "the method of intelligence"; the what, why, and when of schooling are found "in the potential of the individual learner"; the tasks of learning must be organized around "the significant problems of a changing world society"; the learner must be introduced to "the central concepts and methods of inquiry" of the several disciplines.

Child, culture, subject matter, discipline, method—these and more are the stuff of schooling. Schoolmen must not wait for more compelling statements of goal, essential though it be that men of wisdom persist in the quest for them. Likewise, schoolmen must not wait for more precise clarifications of means, for the grand synthesis of method, essential though it be that men of science intensify their researches into them. Schoolmen must act daily upon the fruits of these insights and inquiries, depending on judgment refined by schooling and experience, in thee trial-and-error process of improving education.[2]

Ideas about education drift like clouds around the globe, nourishing schools when circumstances of time and place combine to precipitate these ideas over receptive soil. The central theme of this volume is that the concept of mankind spelled out herein has universal application to educational processes. But nations differ in the specifics of schooling requiring immediate attention and, therefore, in their readiness to use ideas. Consequently, it is difficult, if not impossible, to itemize a bill of particulars for educating children around the world. The writer has chosen, therefore, to select several specific assets of elementary schooling that lend themselves to being "disciplined and purified by reason and self-criticism." Educators may disagree over the proposals, but they dare not ignore the problems and the issues posed by them.

FACILITIES

Elementary education embraces the schooling of children between the ages of five and fourteen, and thus corresponds to the span of years normally inferred from the term "child population." For most of the world, the first significant step toward education for mankind is to get the children into schools and

2. James B. Conant, *Trial and Error in the Improvement of Education* (Washington: Association for Supervision and Curriculum Development, National Education Association, 1961).

keep them there long enough for some permanent value to result. Approximately forty-five per cent (250 of more than 550 million) of the world's boys and girls between the ages of five and fourteen are yet to be enrolled in any school, public or private.[3] And large numbers of the fifty-five per cent currently enrolled do not remain long enough to become functionally literate.

It is difficult for persons living in countries where universal elementary education is established to comprehend the magnitude of the world task that lies before us. The future of mankind no doubt depends on ideas, but the spread of those ideas that are to prevail awaits the construction of millions of classrooms and the preparation of millions of teachers for them. The children who will enter these classrooms await, in their turn, humanizing reform in the conduct of elementary schooling, if significant ideas ever are to reach them.

The provision of these facilities and teachers must be guided by an awareness of the fact that tomorrow's schools can and must provide a bastion for individuality in a world of increasing anonymity. A population tidal wave is threatening to engulf a world-wide awakening of the human spirit and its accompanying striving for education. In every large city and in most of the world where poverty prevails, children share such dingy quarters and have so little opportunity to be alone that anything other than a struggle-for-survival concept of self is hard to come by. Certainly, opportunity to contemplate the state of man and his world is missing.

The opportunity to fashion one's own dwelling according to a personal conception of what is pleasing is available to and used by only a small fraction of the human race. The need to

3. UNESCO, *World Survey of Education*, Vol. 2, *Primary Education* (Paris: United Nations Educational, Scientific, and Cultural Organization, 1958), p. 15.

provide, cheaply and quickly, endless numbers of roofs and walls threatens to extinguish man's quest for the beautiful and the utilitarian merged compatibly into his buildings. One remaining chance to blend form, line, color, and material in useful works of lasting architectural beauty is in the construction of public buildings.

Regrettably, the earth's surface already is strewn with stark, prisonlike monstrosities, clearly identifiable the world around as "schools." Forward-looking citizens seeking to change this stereotype through bringing the best in architectural talent to the problems of school construction encounter rough going. Taxpayers equate beauty with cost, even though handsome schools usually cost less per square foot than commercial buildings constructed close by. School design is only beginning to break out of the traditional mold. As a consequence, the "eggcrate" concept is stubbornly yielding to the fascinating possibilities of what architects call "malleable space."

In colorful, airy, spacious schools, providing nooks for the individual as well as assembly halls for the many, yet another opportunity is provided for children to catch a glimpse both of the infinite and of personal potentialities not previously perceived. Schools should be anything but a reminder of the squalid, fear-ridden existence many children live outside of school.

A little thing, this concern for building design? Perhaps. But just as there is an overarching concept of mankind sufficiently motivating to give direction to the whole of education, there is *no* sweeping panacea for attaining it. The character of the education needed is made up of complex, interlocking parts.

EXPECTATIONS

The elementary schools of the world must provide a reasonable balance of success and failure for *all* children. In many countries, twenty-five per cent of each class group receive seventy-five per cent of the failing marks, and up to forty per cent fail and are required to repeat the work of the grade. A steady diet of failure for even hardy personalities is destructive of self-esteem. But these failing youngsters tend to be the least hardy and least advantaged of the child population. What repeated failure does to them must be damaging beyond belief.

Children around the world are more alike than different. The very young in China, Brazil, Nigeria, Nicaragua, Newfoundland, and the United States are surprisingly similar in their spontaneity, joy in laughter, abandon in play. Culture soon begins its relentless work, however, molding toddlers capable of communicating with toddlers everywhere into children scarcely capable of communicating with anyone anywhere. The range of effective interaction is reduced to ethnic group, social class, or even geographic neighborhood.

In any segment of population, closely circumscribed as it is by uniformity in tradition, religion, caste, or socio-economic status, children's native abilities conspire, nonetheless, with environmental opportunity and happenstance to produce differences in their readiness for school fare. The mental-age range in a group of thirty six-year-olds entering the first grade is more than three years. Ability, interest, and energy soon combine to confound the picture of group variability in regard to any aspect of schooling. In the United States, for example, the academic-achievement range is more than three years from top to bottom in a third-grade class, more than four years in the fourth-grade class, and so on. Less than fifteen per cent of a fourth-grade class is at grade level in all subjects at midyear, even when "fourth grade" is defined as a full-year spread in attainment (from 4.0 to 4.9 grades).[4] This picture of gross variability persists even in classes contrived to be closely homogeneous in chronological age and is reduced only moderately through so-called "ability grouping."[5]

These facts and their possible implications for schooling are perceived only dimly by educators and scarcely at all by the lay public. The schools, we know, are geared to adult expectations for childhood education, which have been frozen into the grades and which persist in spite of the repeated failure of some children to meet them. Nonpromotion serves as the adjustment mechanism for children who do not come up to "grade standard." Such evidence as is available suggests that grade repetition does not produce the benefits assumed for it. Nonpromoted children achieve no more during their year of repetition than their promoted, equally slow-learning age-mates. In fact, such children often show up less well on achievement tests *after* a year of repeating the grade than before doing so. As an alternative to nonpromotion, "social promotion" is less than satisfactory, too, because this practice often moves the slow learner into a classroom environment of still greater demand.[6] Children labeled "failure" or faced continuously with little or

4. For further elaboration of these and other data on individual differences, see National Society for the Study of Education, *Individualizing Instruction*, Sixty-first Yearbook, Part I (Chicago: University of Chicago Press, 1962).

5. For a review of research on grouping, see John I. Goodlad, "Classroom Organization," in Chester W. Harris, ed., *Encyclopedia of Educational Research* (New York: The Macmillan Co., 1960), pp. 221-26.

6. Effects of promotion and nonpromotion are reviewed in Henry J. Otto and Dwain M. Estes, "Accelerated and Retarded Progress," in *Encyclopedia of Educational Research, op. cit.*, pp. 4-11.

no prospect of success come to regard themselves as failures. Such children cannot be expected to develope a wholesome regard for self and fellow man.

This is no plea for rewarding any or all effort, however puny. Nor is this an argument for relative standards in judging human products. Rather, the writer envisions an elementary schooling that probes beneath the surface of immediate accomplishments to find and guide the processes rapidly becoming characteristic of the person. How is each child perceiving himself, his world, and his place in that world? If he perceives each day in school as failure, the school fails the child, and the child, in all probability, will fail mankind.

School expectations are an aspect of failure. Controlling agencies for schools and professional educators translate general expectations into specific content or skills to be acquired at each grade level. Thus, in the United States, learning to read is a task for the first grade and manipulating common and decimal fractions a task for the fifth and sixth. Expectations that have been translated into specific requirements are not easily changed: this topic for the second grade and that one for the fourth. However, there is little evidence to support the grade placement of subject matter. Much of what is taught at one level could be interchanged with what is taught at another or even eliminated. Sequences of learning tasks as they are prescribed provide inadequate assurance that all children will be challenged appropriately.

Three prongs in the advancement of modern education offer promise for modifying the arbitrariness of elementary-school expectations and for devising curricular sequences likely to be reasonable, realistic, and conducive to the development of divergent as well as convergent thinking. These are *teaching machines, modification of graded school structure,* and increasing *attention to the nature and cultivation of creative talent* in children.

Teaching machines force attention to the programing of subject-matter sequences according to the syntax of that subject matter, where it has been defined, and an awareness of problems and rates of pupil progress through it. The absence of such syntax quickly becomes clear in the process and thus focuses attention on the pedagogical requirements of subject-matter organization. Consequently, the programing process always must be closely aligned with realities of both subject-matter structure and differences in children's learning rates. The teaching machine clearly shifts emphasis away from the normative expectations of school grades to the more absolute expectations set by experimentally ordered subject-matter sequences.

Several other virtues in teaching machines become apparent. Limitations in budget and personnel frequently restrict elementary-school offerings to a narrow range of subjects. Children's burgeoning talents go begging because the diverse array of teaching talents necessary to their cultivation is not available. But a dozen teaching machines programed for foreign languages, more advanced mathematics, or aspects of music could very well assure the "branching" needed by an eager group of youngsters but beyond the grasp of a single, human teacher. Teachers are burdened, too, by marking countless "exercises" performed by children in the name of drill. The self-correcting teaching machine removes this arduous burden, freeing the teacher for more creative pedagogical activities.

A nongraded school is one in which the grade labels (first grade, second grade, third grade, etc.) have been entirely removed from a minimum of two grade levels.

The nongraded school is designed to implement a theory of continuous pupil progress; since the differences among children are great and since these differences cannot be substantially modified, school structure must facilitate the continuous educational progress of each pupil. Some pupils, therefore, will require a longer period of time than others for achieving certain learnings and attaining developmental levels.[7]

Such a scheme of school organization does not in itself improve curricular sequences. But it does turn one's attention to differences among learners and the need to differentiate expectancies for them. Instead of rewarding the bright pupil for his easy attainment of a common requirement, the teacher directs him to the next tasks, *even if they are tasks normally reserved for the next grade* in the graded pattern of school organization. A child may work at several different levels in as many subjects; it is not necessary for him to be in a single "grade." In brief, the nongraded school represents another attempt to recognize the hard fact of pupil individuality in relation to subject-matter sequences.

Elementary schools tend to approve a rather narrow range of child behavior, just as they tend to set rather arbitrary, graded expectations of accomplishment. Children are rewarded for "right" answers, recall of material taught, and for relatively low-level cognitive skills. Most children seek to become proficient in that which is likely to be rewarded. Consequently, the schools may be inculcating what psychologists and sociologists call "convergent" behavior at the expense of developing perhaps more important "divergent" behavior. Studies into the characteristics of creative scientists and artists suggest that the schools may need to encourage traits not always valued (and sometimes not even tolerated) in the classroom if an increasingly large proportion of tomorrow's adults are to be capable of molding better

7. John I. Goodlad and Robert H. Anderson, *The Nongraded Elementary School* (New York: Harcourt, Brace & World, Inc., 1959), pp. 52-53.

cultures for mankind instead of merely adjusting well to existing cultures.[8]

CURRICULUM

The problem of curriculum is to economize scarce learning potential by making the most judicious and appropriate selection of study content. Human intelligence is too rare and precious a thing to squander on a haphazard program of instruction.[9]

For what and from what shall content be selected? These are not decisions for teachers alone to make. And, clearly, these decisions are in large measure made before teachers step into the classroom. Society tends to allocate to schools the preservation of certain tendencies considered essential to survival. Ideally, these are tendencies thought essential for the survival of mankind. But when nations are locked in physical or ideological combat, the schools become instruments for inculcating those tendencies thought essential only to the survival of national interests. The struggle for national survival around the world is now being felt by children who are engaged in school activities brought home to them because of world crisis and conflict.

Nations make predictions about the future that have grave consequences not only for the future of that nation but also for the future of millions of young people living and yet to be born. As a consequence of the predictions made at least by major powers, school time devoted to science and mathematics expands, and school time devoted to the humanities and the social studies shrinks. Clearly, then, this science and mathematics must be

8. For a research report and discussion on problems encountered in identifying and encouraging creativity in the school setting, see Jacob W. Getzels and Philip H. Jackson, *Creativity and Intelligence* (New York: John Wiley & Sons, Inc., 1962).

9. Philip H. Phenix, *Philosophy of Education* (New York: Henry Holt and Co., Inc., 1958).

humanized by a unifying concept of mankind or the attributes needed for a world still surviving decades hence will be missing.

Subjects stand in competition with each other for a place in the curriculum. Which, because of its root nature, should take priority in the resolution of highly critical human problems? Sometimes we like to believe that subjects that take for study the very nature of man are themselves more virtuous than others in promoting man's humanity to man. But we have no highly viable evidence as to the prior virtue of one field over another.

I have never been able to regard seriously partisan arguments that the study of any particular aspects of man's folly-ridden history will determine whether the scholar ends up with mature wisdom or with the pseudo-erudition of an idiot-savant. The conflict between education as we have known it and maturity as we can envisage it depends upon something more profound than whether we master the history of an art-form called painting or an art-form called science. There is no educator who does not know scholars who lack the least quality of human maturity and wisdom, yet who are true masters of their own fields, whether this field is the humanities, art, music, philosophy, religion, law, science, the history of ideas or the languages by which men communicate ideas.[10]

The problem of content selection is further complicated by the fact that the products and methods of man's inquiries far outstrip the capacity of a single man to know them. At the theoretical level, men fashion constructs by which only a few scholars communicate. The layman's facts are facts no more. The new facts, pouring out from the empiricists' testing of the new theory, confound the layman and compound the work of teacher and curriculum maker. The resulting pedagogical problems are not merely of encompassing fresh accumulations of

10. Lawrence S. Kubie, *Neurotic Distortion of the Creative Process* (Lawrence: The University of Kansas Press, 1958).

knowledge—awesome though these tasks may be—but of making instructional order out of quantitative chaos. Utmost simplicity is called for. But superficiality is but a short step from simplicity.

Four kinds of curricular disciplining are called for, remembering that "the starting point is to make provision for developing those capacities which are fundamental to man as man."[11] The first calls for precise clarification of goal; the second for comprehensive selection of content from all major realms of human experience; the third for utilization of truly fundamental processes and principles for organizing content; and the fourth for adequate breadth in evaluating pupil behavior. We shall attempt to illustrate briefly each of these disciplining processes, beginning with a well-publicized statement of school purpose.

Clarifying Educational Goal
The purpose which runs through and strengthens all other educational purposes—the common thread of education—is the development of the ability to think. . . . To say that it is central is not to say that it is the sole purpose or in all circumstances the most important purpose, but that it must be a pervasive concern in the work of the school.[12]

Now, thinking is a complex process. We know surprisingly little about it, or about what subverts it, or even whether it *can* be taught. However, in order to think, a child must possess information. This is so clearly evident that elementary schools too often begin and end here. And so the school day becomes a deadly recitation of inert facts—which, ironically, may be fact no longer.

11. Philip H. Phenix, *op. cit.*, p. 60.
12. Educational Policies Commission, *The Central Purpose of American Education* (Washington: National Educational Association of the United States, 1961).

Inquiry into the knowledge possessed by children reveals startling distortions in their comprehension of what they so glibly recite. What they appear to comprehend they frequently do not draw upon in confronting problems calling for application or situations demanding judgment. In short, they do not or cannot think. If tomorrow's adults are to possess the "power of self-transcendence" that is thought to be essential to the preservation and cultivation of mankind, then the curriculum of today's elementary schools must assure development of the full range of processes involved in the mother process, thinking.

Selecting Curricular Content

About what are children to think in today's schools? The early years of schooling must begin with things close to the child: sounds and colors, trees and rocks, winds and rains, peers and adults. To become aware of and sensitive to immediate surroundings is to take a first step toward identifying with mankind.

It is difficult to realize how much of our diurnal experience is what William James called "a big blooming buzzing confusion." It is hard to realize how much of it is a semi-stupor. Life has often enough been described as a waking dream. But not much of it has the vividness, though a great deal of it may have the incoherence or the horror of a dream. For most people most of the time it is a heavy lethargy. They have eyes, yet they do not, in any keen and clear sense, see. They have ears, yet they do not finely and variously hear. They have a thousand provocations to feeling and to thought, but out of their torpor comes no response. Only the pressure of some animal excitement, instant and voluminous, rouses them for a moment to an impulsive clouded answer. Life is for most of us what someone described music to be for the uninitiate, "a drowsy reverie, interrupted by nervous thrills."[13]

13. Irwin Edman, *Arts and the Man* (New York: W. W. Norton & Co., Inc., 1928).

The second step is to learn the use of tools and symbols that, first, give man power beyond that of his unaided hands and, second, bind him to time and space. For man, beyond all other creatures, has the inherent capacity to bind himself to all cultures; to experience the joys, tragedies, heartaches, and accomplishments of all mankind. To fail to develop these capacities is to become something less than a man ought to be.

The third phase in childhood schooling brings the learner face to face with what his primary senses of sight, vision, touch, hearing, and smell do not reveal, but which are very real. Molecular structure, the Bill of Rights, a man's hate for his enemy—what are these, if not real? And so, through the study of art form, cellular behavior, man's quest for freedom, and linguistic patterns, the child learns that culture is not nature, but nature cultivated. Because no single ordering of man's experience clearly is superior in educating for mankind, the curriculum must assure balance among the major fields of knowledge and their methods: the humanities, the social sciences, and the physical and biological sciences.

These curricular progressions are spiral rather than serial in character. They are encompassed as in an envelope by a learning-teaching process of rational inquiry about which we shall have more to say. This is a process involving choices and the moral responsibility for making them wisely.

Organizing Curriculum Content

The third kind of curricular disciplining central to elementary education for mankind requires that in organizing specific content for instruction we pay attention to the fundamental processes and principles of productive learning. The school curriculum should be planned to reveal continuing threads—ideas, generalizations, principles, concepts, methods—

by means of which specific learnings might be related effectively one to another. These threads are derived from at least three sources: the developing characteristics of children, the subject-matter disciplines, and the nature of society. We shall illustrate a central problem of order in the curriculum by discussing the second of these sources.

From the subject-matter disciplines come both the method by which the fields have advanced and the generalizations or observations deemed significant for general dissemination. These methods and generalizations tend to be more lasting and more broadly applicable than the specific data they utilize or explain. Consequently, they are of more permanent value for curriculum planning, especially in a time of rapid accumulation of knowledge.

However, the elementary schools have tended to stress specific bits and pieces of knowledge because they can be packaged attractively for instructional occasions. Research into the alarming rate at which youngsters forget information that they have not organized or related, and recent experimentation with children's ability to comprehend fundamental methods and principles, force a new look at the variables and constants of the elementary-school curriculum. In the past, specific content has tended to be constant. Teachers and pupils alike have been left to find unifying principles where and when they could—often at the expense of truth. In the future, specific contents must be recognized as dispensable data in the effort to understand things more fundamental and constant.

Evaluating Pupil Behavior

Elementary schools embrace a narrow range of pupil behavior, just as they tend to provide learning activities designed for only limited aspects of the broad goals they seek to attain.

Too often, schools reward only that which is easily measured. And what is easily measured may be inconsequential in the conduct of human affairs. Children, like adults, see a certain expediency in doing that which is to be rewarded. Consequently, the world's children spend shocking proportions of valuable time on that which is of little importance.

Worse, pressure to succeed in school, increasing the world over, encourages behavior that is antithetical to goals of rational self-transcendence. Children steal answer booklets, copy each other's work, and falsify records in order to appear to have attained minimum standards set by the system. Education, the individual, and mankind are corrupted. Little wonder, then, that we have much-schooled men devoid of self-understanding and good will toward humanity.

To be effective, reform must take place simultaneously in classrooms and schools. The intimate setting of the classroom provides the daily cues that tell the child whether he is valued for what he is and can become or for appearing to be what he is not. The narrower the range of approved behavior, the greater the pressure to deceive the teacher and, in time, one's self.

The school, in turn, determines the variety of academic races that are to be run and, to a degree, the rate at which they are to be run. The school must not be all things to all people; it is not the sole educational agency. Nonetheless, a narrow prescription of races to be run under school auspices, together with a sharply defined time span for completing, limit dangerously both the talents that will flourish in tomorrow's world and the number of persons who will possess them.

Finally, societal concept of school function determines *who* will be educated. Some societies appraise the quality of their school system by evaluating the academic competence of those who complete it. Through rigorous testing, all who do not measure up are weeded out; only the most hardy (not necessarily the most able) survive. If the quality of a school system were to be determined by evaluating children both retained and eliminated by that system, using a wide range of characteristics deemed essential to individuality and universality, childhood schooling around the world would experience a purifying enlightenment.

METHOD

Teaching seeks to develop that which is already waiting. The first principle of method, then, is to find out what is there in the person. This is not where most teaching begins.

Most teaching begins with determination of what is to be brought to the learner. But how can this step be taken with confidence and precision, when we know not where the learner is? How many lessons are wasted, how many hours spent in boredom or frustration, because the teacher failed to determine first how much or how little of what he sought to offer already was possessed by the class!

There is little agreement on the kind or amount of scholarship required in the elementary-school teacher. The debate over requirements for teacher certification continues to be largely a political one, inconsequential data on what makes for good teaching being used only to camouflage this fact. Certainly, however, excellence in the teaching of children requires a transcendence of scholarship. The scholar who also teaches often wears his scholarship as a mantle. This may be desirable for the teacher of adults, who now should have some insight into what they want to know and so be attracted by the brightest mantles. But the teacher of children who is also a scholar must wear his scholarship as a vest, half hidden under his jacket. That vest should give him patience and understanding but not dazzle and confound the children as he moves into their lives.

The good teacher comes into the situation looking for clues to the child's drives. What is the child seeking? How can he be helped toward his goals and the envisioning of new goals, instead of merely converted to the goals adults have for him? How can the teacher, seeking to close a gap between what he sees in the child and what he wants the child to become, be helped to remember that under what he sees and may not like are the forces of man as man? To be unable to accept these is to be poorly qualified to teach.

Children seek to be respected and be worthy of respect, to relate themselves constructively to others, and to identify with what lies outside of their own immediate being. But these good ends often become hidden under layers of corrupted human interpretation, both self-interpretation and the interpretation of others, each layer like a coat of too-thick paint. In time the searching teacher has to scrape off a formidable amount of paint to discover what lies waiting: the clear, fine, beautifully grained wood that is underneath. In the scraping process, conscientious teachers become angered that human beings should have so corrupted what is basically first-rate, forgetting that the corrupting process probably was effected by persons whose ends were good. In their anger, however, they must not give up the search for what lies beneath, thus yielding to the easy temptation to brush on still another, perhaps brighter, coat of paint.

Teaching seeks to stir that which is already waiting into a fresh becoming and an awareness of that becoming. A second principle of method, then, is to provide a setting in which children's goals and what stands in the way of movement toward those goals may be perceived, examined, and, perhaps, articulated. With these goals at the conscious level, there is a rallying point for educational endeavor, and progress is rapid. Children begin to perceive personal potentialities not previously imagined or believed possible. They begin to accomplish things that belie their own previous, limited expectations. Then they should—and sometimes do—thrust out their chests proudly and proclaim, "Look, look what I have done—and I did it all by myself!"

It is sad that they do not often feel this way or dare not say so. Teachers, regrettably, because of their own needs to be wanted and to be identified with others, do not always understand the true basis of self-fulfillment through teaching. Knowing that he has been a force in a child's becoming, it is not easy for a teacher to stand by complacently while the child crows like a cocky little bantam rooster. Shocked and abused, the teacher retires to lick his wounds. "Did it all by himself, did he? The ingrate! Doesn't he see how much of what he has now become is because of me?"

But what is the goal of teaching? Is it not to bring forth just such becoming? If so, then the process of education is corrupted once again when the child must credit the teacher just before tasting the fruits of success. In so doing, the child is denied his moment of self-fulfillment and, ironically, the teacher is denied his. The child's passage to freedom is blocked. The hand grasping the teacher as it would a crutch grows weak and withers; the person is consumed in self-gratification and, ultimately, by self-hatred. Heavy-laden with mankind's guilt is the teacher who must exact "thank you" from his pupils.

Just as education has been impoverished through neglect of its first pedagogical principles, so education has been corrupted through misinterpretation of them. Good teaching does *not* both begin and end with the learner, for fear that he come not to love but to idolize himself, turning in upon such little knowledge as he already possesses. In the same way that the child must be helped to envision the potentialities of his becoming and his own role in that becoming, so must he be helped to develop the wholesome relativism that stems from awareness of the world's history, mankind, and the universe.

With the sense of timing that no amount of curriculum planning can assure, the teacher capitalizes on what the child begins to see in himself and, in so doing, reveals to the teacher. Aware now of where the child is, and how the child's awareness of success aids and abets the teaching effort, the teacher brings the child to what he has not yet learned. Love of self is the beginning, not the end. But without that beginning, the end comes not into view.

Leo Tolstoy, in *What Men Live By*, said:

I know that God does not desire men to live apart from each other, and therefore, has not revealed to them what is needful for each of them to live by himself. He wishes them to live together united, and therefore has revealed to them that they are needful to each other's happiness.

I know now that people only *seem* to live when they care only for themselves, and that it is by love for others that they really live.

6.

EARL S. JOHNSON

Secondary Education

THE CONCERN that sets our task is this: What good may come from inquiry into the manifold ways of mankind, pursued through comparative cultural studies? How may students come to know better the diverse peoples with whom they share space on a shrinking globe and, in the light of the fruits of such exploration, come to know themselves better because they see themselves in the "mirror of man"?

Such a concern seeks an understanding of mankind, the "universal subject," rather than strange and exotic individuals. It is bespoken in Ernst Cassirer's observation that "humanity is not to be explained by man but man by humanity" and in Goethe's belief that "man knows himself only in mankind." It is, albeit with a sense of guilt, in Cain's immortal question; it is the essence of the Golden Rule found, variously stated, in all the great religions. It is the theme of John Donne's "for whom the bell tolls" and of Whitman's "Song of Myself," which is also the song of all other selves. It is what Martin Buber seeks to understand, in its largest dimension, in the relations of "I" and "Thou"; and George H. Mead's view of the origin of the self is grounded on it.

Thus, it is clear that the process by which students may know mankind is reciprocal: they must know "the other one" and they must know the image that "the other one" has of them. And, to make the matter both more precise and more difficult, each must know how he knows "the other one," that is, by what uses of the mind and from what social, moral, and technological conditions and perspectives.

Robert Burns' words come to mind—and the moral of them, too:

> Oh wad some power the giftie gie us
> To see oursels as others see us!
> It wad frae monie a blunder free us,
>   An' foolish notion.

If it be assumed that the concept of mankind is now taken account of in the curriculum of our secondary school, the reply is "Perhaps," if the humanities are thought to be the area, but a qualified "No" if the social studies in their present status are thought to be the vehicle for its study. Nevertheless, we shall consider the concept as the concern of the humane *and* the social studies, without, however, suggesting that they have or ought to have sole proprietorship of it. On the contrary, if the concept of mankind were elaborated in its widest meaning, each of the three great fields of knowledge—the humanities, the social studies, and the natural sciences—through their course surrogates in the secondary school, would have much to contribute. One might look forward to the day when the sciences, the humanities, and the social studies achieve a genuine and exciting unity of labor in syntheses of various kinds effected through the concept of mankind.

A knowledge of "culture," as the anthropologist understands it, must, of course, provide the substantive ground for the study of mankind through all studies. In the social studies, as they are generally taught, the phenomenon of culture, so conceived, is either little known or is interpreted chiefly to refer either to "polite manners" or the achievements of various elites in the fine arts. Such interpretations have some, although a narrow, validity, but are a far cry from Clark Wissler's view of culture as "the whole round of life."

In the more traditional secondary school textbooks in United States history—whose major concern is with economic, political, and still to a large degree military matters—one usually finds a chapter or two that undertakes a rapid and necessarily shallow survey of what are called "cultural achievements." Chief attention under this heading is given to education, reform movements, and advances in the arts, letters, and sciences. Thus the term "culture" is conceived to refer to only a part of the "whole round of life," something a little more sturdy than a mere decoration but still far less comprehensive than culture viewed as the very warp and woof of a society.[1]

The situation in the secondary school is, however, brighter when account is taken of the work done by such scholars as Robert Redfield, Margaret Mead, Dorothy Lee, Lawrence Frank, Sol Tax, George Spindler, Theodore Brameld, and Solon Kimball. They have done much to encourage introduction of anthropological concepts into secondary school studies. Outstanding among courses in cultural anthropology is the one that Mr. Jack Ellison, of the Francis W. Parker school in Chicago, organized and has taught for ten years or more.[2]

1. See Edward Sapir, "Culture: Genuine and Spurious," *American Journal of Sociology*, Vol. 29 (1924), for a comprehensive treatment of culture: " . . . as any socially inherited element in man's life; as a conventional idea of refinement, and as the general attitudes and views of life that give a particular people its distinctive place in the world."

2. Noteworthy contributions to the journal literature in this connection are the following: Robert Redfield, "The Study of Culture in General Education,"

The course in world history that is characteristically required in the sophomore year warrants special comment. Courses under this rubric usually undertake to treat with man's experience in the framework of nation-states, which are taken as units of the great civilizations. Some of the texts open with a chapter on prehistoric man, usually referred to as "early man." The dominant pattern and theme of such courses, at least as revealed in representative textbooks, is the story of "human progress"—as the account is usually styled. Their final concern is usually to impress students with twentieth-century man's debt to all that has gone before and to which he is now legatee.

It is the view of an increasing number of historians and specialists in secondary school social studies that such courses presume a fund and quality of historical knowledge that is so extravagant as to be unattainable even by teachers; only by remote inference do they provide a world perspective on man-in-society; they are committed, perforce, more to coverage of factual knowledge than to mastering the meaning of the great social changes that are the substance of man's history. Nor do they illuminate the concept of mankind, because they do not examine societies in frames of reference that reveal the common, recurrent, and pervasive aspects of the life of peoples.[3]

Social Education, Vol. XI (October 1947); Alex Weingrod, "Anthropology and the Social Studies," *Social Education,* Vol. XX (January 1956); and Jack L. Ellison, "Anthropology Brings Human Nature into the Classroom," *Social Education,* Vol. XXIV, (November 1960). See also George D. Spindler, ed., *Education and Anthropology* (Stanford: Stanford University Press, 1955), and a forthcoming report by the American Council of Learned Societies on the role of anthropology (and many other of the traditional disciplines, social and natural) in secondary education.

3. See Stanley N. Miller, "The World Cultures Course," *Social Education,* Vol. XXVI (February 1962); and four papers on various aspects of the problems related to world-history courses in *Social Education,* Vol. XXIV (April 1960). An excellent high school text in world history, written by Professor L. S. Stavrianos, of Northwestern University, provides a constant schema for comparative study of nations and civilizations.

Before we offer our approach to the study of mankind we believe that some definitions and interpretations of the concept of "culture" are in order.

Edward B. Tylor, one of the patriarchs of cultural anthropology, understood culture to be "that whole complex which includes knowledge, belief, art, morals, law, custom and any other capabilities and habits acquired by men as members of society."[4] To the late Professor Alfred Kroeber it is that for which man "has a propensity," which suggests that it is coterminous with mankind. Bronislaw Malinowski understands culture to be "that full context of all man's activities . . . the vast instrumentality through which man achieves his ends, both as an animal who has to eat, rest and reproduce, and as a spiritual being who desires to extend his horizon to produce works of art and develop systems of faith."[5]

Malinowski's term, "the vast instrumentality," is uniquely appropriate to our purpose—to show that culture is the great middle principle through which all that man has made that lies outside him, as well as all that which lies within him—methods of thought, technical skills, ideas, and ideals—is related and gives meaning to his self and to his relation with his fellows. Not even Rousseau's "natural man" escaped the impact of his culture, so conceived.

But there is a quality in the phenomenon of culture that these terse and almost epigrammatic definitions hardly convey. For that quality we turn to the late Professor Clyde Kluckhohn:

A culture is not merely a congeries of customs. . . . The way of life that is handed down as the social heritage of every people

4. Edward B. Tylor, *Primitive Culture* (New York: Brentano, 1874), p. 1.
5. Bronislaw Malinowski, "The Scientific Approach to the Study of Man," in Ruth Anshen, ed., *Science and Man* (New York: Harcourt, Brace & World, Inc., 1942), p. 207.

does more than supply a set of skills for making a living and a set of blueprints for human relations. Each different way of life makes its own assumptions about the ends and purposes of human existence, about ways by which knowledge may be obtained, about the organization of the pigeonholes in which each sense datum is filed, about what human beings have a right to expect from each other and the gods, about what is 'good' and 'right' or 'better' and 'worse,' about what constitutes fulfillment or frustration. Some of these assumptions are made explicit in the lore of the folk; others are tacit premises which the observer must infer from finding consistent trends in word and deed. The unstated assumptions (in particular) are ordinarily taken for granted as an ineradicable part of human nature and naive participants in one culture find it hard to understand what normal persons could possibly conceive life in other terms. In other words, many cultural premises and categories are nonrational and defensive attitudes related to them may be decidedly irrational.[6]

What Professor Kluckhohn implies ought now to be made explicit: every culture is a system *sui generis*. This fact may well give to comparative cultural study its most interesting and likewise its most enigmatic and troublesome character. Even so, high school students ought to learn that every culture is like every other, and every one is also unlike every other. Each is a "patterned selectivity," manifesting certain universal forms that tend, in content, to be unique to particular histories and traditions.

At the cost of some simplification, we would refer these common aspects of all cultures to mankind's biological, physiological, psychological, and rational equipment and mechanism, and to the fact that everywhere man confronts recurrent and

6. Clyde Kluckhohn, "Common Humanity and Diverse Cultures," in David Lerner, ed., *The Human Meaning of the Social Sciences* (New York: Meridian Books, 1959), pp. 247-48.

common situations. The latter we are disposed to think of as universal exigencies of human existence. Thus it is that the more apparent universals in the cultures that man has elaborated are not identities in their behavioral *content* but in their *forms*.

Through studies of how these processes work, both independently (if they ever do!) and interdependently in a variety of cultures, students may get an understanding of how cultures are alike and how they are unalike, respecting both the forms and the content that such processes manifest. Thus they may develop some identity, even kinship, with mankind: historic with prehistoric; advanced with primitive; complex with simple; and preliterate with literate.

Our first concern is with patterns or frames of reference that will serve adequately to discipline and direct comparative cultural studies so that the concept of mankind may be discovered and revealed.

That patterns are needed goes without saying, for, lacking them, we have no way to reduce "facts in a state of dispersion" to determinate orders of one kind or another. Perhaps the simplest of such patterns is that which we owe to Clark Wissler's "universal culture pattern."[7] It offers one way of stating cultural universals—in terms of form rather than content. There are, likely, a great many other patterns, each reporting the view of given scholars as to what each conceives the common ground of cultures to be.

Our predilection is for the scheme elaborated by Leon C. Marshall,[8] which undertakes to *identify the universals* in culture in terms of social processes. In skeletal form, but otherwise

7. Clark Wissler, *Man and Culture* (New York: Thomas Y. Crowell Co., 1923), p. 64.
8. Leon C. Marshall and Rachel Goetz, *Curriculum Making in the Social Studies* (New York: Charles Scribner's Sons, 1936), pp. 7-22.

only slightly different from Marshall's original presentation, it reads as follows:

1. interaction with nature: the geo-ecological phase of man's activity

2. adjustment to the resources of the natural world so as to serve man's creature needs: the activity of economizing

3. the elaboration of a spatial pattern of human settlement: the demographic and territorial phase of man's activity

4. biological continuance and the conservation of human life: the demographic and genetic processes

5. the establishment of value standards or norms: the ethical-moral process

6. securing minimum adherence to these standards or norms: the process of social control

7. developing and operating the agencies of social organization: the governmental-institutional process

8. cultural continuity and change: the processes of education and invention

9. personality formation: the summation and focus of all the processes[9]

These processes may come to be seen as the links in the "great chain of being"—when mankind has gained ground, it has been through the play and interplay of these processes; likewise when it has lost ground. It is in the context of inquiry, disciplined and directed by such a pattern, that the idea of mankind may become a working idea.

In such a schema as Marshall's, comparative cultural study could envisage "the whole round of life" through the use of data and methods that help students to comprehend the nature of human affairs: those of the physical and biological sciences,

9. The limitations of this taxonomy for studying the organization of primitive cultures will be treated below.

humane letters, and the social studies. In this view, comparative cultural study would draw upon and draw together materials from all the scholarly disciplines, and provide a working plan for a true synthesis of knowledge about mankind.

But for our purposes here a more modest and limited enterprise is suggested, namely, that comparative cultural study be limited to the perspectives, methods, and data provided by the social and humane studies. What they have in common has been stated with rare insight and literary beauty by Robert Redfield. When asked what the social sciences and humanities have in common, he replied that "they have humanity in common."

Humanity is the common subject matter of those who look at men as they are represented in books or in works of art, and of those who look at men as they appear in institutions and indirect-visible action. . . . As physics is concerned with energy and matter, and biology with organisms and their life processes, so social science is concerned with the way men and women feel and think and act. . . . What matters to us all, what we live for, is sympathy, understanding, imagination, reason, tradition, aspiration, and personal and human association.[10]

Do we have here another set of cultural universals? It would appear that we do, and we find no barrier, except it be the lack of the teacher's knowledge and imagination, to their being woven into the study of cultures from the perspective of the social processes. In this, the art and literature (if of the latter there be any) of the cultures would help effect a synthesis of the social and humane perspectives.

These observations raise the question of the methods most germane to combined social and humane inquiry into the nature of culture and the idea of mankind. Note, *methods,* not

10. Robert Redfield, "Social Science Among the Humanities," *Measure,* Winter 1950, pp. 63-64.

techniques, although in this distinction no slur upon pedagogy, as it is usually interpreted, is intended.

Method, as exemplified in the concepts and apparatus of the traditional disciplines, or in the view shortly to be offered, is slighted to an alarming degree in secondary education. To a very great extent, concepts and general propositions, if given anything more than lip service, are based on the authority of the teacher or the textbook. Learning is, thus, to a great extent, learning the rhetoric of conclusions. The "method of authority" rather than the "authority of method" tends to dominate.

All thinking lies along a continuum that includes fact, logic, and imagination.[11] These "elements" may be seen in terms of a series of interrelated questions: "what and how," or the method of true description and cause and effect; "why," or the method of inference and interpretation, requiring insight that comes both by "knowledge about" and "acquaintance with"; and "what ought," or the method of assessing and valuing. The first two lie within the scope of the sciences, natural and social; all three lie within the scope of the humanities.

The method of "what and how" requires critical scrutiny of evidence and proof of the reliability of statements of fact. It will, in comparative cultural study, run counter to such "truths" as travelers' and missionaries' accounts, laymen's quasi- and folk-wisdom, and, at times, downright and intended falsehood. Thus it will demand skill in the use of the canons of historical scholarship, especially awareness of one's biases and the modes of their intrusion, and ability to use the rudiments of the empirical method.

The method of "why" will require deep and informed insight into the ways and rationalizations of cultures other than

11. See Earl S. Johnson, "Ways of Knowing," *Social Education,* Vol. XXVII, No. 1 (January 1963), pp. 5-10, 35.

the students' own, and the ability to enter imaginatively into them.

While the boundary line between "what and how" and "why" is difficult to draw, that which separates "why" from "what ought" is even more difficult. The latter involve feeling as well as knowing, for both are worlds away from von Ranke's too-simple *"wie es eigentlich gewesen ist."* But to the degree that the "why" and the "what ought" are separable, the latter will require the making of assessments and value judgments about conduct and moral standards in the context of the culture to which such behavior and standards are indigenous, not in the context of the students' own culture.

The continuum that we have in mind runs, when viewed ideally, from the knowing-understanding that we identify with the methods of social study to the feeling-appreciating that we identify with the methods of humanistic study. Or the continuum may be viewed in the terms we owe to Wilhelm Dilthey.[12] "What and how" may be learned through the method that neither requires nor involves the observer's sympathy. This is not to deny that his interest is involved, for we cannot afford to ignore the wisdom of Darwin's axiom, "All observation must be for or against some view if it is to be of any service."

"Why" involves and requires a good deal of the observer's identity with the thing observed, which, in cultural study, would be goal-oriented and/or value-serving behavior. Such activity suggests the method of *Erleben*—literally, "to live with and through another's experience"—thus involving "inner perception" as distinct from the "outer perception" of the method of *Anschauen*.

The assessing and valuing involved in "what ought" per-

12. See H. A. Hodges, *Wilhelm Dilthey: An Introduction* (New York: Oxford University Press, 1944).

mits and requires, through imaginative participation, still more of the observer's identification with the one observed, through both knowing and feeling. Here, the method of *Erleben* is complemented and heightened by the method of *Nacherleben*—literally, "to re-experience or repeat in one's own consciousness [and conscience] the experience of another." Thus, inner perception and inner feeling are combined so as to permit sympathetic introspection and the making of value judgments. It needs to be made clear, however, that this experience does not require the student's real acceptance or endorsement of the behaviors so understood or of the value judgment made about them.

Certainly, the methods of such a continuum require great skill. Likewise, they involve great risks, especially respecting those of *Erleben* and *Nacherleben*. Nevertheless, all are required if students are to master the full range of methods in cultural studies.

Remembering and taking full account of the fact that all cultures are systems *sui generis,* certain expectations about students' understanding may be entertained. Such as the following:

(a) Cultural relativity does not mean that if parents in Tribe X put every third child to death, that it is right for parents in any other tribe to do the same; on the contrary,

(b) it means that any positive or negative custom, any particular "right" or "wrong," must be judged in the context of the culture whose custom it is;

(c) despite differences in its content, morality is universal in the sense that always and everywhere, implicitly, conduct is instructed by principle and not by mere convenience or whim;

(d) the value modalities that may be discovered in variable cultures permit the judgment that there are cultural absolutes but that these, like all absolutes of which we know, are not served *absolutely,* for there is a simple but profound difference between "an idea of perfection" and a perfect idea or act;

(e) moral principles are amenable to change in "right" or "wrong" directions, as these may be understood in the finest and meanest images, respectively, that man has entertained about himself; and

(f) mankind is now little more than a hope, but there is nothing in the nature of either culture or human nature that necessarily prevents its emergence as a conscious social fact.

In concluding this chapter we wish, first, to comment on some of the dangers and difficulties that attend comparative cultural study and, second, to say what we hold to be some of the great good that may come of it. The dangers we foresee are in the nature of dangerous thoughts; the difficulties are of the order of more technical matters. The good of it will come if the dangers and difficulties are not too great.

Perhaps the greatest danger and the greatest good that may come from it is the challenge, if not also shock, to parochial views and values. The intended consequence would be, mild or severe, a form of emancipation—a break in the students' continuity with their past value orientations.

But it is the business of education in societies such as ours to create these discontinuities, even by conscious design, for intellectual and moral growth in advanced cultures comes from the successive breaking and mending of students' relations with the old, the known, and the secure. The objection that such experiences are not for high school youth may be an overriding one. Therefore, such studies should not come until the senior year. Moreover, they should be undertaken only by teachers with adequate knowledge in cultural anthropology and with the capacity of creating, with "supporting love or loving support," a climate in which the risk of shock might be made minimal and the likelihood of recovery made maximal.

We would not minimize the potential shock and harm from too-abrupt and disturbing discontinuities. The experience of one's having his ethnocentrism revealed is not only novel but upsetting. But if one learns at the same time what others practice vis-à-vis their cultures, the shock might be greatly reduced. Teachers can avoid the fear-and-devil-plot-exposure effect in ways similar to those used in the study of vicious and even terrifying propaganda, by approaching the matter in the temper of "Let's see what these fellows are up to and maybe we can beat them at their own game." Just as for propaganda there is also counter-propaganda, so for the exposure of ethnocentrism, counter-exposure is possible.

One wonders, however, if exposure of students' ethnocentrism would have as disturbing an impact on them as would the phenomenon of cultural relativity, especially when it represents also relativity in ethical standards. All of us would rather be absolutely right than relatively right. Even so, a patient and gentle elaboration of the element of choice, of simple human preference, which cannot be eliminated from the making of moral judgments in our world, could be undertaken with the likelihood of sober, and even quite satisfying understanding by senior students in the high school. It can certainly be pointed out that at any time and circumstance, we have to act upon what we *have* as if it were the best and that when we find something else better, *it* becomes the basis for perfection of a new and better order.[13]

13. See Edward Scribner Ames, *Beyond Theology* (Chicago: University of Chicago Press, 1959). Ames holds that even the best and wisest among us live by what he calls "practical absolutes." A British Episcopal clergyman writes in a convincing and charming way about the "relativities" of life: "They are the warm flesh which covers and makes fair the bare skeleton of basic

Another risk or danger is possible, even probable, in students' first becoming aware of human nature and culture as it actually is—a mixture of rational, irrational, and nonrational. But these matters can be approached with good sense, even with humor. If students would learn that a cowboy on our western plains has been known to walk three miles to saddle and mount his horse in order to ride less than a mile for a package of cigarettes, the departures of strange and alien people from what we would consider sensible might come home to students as belonging to the same species of behavior.

There is also the possibility of students becoming cynical, concluding that nothing is *really* true and good, or even that *nothing* really matters. We may hope that such a reaction might be dispelled by drawing upon the wisdom of Whitehead, who tells us that there are "two principles inherent in the very nature of things, recurring in some particular embodiment whatever field we explore—the spirit of change, and the spirit of conservation. There can be nothing real without both."[14]

One more danger comes to mind, the reaction known as that of the smart aleck, which may be a kind of cover for cynicism. Plato foresaw this as a consequence of students' first training in the critical spirit of philosophical discussion. But, no matter, it may appear as well in students' first confrontation with scientific analysis. Plato described the symptoms:

You must have seen how the young, when they get their first taste of it, treat argument as a form of sport solely for the purpose of

---

social necessities. The most lovable characteristics of any society, as of any man, are its accidental, non-essential ones, poor things perhaps, but its own. Where real life and love are concerned the *differentiae* always matter more than the definitions." J. V. Langmead Casserly, *Morals and Man in the Social Sciences* (New York: Longmans, Green & Co., 1951), p. 100.

14. Alfred North Whitehead, *Science in the Modern World* (New York: The Macmillan Co., 1925), p. 28.

contradiction. When someone has proved them wrong, they copy his method to confute others, delighting like puppies in tugging and tearing at anyone who comes near them. And so after a long course of proving others wrong and being proved wrong themselves, they rush to the conclusion that all they once believed in is false.[15]

The "cure" for such a reaction may have to wait upon the healing balm of more mature years.

Some final general comments may throw some light on the dangers that have been pointed out. Students' experience in anthropologizing their own culture is, *pari passu*, a threat to *the self*. The threat comes, as has been implied, by too-sudden and too-upsetting awareness of, and naked attention to, "external connections" of various kinds, of which they have hitherto been unconscious. What happens in this process is the shock of exchanging simple hypotheses and intuitive methods of understanding for methods of more rigorous analysis.

We conclude, then, that if comparative cultural studies are made from the perspectives and with the methods we have suggested, such enterprises ought to be undertaken at not too fast a pace and with care that their impact be not too strenuous.

Among the technical difficulties, pedagogical for the most part, the following come to mind.

There is the problem of the taxonomy or classification that "fits" a primitive culture in which we should not expect to find the same compartments of experience that characterize our culture. For instance, such concepts of ours as economics, religion, art, or politics have a large element of "cultural arbitrariness" in them and are not found with equivalent distinctiveness among less advanced cultures. Cultures are, as we observed, systems *sui generis*.

15. *The Republic*, VII, 539 A.

Even when students learn that their own culture will not "match" certain others, they may arrive at a more critical view of what were for them commonplaces. They may, for instance, discover that ethics and economics may be much more closely related than they had supposed.

The choice of cultures for study is a technical matter of not-too-great difficulty. If one wishes to pair cultures in terms of primitive-primitive, primitive-advanced, and advanced-advanced, then one may analyze the Indian tribes of our own continent, village life in the nation-state of India, the "hollow folk" of the Kentucky valleys and the hillbillies in our mid-southern states, as well as enclaves of such people in northern cities; the coffee culture in the central mountains of Puerto Rico and the cane culture on the coastal plane of the same island society; a village in Guatemala or in a Haitian valley; a country town in Iowa or Kansas in the middle nineteenth century and today; a sharecropper community, white or Negro, in the Cotton South; mountain tribes in Tibet or Iran; or feudal villages in east or west.

But if the choice were the pair "primitive-advanced," it might be possible, in microcosm, to bring students to realize the significance of the great historic transition from associations sentimental, intimate, and kinship-like in quality (the *Gemeinschaft*) to associations rational, impersonal, and legal in quality (the *Gesellschaft*). The drama of this transition is now being enacted in almost all the continent of Africa and symbolizes what is involved in the dominance of the *Gesellschaft* type of institutions over the *Gemeinschaft* type, or the "advanced" over the "primitive."

The problem of finding literary surrogates for field experience is, of course, insolvable in many communities, though schools such as the Verde Valley School, Sedona, Arizona, have pioneered in this respect. But with the growing body of monographs in cultural anthropology, much can be done to insure a quality of intimacy with the manners and morals of other peoples. An album of phonograph records entitled *The Ways of Mankind* is available by purchase or rental.[16]

Finally, under the heading of difficulties, there is the fact that anthropological studies are, in large part, about small, primitive, and isolated peoples. If they are the focus of study, there is no problem. If, however, the methods of anthropological study are to be applied to larger social units, the writings of such scholars as W. Lloyd Warner and the Lynds are available. In fact, the anthropological approach to the study of modern societies is becoming more and more the practice.

We noted earlier some of the insights and understandings that might be anticipated from such studies as have been suggested. To those, others might be added, and respecting all of them, the "long view" as suggested for today's education cannot solve today's moral and intellectual problems:

(a) Students may come to realize that perhaps the greatest troubles and some of the gravest problems we face as a nation have their origin in what is both admirable and dangerous—which is impatience to improve the lot of our fellow men at our pace and by use of their own criteria as to what they ought to do and be.

(b) Images may be formed of a more orderly world, but with the clear realization that no stable moral order is possible without informed and dedicated account being taken of the realities of economics and politics.

(c) The circle of youths' loyalties may be enlarged, not on

16. The entire album of ten recordings may be obtained from the Audio-Visual Center at Indiana University, Bloomington, Indiana. An excellent resource for teachers is Walter Goldschmidt, *Exploring the Ways of Mankind* (New York: Holt, Rinehart & Winston, Inc., 1960).

the basis of shallow sentimentalism for "lesser breeds without the law," but through critical insight into the social significance of the revolution in communication and transport that now makes the whole world one.

(d) Youth may abandon romantic conceptions of cultural pluralism but hold firmly to the *principle* of pluralism, to the end that they may learn to respect a decent diversity of social systems.

(e) Studies of underprivileged and backward peoples of the world may reveal the role that science and technology, applied at the roots of ignorance, disease, and poverty may play in the betterment of mankind, but not without the motivation that love and an image of the potential dignity of man provide.

(f) Youth may understand that the confusion in our world is due not so much to a Babel of Tongues as to a Babel of Symbols, which affirms the presence of frightening and divisive disagreements about the meaning of justice, freedom, individuality, and human worth.

(g) By reason of all the outcomes we have permitted ourselves to anticipate, there is one that includes and yet transcends them all. This is a profound understanding of the *epic of man,* a deep and lasting feeling for the great human adventure wherever and whenever experienced.

Thus we may devoutly hope that such studies as have been suggested may "frae monie a blunder free us /An' foolish notion."

7.

HORACE M. KALLEN

Higher Education

I.

AS THE EXPRESSION "higher education" figures in common English usage, its connotation signifies more than its denotation. The denotation is the concern of those who, in one capacity or another, earn their living at "higher education"—from admission officers, recruitment scouts, presidents, deans, and professors, to charwomen and campus police. Their jobs serve the day-to-day upkeep, repair, development, security, and financing of the manifold fields of a configuration of properties and persons—classrooms, libraries, laboratories, museums, observatories, chapels, armories, hospitals, athletic stadia, dormitories, campuses, other grounds and buildings, instruments and possessions, and, ultimately, students, for whom the institutions compete, and who compete for them. We call such collocations "colleges," "universities," "institutions of higher learning." Their beginnings, histories, and first intentions are as diverse as those of the men and women who live in, on, by, from, or for them. Their relations with one another are for the most part more competitive and emulative than co-operative, and such co-operation as they practice often turns on motives of economy and common defense. They vary in form and function from land to land and within each land. But all purport the same end in view: in the course of two or four or more years to develop students into "educated men" or technicians, or "scholars." All mark the formal completion of the process by degrees of diverse sorts, from B.A., M.A., and their variants, to Ph.D., D.Sc., and *their* variants.

The connotation of "higher education" relates to the prevailing climate of opinion in a society, relates to how it imagines, forms, and acknowledges its elect. Thus, to speak of any American as a "college man" is to endow him with superior status: to speak of him as a Harvard man or a Yale man or a Michigan man is to specify levels within the status, even though the distinctions could well be invidious and the Harvard man less "educated" than the Michigan man, even though the college degree need not signalize an achieved education at all.

The potent word of the phrase is "higher," not "education." And "higher" is a relational, not an absolute, qualification. Often the adjective stands for something scarce that everybody wants and strives for but only the more privileged, the richer, the stronger, the more influential and, by metaphor, the abler succeed in getting. *What* this something is may be of no particular relevance; to win and possess it is to achieve status, to gain prestige and distinction, to figure as one elected by fate or fortune to achieve a higher order than the unelect.

In other connections "higher" may stand for a status that cannot be achieved, a position in a stable hierarchy of rank and privilege to which one is born and which one holds regardless of achievement. Hereditary membership in "upper classes," signalized by deference that, say, titled people enjoy even in democratized societies, would exemplify this meaning of "higher";

so would the entail-like privileges of "upper classmen"—"upper" by chronology—vis-à-vis "freshmen."

In still other connections "higher" signifies the relations of wholes to their parts when the wholes are believed to be organic unities. Then the whole is somehow prior to, and above, its parts and determines their nature and function with respect to each other and with respect to itself—their unity, as distinguished from the diversities that it sets and holds in a single order of ratings or ranks. Such an order is a presumably inalterable hierarchy, with power and authority flowing from a central apex downward and outward in fixed patterns. This idea of whole-part relations replaces the pre-Darwinian notion of entelechy.

Of course, the same wholes may be understood not as organisms but as organizations. In organizations the parts do not derive from the whole nor are they at its command; the whole is a formation entered into by the parts. They are the creators, the causes, the controls. They embody the diverse and singular ends to which the whole they have shaped up is a common and collective means. The relations by which they constitute the whole are external and passing. Anyone who assumes them may discard them, and in every enterprise and institution, many continually do. Should very many do this, the whole would perish, while the parts would survive, to enter perhaps into new wholes. Because this does not very often happen among the families of man, because the individuals, whose lives sustain the wholeness of any human group, enter or leave it singly or in small companies, because, therefore, the whole seems to go on although the parts go out, organizations are taken for organisms, conceded organismal powers over their parts, and attributed an immortality denied to the individuals from whose life, and only from whose life, they live. First and last, nevertheless, the "higher" partner of the relationship is the part. Each, in the nature of things, is the end in itself to which the whole is the means. Among "institutions of higher learning," the confusion of organizational with organic relationships is an overflowing well of perplexities and predicaments.

Yet again, "higher" may signify a status not due to position in a hierarchy of power and privilege nor to relationships within an organizational or organic whole. "Higher" may signify a status established and maintained by a free decision that some person or place or event or thought or thing is precious and to be cherished and exalted "above" all others; that the others are to be rated and ranked in the degree they do or do not measure up to this now-paramount value. So tradition distinguishes a person's life as "higher" and "lower"; moralists distinguish codes of conduct in those terms. Ultimately, the matrix of all the meanings of "higher" is the quality of our awareness when, whatever the body's position, the head is bent backward, away from the trunk and the feet, and the look is "up"; the matrix of all the meanings of "lower" is the quality of our awareness when the head is bent forward, toward the trunk and the feet, and the look is "lowered," is "down." Quite likely, these are the common core of all meanings of "higher" and "lower"; they may indicate why the tendency prevails to treat their singularities as interchangeable and to use their differences indifferently.

Broadly taken, this has been the case with "higher education." Among English-speaking peoples, and among Western peoples generally, especially among those whose economy is postulated on industrial technologies and the literacy these require, "higher" purports an educational pyramid, the base of which is the kindergarten and the apex the graduate school, with elementary and secondary schools, colleges and universities in between. In free societies the apex tends to flatten and spread into an ever-broader plateau.

The tendency is most conspicuous in the United States, a wide-ranging organization where the interdependence of political equality, responsible citizenship, and equal opportunity with *ad hoc* education became early an article of the democratic faith, to be unceasingly implemented in programs of public education. A consequence is that Americans count today almost four million "credit students" in some two thousand individual "institutions of higher learning" public and private, together with their two thousand presidents and fifty thousand administrative officers (deans and counselors and health officers and athletic coaches included). The forecast for tomorrow is ongoing increase of the entire establishment in all its divergences of code, creed, structure, function, and government.

Traditionally, colleges and universities have been communities of teachers and pupils living together under a common rule and order of precedence constituting "gown," and variously in conflict with "town." Less traditionally, the teachers tend to be absorbed in "town," colleges to be communities of students mostly, permitted some self-government under the supervision and policing of college authorities and essential items in "town's" economy. Now, with the multiplication and expansion of academic establishments, fewer and fewer students live together as communities; "college life" becomes ever more a matter of classes, classrooms, academic ceremonials, and athletic spectacles; "gown" is dissipated in "town." Here and there scholars are selectively joined into communities of their own, whose intent and structure come closer than any other to John Henry Newman's "idea of a University": "an assemblage of learned men zealous for their own sciences and rivals of each other, brought by familiar intercourse and for the sake of intellectual peace to adjust together the claims of their respective subjects of investigation and to learn to respect, consult and aid each other."

The sequences of the expansion of original academic life into the community at large may be observed in synthetico-organic commu-nazi aggregations like the Soviet Union or China no less than in freer societies such as Great Britain, France, and the United States. Both the leaders of the latter and the rulers of the former have recognized that the ultimate weapon in the war for survival that they wage with each other is education; they are aware that victory will come to the combatant whose generations have mastered the most reliable arts of survival at war, whether hot or cold, and, even more, in peace.

For them "higher education" has analogous meanings and roles. They diverge radically from the roles and meanings attributed by Socrates, articulated and implemented by Plato, revised but not altered by Aristotle, codified by schoolmen, displaced by the men of the Renaissance such as Castiglione and Erasmus, by the men of the Reformation such as Luther and Calvin, and since the age of Rousseau, Condorcet, Franklin, and Jefferson, pushed, at a slowly quickening tempo, by the mechanic arts and sciences from the center to the peripheries of the educational enterprise. The meanings still diverge radically from the "higher education" of the Jews' Talmudical academies, the Moslem *al Azhar*, the Buddhist monasteries of Tibet or Burma or India or Japan, or the Christian ones in Israel and the Western lands. All look "up" and move "up." But the "up" of the one is the deprecated "down" of the other, and the way up to a *vita contemplativa* is at the same time a way down from a *vita activa*, and vice versa. The levels of living truth of the former are judged levels of suicidal error by the latter, and vice versa. As the former are postulated on one creed or another, asserting that mankind continue to live when they are dead, their aficionados insist that the suicidal error is their opponents'. So far as the historic record verifies either claim, it provides no direct witness from the living dead but does testify to the perduring assertion of the living that the dead do live, and thus discloses a quality of the living's own struggle to live on, to outlive all foes and rivals that might prevent them.

This, reduced to its simplest and nakedest terms, is what all education is for and about, from kindergarten through graduate school. This is what all the hullabaloo regarding the *what* and *how* of education is about. With respect to this it is that the distinctions between "liberal," or "general," and "professional" get established and the issues of the religious and the secular, the sciences and the humanities, vocation and culture, get labored. Each of these terms signifies an assembly of diverse concerns, set over against each other in a rivalry for the minds of the generations to come. One need only to look at any person's or people's history to grasp that what it records is a congeries of struggles of Selves for survival, struggles with one another of both individual Selves and of the group Selves whose identities are organizational Wholes compounded by interindividual relations—struggles of families, communities, nations, churches, states, alliances, joined together in all sorts of interpersonal and intergroup configurations of conflict and concord, each striving to preserve itself.

Ask of any victor in the struggle what is the Self that is being preserved, that bias that outlives its rivals and foes; ask what his survival is and you learn that it is still a striving, still struggle, but against still other opponents. Everybody's struggle for survival is a struggle to go on struggling. Should any stop struggling, he stops going on; his identity as this-person-and-no-other contracts, lapses, and he dies. His education, finally and particularly his "higher education," purports to invest him with the faith, and the vision, and the knowledge wherewith he can achieve this identity more bravely and more abundantly than ever before. (It purports to disclose to him how to make his living and how to live, and live on, as this identity.) Its revealers and mentors are the men and women who teach and inquire, their books, and other tools of teaching and inquiry. They are the vital organs of an educational establishment, and the proper role of its administrative hierarchy, from boards, trustees, and presidents down and out to maids and garbage collectors, is so to manage the housekeeping of their institution that the teaching and inquiry will maintain an optimal range and tempo. For as housekeeping is to home life, administration should be to academic life. Should be, but isn't. All too often the means changes places with the end, and the educational enterprise is made an instrument of administrative expansion, in apt conformation to Parkinson's law.

The inversion is intrinsic to educational enterprises of servile states such as the Soviet Union and its dependents, since among those the power structure is such that teaching and inquiry must conform to prescribed doctrine and are subjected to an authoritarian discipline. But the inversion is noticeable in every establishment with an educational function under authoritarian auspices.

In the perspectives of this view of "higher education" I now ask: What would "an understanding of mankind" contribute to the equipment for survival of A.B.'s, M.A.'s, Ph.D.'s, and the rest, whether in free societies or servile states? But first, indeed, what happens to a person when he understands anything? How does he "understand"?

II.

The questions are hardy perennials, and the history of culture records a number of standard answers. First philosophers, then psychologists purporting to be scientists without philosophical preconceptions, produced answers. Some, like Plato and Aristotle and their secular and sacerdotal epigons, like Immanuel Kant and his, have endeavored to signify "understanding" within a conspectus that included such terms as "reason," "intellect," "intelligence," and their ilk. Some, like John Locke and Baruch Spinoza, have held understanding important enough to use the word in titles of books of theirs. After Darwin and the recognition that human existence is an ongoing struggle for survival in an interplay of spontaneous variations and natural selections resulting in "the survival of the fittest," writers, among whom Herbert Spencer was the first, set understanding within a conspectus of this struggle, assigning it a prime role and a paramount survival value, hence a value derivative and secondary, grounded in the sequential process of the struggle for survival. This came to be called evolution. And with the idea of evolution science restored to faith—but faith as a humanized animal disposition—the primacy it had attained in the religious.

Religionists, like Martin Luther and Ignatius Loyola, have built understanding on belief. Both were insecure and anxious about the kind of life they would live when they were dead, and both sought to make sure it would be a good life—each according to his kind. "*Glaubst du, so hast du, glaubst du nit, so hast du nit,*" said Luther. Loyola devised a system of "spiritual exercises" and ordained a discipline of faith that would render ineluctable for the true believer who had taken the vows of his Society of Jesus "to praise all the precepts of the Church, holding the mind ready to find reasons for her defense and nowise in her offense"; would render inevitable for the believer "to make sure of being right in all things" by cleaving to "the principle that the white I see I should believe to be black if the hierarchical church were to rule it so." The submission and obedience of the believer to his superiors, especially to the Pope, were to be absolute. He was to become "like a corpse which can be turned this way and that, or a rod that follows every impulse, or a ball of wax that might be molded in any form." By virtue of this utter self-surrender, he would become a commando of his Church, conquer the world for it, and so save his own soul. Seeking reasons for the defense and nowise in offense of the Church led to a new use of logic—to a mode of reasoning and style of argumentation lumped under the term "casuistry." As a formation of understanding, it aroused the ire of Blaise Pascal, who exposed its principles and practices to shame and laughter. But Pascal was also eager to make sure about where and how he would live when he was dead, and he devised the oft-cited Pascal's wager, which is not without a near relationship to Jesuit probabilism. An English Franciscan had, some centuries before, imported a similar way of betting without taking any risks. The friar was called Alexander Neckam. He told how a doubter at the Sorbonne was won to the faith. "If you believe in the resurrection and it is true," the believer advised the doubter, "you will be rewarded for your faith. If you believe in the resurrection and it is not true, it does you no harm. If you do not believe in the resurrection and it is true, you will be punished for your heresy. Therefore, since you run a certain risk in not believing, and no risk in believing, why not believe." Neckam says the doubter was convinced and lived and died in the true faith of the Church.

The role here of the article of faith and of the code that

it underlies is to liberate the believer's hopes and to dissipate his anxieties and fears. He bets his life on it and trusts it unto death, although it has no free, independent, confirming evidence and must create for itself a confirmation that ceases to confirm if the believer turns infidel. *Credo ut intellegam!* St. Anselm said it: "For I do not seek to understand that I may believe, but I believe in order to understand. For this also I believe that unless I believed, I should not understand." Understanding follows from believing, as against the believing or conviction that follows from understanding.

By and large, this holds with even the most empirical and perceptive writers. They compose discourses in which conclusion follows from premise duly and in good order, each a neat, clean configuration of abstractions, a clear and distinct structure, a work of logical art, but with no indication of what started the work, nor how the artist himself, or another living person struggling to live on, came to experience that moment of belief and conviction that "understanding" signifies. Perhaps understanding as experience is ineffable, and philosophers and psychologists can only talk *about* it, not being able to bring acquaintance with it. They can point to its occasions; they can even recall and record sequences that understanding may be said to consummate.

But they do not uncover to perception that which takes place in the experience of a living person when he "understands" amid his struggles to keep on living in a circumambience of diverse and diversifying persons and events, thoughts and things, similarly engaged. There, understanding is one happening in a stream of others that compound into a person's existence from birth to death. Of this indefinite and not-to-be-measured total, his own autobiography or another's biography of him can select, encompass, and impattern but a portion, at most an inconsiderable portion, and project the result as his singularity and character. The result must needs be an abstraction, as his understanding of "understanding" is an abstraction, from the event "understanding," and from its eventuation.

All our lives we experience happenings we do not "understand." Each, simple or complex, confronts us with a singularity somehow strange, new, unattached, obstructing or barring the works and ways of which our Selves-preserving-ourselves consist. We encounter it as a challenge to one or another of these activities. Before it we stop, rendered for the moment alone, upset, and lonely; perplexed and anxious; shaken with insecurity. We feel we must either flee the challenge or face and destroy it, or else overcome and harness it up to the service of the works and ways it bars and threatens to cut off. To harness it up is to deprive it of its singularity, its freedom and independence, to transvalue it into an effect by assigning it to a cause from which it must needs follow, and to a place in a sequence whence it cannot escape.

Even the freest, most independent being we can imagine gets thus harnessed up. The common word for such an absolute is God, and the tradition defines God as *causa sui,* the effect that is its own cause, the cause that is its own effect, a One that is beyond understanding, a sole, singular, unique, free, and independent One that, even when qualified as first cause, is also qualified as first effect, *causa sui,* and, in being so qualified, "understood." Without some such harnessing, God becomes indistinguishable from pure chance, from the spontaneity, the anarchy, the wildness, the tohubohu of existence. To imagine God as an activity of determination, if only of Self-determination without alteration, is to harness God up, to tame the aboriginal wildness and anarchic spontaneity of existence, to turn it into "reason" and thus bring it to order and use. So to harness is to understand.

Where we thus understand anything, we have removed its autonomy and freedom from it, demoted it from the miracle absolute that challenges and threatens to rupture the closed circlings of doings and feelings we struggle to preserve, to a superstructure supported by a foundation. When we so understand anything, we have fitted it together with other objects and reduced it from a unique whole to one of a variety of parts in a larger whole. What we have done—say discovered, or produced, or created—we may later appraise as a mistake, an error, or an illusion; it may in its turn upset us, bring on puzzlement, insecurity, anxiety, challenging survival. But for the nonce, we have "understood," and the event is suffused by feelings of relief and gladness, of living on without the strains and strivings, the searchings and seekings, the tryings on and fittings and refittings, which "understanding" has finished off. We enjoy the serendipity of having gotten ourselves free from all that; of having gained for ourselves, vis-à-vis the understood object, the freedom and independence that understanding it has deprived it of. For the nonce, we live on, think on, with untrammeled fluency. As experience, understanding is a mood specific to a person and the situation he has understood. Its formation is a happening as singular as a thumbprint, and no matter how much we work at understanding, it is ultimately as little amenable to generalization. The feel of it may come suddenly, or may mount into a sentiment that consummates our overcoming of challenges and razing of barricades. William James called it "the Sentiment of Rationality": "This feeling of the sufficiency of the present moment—of its absoluteness—this absence of all need to explain it, to account for it, to justify it, I call the Sentiment of Rationality." It arises in us whenever we succeed in envisioning aggregations of diverse and diversifying existences —each struggling among the others for its own survival—as configurations ordering them into relations with one another which render them parts of a new whole; an ordering that makes the relations simpler, easier, and more rewarding than those that turned on segregate identities of singulars struggling to maintain themselves and survive.

Our modes of knowing and learning alike the philosophic, the scientific, the nonscientific, and the antiscientific—all our quests for "laws" of nature, of God, of God's nature, or of nature's God—are strivings after "understanding" as this experience. They are ever-diverging treks from moments of insufficiency to moments of sufficiency that, in their turn, lapse into insufficiency. Thus the content of an experience that at one time we find so adequate, so complete and perfect in and by and for itself, that it calls for no ground, no goal, no support, and no justification renders the experience sufficient in itself, and yet an insight, an understanding, rational intrinsically, may at another time reflect the experience as the uttermost of irrationalities. The configuration of a sentiment of rationality may be excommunicated from rationality and outlawed from understanding by every idea of reason and understanding that tradition preserves. Yet the absurd and outlawed which thus passeth understanding may be that whence flows the understanding of everything else, including understanding. Nothing could defy the rules of reason and the laws of logic more absolutely than Tertullian's *Credo quia absurdum est, certum est quia impossibile est.* The certainty and absurdity he believes in is a miraculous event, an utter singularity of grace and liberty that challenges all order and disrupts the cosmos. It is that which Neckham's student and Blaise Pascal bet their lives on, which Luther, Loyola, and their congeneric successors committed themselves to. The bets, the commitments, are acts of faith, hazards of Kierkegaard's "leap," of William James' "will to believe." For the nonce, these acts of faith consummate in victory an arduous struggle against an age's formation of rules and laws that render absurd and null the ongoing survival that the believers struggle for, which deny them immortality, form barricades to their living on when they are dead. Vindications of survival in the struggle to go on struggling, the absurd and null become sufficient for the present moment and are thereupon employed by each anxious and despairing believer to ground and to arrange duly in his own good order—employed, that is, to fit together as parts of a historical and dramatic whole —the entire sequential aggregation of the course of human events, and so bring their own absurd singularities to rational understanding.

Reason is here the conformation of irrationalities to one another; it is the moment of peace in the universal Hobbesian war of all against all. Understanding is the perception of the moment of peace, whether it comes in the formation of the cosmos, achieved freely by the ongoing reciprocal adjustments to one another of absurd, no-longer-analyzable bits of original and originating nature that give rise to the scientists' "laws of nature"; or whether it comes as conformation to the overruling absurdity of man's impulsion toward survival and the strugglings that express it. Let the understanding be Tertullian's or Spinoza's, Kant's or Spencer's or Auguste Comte's, Anselm's, Ignatius Loyola's or Martin Buber's, Karl Marx's or Søren Kierkegaard's or Albert Einstein's. Each is the formation of a sentiment of rationality whose impatterning nucleus is an act of faith, a belief, on which ultimately the believer, if he be a true believer, bets his life. Was not Bacon's *Advancement of Learning* placed on the Roman Index and banned by the Roman Inquisition for undermining the one true Faith, because it threw doubt on the autogenic evidence that "supports" and "confirms" it?

III.

Our query now becomes: Can whatever "mankind" signifies as fact, idea, ideal, or direct experience be rendered the object of a belief on which a graduate of an institution of higher learning will then have learned to bet his life? Can a college or university teach him such a commitment to "mankind"?

One signification of mankind the learner does not need to be taught. This one he brings to school with him and he needs, if anything, to unlearn it. This meaning is the face-to-face relations with the other persons among whom the learner has lived and grown. First, and most intimately, his family, his *kin*. Then, in ever-extending and emptier range, his schoolmates, his playmates, his workmates, his classmates, and so on. Together they form his *kind*. They are whom he addresses as "folks." He and they speak much the same language, avow the same creed, and judge each other according to the same codes of eating and drinking, playing and working, loving and fighting, and communing with their divinities. They are like-minded and alike. They are *the* people; they *are* mankind, and the test and measure of all who, similar otherwise, claim to be of the same kind. If the latter fail the tests, if they are unlike in these respects, they are not mankind—at least, not quite mankind. However like oneself they may be in bodily form and bodily function, their unlikeness in style of life and expression shuts them out as kin and kind. Their females may satisfy lust but cannot become wives; their males may serve in other ways but cannot become comrades or peers. Because of that unlikeness they fall short; they are other than human, or if human, they are an inferior breed of humans—Yahoo human; they are barbarians, they are gentiles, they are pagans, they are infidels, they are foreign devils, they are non-Aryans, they are *hoi polloi,* they are the masses, they are bourgeois, they are coloreds, and so on, to no end. Among college students, Greek-letter fraternities and clubs continue the invidious exclusions.

On the record, even the most submissive and acquiescent of the different concede such reduction to animal bodies only to superior animal force. They endure it, but do not accept it, and they sabotage, evade, and frustrate it in every way they can, often by laughing at it among themselves, turning it into caricature and farce. Among their own kin and kind, they are sure that, as they are, with all their unlikenesses on their heads, they are as good as their betters and better, and they design a future when they shall become the stronger and be freed to manifest their own exclusive humanity. Such designs serve as utopian visions that compensate the actual plight; they render it more endurable, but hardly alter it. Sometimes the designs become creeds and codes that are enacted, programs of revolt and reconstruction, strategies and tactics and logistics of the believers' struggle, against preponderant power, to live on as themselves mankind in peace, in freedom, and in abundance.

In the degree that such struggles are successful and the victories bring the unlike to equality with the kind that penalized them for their unlikeness, the meaning of "mankind" as direct experience changes. It can no longer denote one and only one kinship with one and only one style of life. It is recognized, however grudgingly, that there are now many, each different from the others and struggling among them to live on in its own way by its own works.[1] But the relations between the different can-

1. Spinoza said it for his own embattled time in his Theologico-Political Treatise, the sixth chapter: "The power of Nature is the power of God, which has a

not be, if they ever were, face-to-face relations. They must be signified by images and conceptions, instead of perceptions, and be carried by signs and symbols, which apply indifferently to the different. Such an application effects a symbolic identification of the different, although not any actual identification. It creates an idea of mankind, an envisionment of the unlike as like, a transvaluation of the many into one. Its survival value is to shift the relations between the different from the mutually destructive rivalries of war toward the friendly and creative rivalries of peace.

Where the shifting is consequential—as the formation of communities, cities, city-states, peoples, nations, and other interpersonal and intergroup societies witnesses—the relation of the unifying concept to the experiences it gathers and abstracts from becomes inverted. Actually an effect, it is transposed into a cause; the *idea* mankind is endowed with transcendent existence and power. It is hypostatized into the single underlying archetype of which the manifold mankinds that are men's experiences are divergent and imperfect expressions. In due course this cause as peoples' *terminus a quo* is assumed into their *terminus ad quem:* the divergent many are destined to converge back into the oneness from which they have lapsed. This assumption of the idea of mankind exalts it into an *ideal;* it devalues the actually

---

sovereign right over all things; and inasmuch as the power of nature is simply the aggregate of the powers of all her individual components, it follows that every individual has a sovereign right to do all he can; in other words, the rights of the individual extend to the utmost limits of his power as it has been conditioned. Now it is the sovereign law and right of nature that each individual shall endeavor to preserve itself as it is, without regard to anything but itself; therefore the sovereign law and right belongs to every individual. . . . Whatsoever an individual does by the laws of its own nature it has a sovereign right to do, inasmuch as it acts as it was conditioned by nature and cannot act otherwise."

diverse and diversifying multiplicity of mankind into "appearance," it transvalues the imaginary oneness of the many by origin and by goal into "reality."

On the record the transvaluation contradicts all that the diverse families of mankind have learned in their struggle for survival, and all that their plight here and now communicates. The idea of mankind's unity signifies no fact; it only projects an ideal. As ideal, it is an expression of faith, "an evidence of things hoped-for, a substance of things not seen"; it serves the peoples of the world as consolation and compensation for their actual plight, but does not change it; or else the ideal serves as a design and road map, a plan of unification whereby the many may make themselves or be made one, articulating the knowledge and know-how that can translate faith into fact.

For facts are not the beginning of knowledge and know-how; they are the conclusions. Their beginnings are impressions, imaginings, experiences, ideas, commingled, from which a person chooses one to assert, to bet on, and to try out for future consequences. His selection is by no means a sure thing; to become that it must be tested, verified, confirmed, and agreed to by others. Always the question is asked: What are the facts? Literally, fact is the completion of act; it is the consummation of a process of production agreed upon by the questioners. In litigation fact is the issue: lawyers stipulate, examine, cross-examine; each makes a claim on which he bets; finally judge or jury brings in a verdict—literally, a "truesaying"—that such and such is the "fact." But the verdict may be challenged by appeals until one is given that cannot be appealed. In scientific inquiry, alternatives of belief are taken for working hypotheses; experiments are set up to enable them to work out freely and independently, to achieve verification and confirmation by their consequences.

Without them, they are faith, not fact. With them they are fact incarnating faith, and still requiring reconfirmation and revalidation.

So the idea of the unity of mankind is an expression of faith, not a consummation of fact. True, physiologists, anatomists, anthropologists, and the other students of man call attention to repetitions and resemblances that they identify with one another, as is the unifying wont of scientists. But insofar as this identity of the different is validated, it is rather their animal than their human identity. If the different families of mankind do indifferently participate in a common nature, it is their animal, not their human, nature. In practice, if sometimes not in theory, males and females, of any human group anywhere, mate and produce offspring at longer intervals than most other animals, and usually one at a birth, not litters. Their generations go through analogous cycles of bodily change, from conception, through infancy, maturation, and senescence, to death. But animal sequences are much shorter, animal lives are briefer, and they come to adulthood much sooner. Human infancy remains helpless and dependent while animals have already gotten families in their turn. Without prolonged care by, at least, the mother, the human infant would perish. They learn from caring, and in due course, on their own, from experience. Their capacity to learn, so much more extensive than that of other animals, is their equivalent for the organs of defense and offense—claws and fangs, horns and hoofs, carapaces, poison glands, and quills that animals are equipped with and employ by "instinct." Their superior animal advantages are also their limitations; they can learn a few tricks, but are not capable of producing the enormous changes in themselves and in the world around that the human animal produces. Those grow and accumulate because each generation learns from the older one and changes what it has learned by adding to it.

Some add little. As nearly as the nature of life allows, their future repeats their past. Others diversify as they live on; their future changes their past, which it keeps presently joining. Others may lose their past through disease or accident, or may be robbed of it by the sadism of other men, like Jews in Nazi concentration camps who were so maltreated that they forgot all that they had learned, and their individualities contracted to animal cravings and functions. They were dehumanized and their survival became sheer animal survival. By and large, body for body, sense organ for sense organ, the natural primitive and the Hitler-made primitive could be identified, but identified in their common animal nature, not their common humanity.

At birth, no man-child is human. It is humanized as it grows up and grows older. It learns humanity. Its humanization is postulated on its animal nature, but is at once a modification of that and a divergence from it. Although its survival as man depends on its survival as animal, the two are not the same. Survival can consist in the ongoing exercise of the animal functions, the body preserving itself without the body's mind—without the doings, sufferings, believings, and knowings wherein it becomes a Self aware of itself. Not for their animal nature do people attack and destroy each other. The warfare is upon their human nature, upon an identity that such words, say, as American, Russian, Englishman, Chinese, Frenchman, Hindu, African, signify: an identity established in a singular configuration of creeds and codes impatterning thoughts and things and works and ways that repeat, yet alter as they repeat, in the struggle of that pattern to preserve its differential identity against the others.

One name for such configuration is culture. Another is mind, or spirit. However else theologians and philosophers may signify an individual's mind or spirit, it is commonly identified in terms of *what* he minds and *how* he minds it. And we identify a group mind or people's spirit similarly. Each is a field of interest and activity, a region of the person's circumambience, with all the parts of which he has made himself so intimate that he moves among them, cultivates, uses them, freely, easily, with assured mastery. Because of this way of minding what he minds, we speak of his "having" a mathematical mind or a musical mind or a legal mind, or a political or a literary mind or an international mind. Or we speak of his being "typically English" or "so French," or "true Catholic" or "fanatical Communist," and so on. Of course, every person achieves, as he grows up and grows older, many minds. Some fields he enters and leaves, or they fall away from his concern. His interest in others perdures. But it manifests an order of preference and commitment, with one or two dominant, the subjects of his ruling passion, the rest making an ordered recessional.

Conflict of interest, conflict of mind, is intrinsic to every person's plight, a quality of our "human nature." Personality and character, mood and style of life, become, then, consequences of the manner and degree in which an orchestration of one's many minds is achieved. In terms of personal history, they are designs for living. Each of us forms, aware or unaware, an ideal of self-hood—an image of the identity we want to be and crave to believe that we "really" are, and which we strive to disclose by means of such an orchestration. We either gain comfort and a precarious redress of our own imbalance from the image but no more, or we commit ourselves to it as our life plan, the human identity for whose survival-in-struggle we struggle. This identity seems related to our bodies as a flame to its candle. The flame is the candle burning up. It can be put out, and the candle kept for another burning. But if the candle is consumed, the flame is no more. So our identities come to flame up and burn out. Each is, they say, a formation of changes that start with conception.

Each is then a quantum of energy compacted in our genes like solid fuel in a rocket and spending itself in waves of change. Eating and drinking refuel what they may, but never enough. As the years pass, our forces diminish, our tempo slows, until at last the wick chars and the candle of our existence has burned itself down to the deliquescing bodily residue we call death.

What we knowingly survive as, so long as we survive, is a singularity of remembrance, is the congeries of events succeeding and commingling as a past growing—growing because the future joins it, from conception to death. Inward to the succession is the ongoing resistance to the process of spending, the craving to spend without diminution, to keep growing up without growing old, never to die. So the families of mankind everywhere live on in the belief that not the Self, only the body, comes to death; that the Self continues alive when the body no longer has a future. Our mortal part is our animal part; our human part is deathless. This faith is the substance and evidence of immortality. It is an idea hypostatized into an ordeal, a survival value with which the families of mankind, each according to its own kind, compensate themselves for death and assure themselves of everlasting victory in their struggles for survival.

The patterns of this assurance cannot be attributed to our animal heredity. The import of that heredity is death, not deathlessness. Animals have no idea of deathlessness or death. Deathlessness is a creation of our cultural heritage, a traditional aspiration of communities of men living out their personal lives together in minding the world around them, fitting their environment to themselves by altering its forms and creating from materials that outlast their creators new ones that shall still their fears and gratify their hopes. We call the creative *know-how* arts, crafts, skills, technics. Together with the faiths they work out (we call those sciences) and the tools and weapons and foods and garments, the shelters for people and the shrines for gods, together with the common remembrances of their works and faith that chronicles and tales and songs and prayers and dances and drawings embody, they make up each community's characteristic cultural heritage. Animal heredity cannot account for their diversities. No man can change his own. Its substance is the sequential energy of the genes that start him off. Such starts both initiate and maintain the breed, generation after different generation, and none of them can ask to be born or choose the genes of his own happening. Between animal heredity and cultural heritage the gap is wider and deeper than between Mendel's "laws" and chemical properties of living matter; different complexities of organization are like biological mutants, and while the more elaborate implies the simpler, the reverse is not the case, except developmentally as an evolution of organism from organization by way of spontaneous variations. To define a community of culture anywhere in the world in terms of its animal heredity is not to define it as it is humanly constituted. That, however largely repetitive it be, is a reworking of its cultural heritage. Ideas of "race," of "class," are such reworkings, Hitler's and Stalin's elaborations being but a current phase of an ongoing series. The commu-nazi transvaluations of persons and their relations do not conceive the human being as a biological existence; they conceive him as a cultural value to be conserved or destroyed. His humanity is his culture and so lives on.

That it shall live on does depend, as has been remarked, on this certain animal capacity that the nonhuman animal largely lacks—the capacity to learn—the capacity to acquire characteristics no animal, human or not, is born with. The institution of education, with its hierarchy of schoolings, is everywhere postulated on this capacity and is variously designed to actualize, to channel, and to consummate it. The idea of mankind being the orchestration of peoples that it is, can it be learned in each culture so that it will suffuse the minds of every culture, including the totalitarian? Can youth learn it, can age teach it, whatever "culture" may mean to learners and teachers? There are the meanings that, ever since Tylor, students of human societies have given it. There are the meanings that, ever since Matthew Arnold, writers and talkers and cultivators of the "humanities" and the liberal arts continue to give it, heedless of the fact that the former is groundless without the latter. They take the latter for an independent variable, and distinguish within it two more, which they segregate from one another. The first they signalize as "high culture," all excellence; the second as "mass culture," all philistinism, mediocrity, and vulgarity. "Higher education," they urge, must needs impart the former, shut out the latter. Can it do so, and teach "the idea of mankind" as well?

IV.

The notion of a "high culture" that it is the role of "higher education" to transmit, duly and in good order, is a mutation of the invidious Greek notion of *Paideia,* and of the image of the free man that it cultivated. This image is postulated on slavery and war as intrinsic to the human enterprise. So Aristotle declared (*Politics,* 1256): "War is strictly a means of acquisition, to be employed against wild animals and inferior races of men who though intended by Nature to be in subjection to us, are unwilling to submit; for war of such kind is just by nature." Hence, the free man is basically the fighting man, thence the master who passes judgment, serves the gods, strives to discern and contemplate the eternal and design the state accordingly. This image of the free man had been Plato's before it was Aristotle's. For both, it was an idealization of an actual ruling class, an elite minority, set over against a majority of farmers, traders, artisans, manual laborers, and slaves excluded from the responsibilities and privileges of citizenship.[2] The culture of the rulers had to be intrinsically of another dimension than the culture of the ruled. The latter worked without living; theirs was a producer culture and their arts were servile arts. The former lived without working; theirs was a consumer culture. They were free men in virtue of it. Their energies were neither tamed nor harnessed to the exigencies of animal survival. Their arts were "liberal arts," an exercise and perfection of their powers by conquering "inferiors" and harnessing them up to their superior uses. They were "the end"; the rest were the means. The "gentlemen of leisure" of later ages were still an elite who could live without working but no longer exercised their liberty on the crafts of warring and ruling: they engaged instead in the enjoyment of the "liberal arts."

Almost one hundred years ago, in Victorian England, an inspector of schools, a poet, critic, and admirer of the Greek *Paideia* for its "spontaneity of consciousness" and its "disinterested play of consciousness," published a book entitled *Culture and Anarchy*. Its author condemned "the gentlemen of leisure" of his own age and country as barbarians, their merchants, manufacturers, and moneymen as "philistines" (he borrowed the

2. "The citizen, the good man and statesman," Aristotle declares, "ought not to learn the crafts of inferiors except for their own occasional use, else there will cease to be the distinction between master and slave." (*Politics*, III, 4). "In good states no citizen should be a farmer or mechanic. For civic virtue requires leisure." (VII, 9) ". . . leisure is the first principle of all action. It is better than occupation in the end." (VII, 4) Hence "no husbandmen or mechanics are to be priests, for God should receive honor from citizens only." (VII, 9) "Paid employments are vulgar. They absorb and degrade the mind. Some liberal arts are quite proper for a free man to acquire, not to follow them too closely to attain perfection in them. . . . Learning for its own sake, or of friends, or with a view to excellence, is not illiberal. But if it is done for the sake of others, the same action is menial and servile." (VIII, 2)

term from Heine), and the great majority as "populace." He was deeply concerned about the education of his fellow countrymen, but did not know how to project his concern as an issue of pub- lic policy. Paradoxically, his concern was entirely un-Greek. He wanted for all the people what the projectors of *Paideia* wanted for a few. "Culture," Matthew Arnold wrote, in *Culture and Anarchy:*

. . . is for all the people; beauty and intelligence viable to everybody. But it must be real thought and real beauty, real sweetness and real light. Plenty of people will try to give the masses intellectual food fit for the mass mentality, plenty of people will try to indoctrinate the masses with ideas that constitute their own creed. But this is not the working of culture. For culture does not try to win the masses to this or that sect. Rather it seeks to do away with classes; to make the best that has been taught and known in the world current everywhere. The great men of culture, the true apostles of humanity are those who are able to diffuse the best knowledge, the best ideas of their time, who humanize knowledge by broadening the basis of life and intelligence outside the clique of the cultivated and the learned into the market-place.

Culture and Anarchy was "literature" in Arnold's sense. It was a criticism of the life of its time. Its author attributed to that ways of living and thinking that he felt were competing and competing successfully against the ideal ways he postulated for himself and his people. It seems never to have occurred to him that he was as sectarian as those he condemned; that his "best" and "real" could be their "unreal" and "worst"; that, in terms of actual mankind, "real" and "best" denoted the manifold and antagonistic values of the global miscellany; and that knowl- edge therefore gets humanized and the basis of life and intelli- gence broadened when each recognizes the indefeasible plurality as the human condition and endeavors to orchestrate their diversity into a world-wide sporting and peaceful competition in the market place of values.

Sectarianism is universal and endemic, however. It increases and multiplies. The epigons of our "critic of life," each a missioner of his own "bests," have only bettered his example. In the almost century since Arnold preached his gospel, his "barbarians" have receded below the horizon—perhaps they have been absorbed into the "bourgeois" who replace the "philistines"; his "populace" have been rechristened "the masses" and described as unable to take in the real culture of "the best that has been known and taught" that Arnold declared is for all the people. Western literatures with a vocation for criticizing life ascribe to them a "homogenized culture" peculiar to their kind—"mass culture"—deplore it, denounce it, and would keep it segregated from the "high culture" of their own exalted preferences. Iron-curtain literatures are organized in cartel-like academies and syndicates. Much of what is "high culture" for the Western ones is for these "academicians" corrupt, decadent, "bourgeois"—to be penalized whenever its kind happens among them. Their own "high culture" is designated "socialist realism," is conformed to their Communist creed and code, and guarded from wandering off the strait right path by party policing and censorship.

In the West, where men are free to change their minds, taste is mobile, interest follows curiosity, "mass culture" is less a matter of *who* and *what* than of *how.* "Mass culture" is a matter of mass production, and mass production is essentially *re*production. It is a consequence of the invention and perfection of media of communication that enable an unceasing repetition of identicals. Once an idea or an image has been uttered by a scientist, a painter, a poet, a sculptor, a musician, a dancer, a philosopher, or a politician, the printing presses, the recording discs, the cameras, the motion pictures, television, radio can repeat it "live" as it occurs, and again repeat it endlessly in any place, at almost any future time.

The media of communication have thus rendered the economy of ideas an economy of abundance—abundant not alone as the repetition of identicals, but abundant also as the multiplication of diversities for repetition. The historic letters, arts, and crafts of "high culture" are now part and parcel of "mass culture" and, as never before, objects of enjoyment, study, and appraisal by multitudes. Arnold would agree that there has been improvement.

The critics, however, challenge the consequences of this cultural economy. They focus their attack on television as the most widely used of the mass media. They point out that these absorb more young people than old—high school and college youth notably. This puts them square in the middle of problems of "higher education" and gives them a critical relevancy to the idea of mankind.

Some platonizers would like to see this new cultural abundance paid for and controlled by the state; certain Americans would like television to be tax-supported at least as the public schools are tax-supported, and regulated for matter and medium as a school curriculum is regulated. Others would have at most a central distributing, if not a central production, agency—a distributing agency like a department store, offering an endless variety of entertainment and instruction for the consumer to choose from and pay for. This, they urge, would be an improvement on the economy prevailing in the United States, where the consumer does have choices, but only very limited choices; where he does pay for what he gets, but believes he is getting it for nothing. In this economy—and the comment applies as well to slick paper periodicals and the newspapers—instruction and entertainment are bought and paid for mostly by manufacturers of cosmetics, drugs, foods for men and beasts, motorcars and their accessories, and the like. These "sponsors" use the articles of "high culture," when they do, as means to sell their goods with a profit. The larger the number of buyers, the greater the profit; the larger the number of viewers and listeners, the larger the number of buyers. So, first and last, the consumer pays.

To make sure of numbers, the sponsors employ professional calculators who assign "ratings" to the shows they sponsor, and the ratings reappear in their sales records. Seeking the highest possible rating leads to skulduggery that becomes scandalous; it reduces the matter sponsored to a stereotype directed upon the interest of the greatest possible number of viewers; thus it rules out the truly new, the truly important, the honestly controversial. The sponsor won't bet his money on engaging the viewer's mind; he will bet only on diverting and bewitching it.

So, this form of mass culture is related to the masses like scratching to an itch. The more you scratch, the more it itches. For in free societies the masses are no longer the laboring classes of the servile states. They are aggregations of free men, whose lives are consumed in working and in restoring the energies expended in working. More and more their personal histories are qualified by leisure, less and less by labor. Western mankind is in the process of the third of its industrial revolutions—its electronic revolution. Now production becomes a mechanical operation culminating in a product untouched by the human hand, and thinking becomes a mechanical operation untouched by the human mind. Workmen are taking on the role that Deists assign to their God: they set the machine in motion with a word or a flick of the hand. They scan a dial; they push a button; the automatic mechanism does the rest, and does it more precisely, more speedily, more surely and abundantly, than any merely human mind—or any merely divine one made in the image of the human—ever could. Automation takes their employment from more and more laborers; it also deprives the employed of their vital function; it imposes on them an unnatural passivity and frustrates their "instinct of workmanship."

The letters and arts that they prefer to take up their leisure with are those that provide them with the greatest possible variety of participation in vicarious activity, the most acceptable compensations in image and idea for the boring fact of inaction in reality. Westerns, sports, comic strips, whodunits, soap opera, and slapstick, with their violence, their sentiment, and their ethical and aesthetic commonness, figure far more largely among their choices than the items of "high culture" also offered them. "This," the spokesmen for the "sponsors" reply to the critics, "is what the people want; we give them what they want."

No candid student of letters and the arts will fail to recognize that much of what the elite get who patronize "high culture" is no less violent, nor less sentimental, less clowned, than the content of "mass culture." The difference is not one of content but of form. In their earlier expressions hardly any of the works of man manifest the finish, the style, and the sort of "rightnesss" that a constant reworking and reshaping gives them. As practice makes perfect, so mass culture undergoes reformation into high culture. The destinies of Superman, Li'l Abner, Little Orphan Annie, Dick Tracy, and Father—whom his offspring are "Bringing Up"— of Matt Dillon, Wyatt Earp or Wells Fargo or Paladin and their rivals, need not be a lesser immortality than that of the heroes and villains of pagan and Christian legend whom the arts remember and celebrate. Many survive their inventors and become perennial symbols of action and passion, whom their viewers pleasurably hope for or fear. Repetition brings familiarity, discrimination of quality, judgments that become deliberate and reasoned, like their judgment of a baseball pitcher or a prize fighter. Unreflecting perception gets refined into critical observation and aesthetic understanding. The professional critics get confirmed or refuted by the choices of the masses. The producers for these multitudes of unidentified, therefore "faceless," people, find themselves willy-nilly making changes to meet the exigencies of the changing "anonymous" judgments—changes that seem slow, directed less to theme or content than to style and form, as might, when one takes the history of the arts into account, be expected.

Now amid the circumambience of this formation and re-formation of its mass culture, a country's colleges and universities struggle to carry on and grow. They are the institutional repositories, its conservators and transmitters, of its "high culture." They carry its "great tradition" of faith and works. In many lands they are also expected to increase and enrich it, to cultivate a "creativity" consistent with it. And often they do, even the least of them, according to its kind and degree. All signify, to the most unstudious of their students, a road up and away from their primary intellectual or social milieu. All facilitate some mode of social or spiritual mobility. Rarely indeed does any youth enter college with more reliable knowledge, more discriminating taste, or sounder judgment than when he leaves it. College changes youth without, apparently, youth's changing it. Whatever degree anyone graduates with, it does signalize, within the boundaries of a nation's culture or a religion's creed and code, a widened horizon, a less prejudiced understanding, a more diversified mind, and a more informed faith than he entered college with. Indirectly or directly, he has been "educated."

Although it has long been a custom among academic authorities to take account of the indirect educational processes

—usually to deprecate and purge them—their vocation is the direct ones: the configuration of classrooms, laboratories, libraries, teachers and teachings, researchers and researchings. These tend jointly and severally to postulate their works on an idea or concept of man generated and nourished by the whole national culture (for example, the American Idea, in the United States) or the religious creed. Aware or unaware, they pursue youth's commitment to their Idea and youth's readiness with knowledge and skill to fight tomorrow's battle of the books for it, to replace the ranks of their elders in the unceasing strife of the ancients against the moderns, and in their turn struggle to have the Idea outlive its rivals and competitors, generation unto generation.

Globally, the number and variety of such symbolic projections is legion; each has its local habitation and name, its syndrome of signs and meanings that living men and women learn and use in defining the Selves they envision as image and would like to become as fact. Since the diversity of spirit and culture that these projections symbolize is actually irreducible, identifying them with one another in reflection or imagination is self-deception. The "idea of mankind" as one sole, composite image or single concept falsifies the truth and imperils whatever unification is achievable. To be consequentially valid and verifiable, the idea must needs present mankind as a configuration, not a figure. At best, it signifies an orchestration of cultural diversities, a precarious harmony of them supervening on discords and dissonances whose return is ever imminent. Pax Romana, Pax Dei Ecclesiae, Pax Britannica have been undertakings to maintain such a harmony by *force majeure*. The designs of Marsiglio of Padua, of Immanuel Kant, and of the authors of the Universal Declaration of Human Rights, and lately of Grenville Clark, remain much more compensatory ideals than consequential plans of action. The covenant of the League of Nations was shattered by members sworn to maintain it and follow its statutes; the covenant for the United Nations Organization is in imminent danger of similar rupture.

V.

Can the schools of the world so modify their teachings that the idea of mankind as an orchestration of cultural and other diversities will be joined to their ongoing curricula, sincerely taught, and genuinely learned; taught and learned, indeed, to such effect as to reverse history and bring the process of orchestration to lasting dominance? I believe it can, but only as each student's learning of the idea freely renders it a central dynamic in his image of himself. On the record this has not happened with any comprehensive idea of mankind, monistic or pluralistic. Perhaps it cannot happen. Or has education been in such wise practiced that it could not happen?

A look at the practice of teaching and the theories of learning might provide more acceptable support for the second alternative than the first. In colleges and universities, teaching —pedagogics, information, and communication theories notwithstanding—remains still pretty much a series of soliloquies spoken in public; learning, save perhaps on athletic fields, continues to be, as is natural, much like feeding, an activity of intake and output, however cooked or raw the diet. Neither experiment-based nor speculative theories of learning seem to much effect actual transactions between professors, students, and subject matter. The latter is taken for a fixed body of knowledge capable of being indefinitely repeated. Professor and student take each other for unaltering identities, and their business together as the transfer of a slice of the unchanging body of knowledge from the first to the second.

But neither immediate experience nor biographical record confirms the takings. Of course, we do feel and know that we are we. Each of us his whole life long experiences himself as *this* Self and no other—but a *this* of diversifications identifying each with the others. The sameness we are aware of is a present passage and commingling of feelings, perceptions, images, ideas; a perduration wherein moment by moment the past grows as the future appears, combining its newness with what is no longer new, and altering it, making it new again. What else is our present, what else can it be, but the past we are, being altered by the future not yet ours, becoming ours only as it becomes past? What else, then, is any human existence but such a stretch of time, from birth to death, one's today a changing of one's yesterdays? The struggle for survival is a struggling to keep this change going on, to keep on being—that is, to preserve the past by altering it, to become. For mankind existence is remembrance; to forget one's past is to forfeit one's Selfhood; it is human as against animal death; but to preserve this past as mere persistence, as repetition without alteration, is also to forfeit Selfhood, to be at a standstill, to have become a breathing fossil, as often happens in aging. What is *humanly* alive is an individual past growing by changing, growing up and growing older in the spirit and the flesh by ongoingly minding together ever more freely and surely an ever-increasing diversity of persons, thoughts, and things. In terms of its consequences, such changing is learning; struggling for survival is learning. Learning is the change of himself that a human being achieves in order to preserve himself. He keeps being himself only as a sequence of experiences of which the latest comprises also those that have gone before, whether or not in the order of their succession. The sequence is his identity, and it is his past struggling for a future. Its survival is ever future—ever-unpredictable variation within predictable repetition striving among, against, and with other such singulars, to live on and to outlive their foes, their rivals, and their competitors and, for that matter, their friends and lovers as well.

Hence the clichés that human beings live by learning, learn by living, and that soon rather than late failure of the one is atrophy of the other; that human societies educate to survive, survive as they educate, and do so by means of unceasing reformation and reciprocal suffusion of their sciences and arts into the knowledge that is power. But on the record, in many societies reformation is displaced by repetition, suffusion by isolation chosen or imposed. The end of repetition and isolation is fossilization. It is a dead end with extinction for its *terminus ad quem.*

Survival as living on, as outliving, is always learning, open-ended education. So, we keep learning from "experience," which educates us regardless of any art or science of education, by methods of trial and error. Such learning is said to be done "the hard way," in a "University of Hard Knocks." It is usually contrasted with the learning done in colleges and universities, which are designed to better it, to educate purposefully, according to plan, and to render learning safer, speedier, less painful, less arduous, less costly. Whatever their special goals, each institution purports a science, an art, and rationalizing philosophy on which it bases the *what* and *how* of teaching.

Whether, and how much, any learner freely shares the goals that his teachers set for him or accepts the way to them the teachers prescribe is an open question that psychological denominations and academic authorities are always trying to close. Studies diversify, theories multiply, and the world's hucksters and traders have shown themselves readier to gamble on variants than the world's teachers or preachers. As I read the record, certain assumptions are unconsciously shared by all experimenters and all teachers. Learning, it is commonly assumed, spans a stretch of time; it is directed toward the future; it is achieved when one or another way of doing, feeling, thinking has been permanently added to those already constituting the personality, added without displacing any, or added by displacing some particular one. In the latter case—and this is the prevailing condition for much human learning—*un*learning is a constitutive part of the learning process. The differences between the schools turn on the sequence of skills into which they analyze the process and the kind of cause they use to account for it.

But alike, when new and old are only being juxtaposed, and when the new is displacing the old, resistance becomes manifest. In the former situation, even when a learner is eager and willing and his curiosity is intense, his decision to mind something different, new, and strange encounters first the inertia, then the resistance, of his ongoing old ways, with their confluence (syndrome) of intimacy, warmth, functional smoothness, and satisfactoriness. One might say that the past strives for its own survival as only past, and resists the alteration that "future" means. The learning experience, then, is an experience of resistance and effort to overcome resistance, to seek relief from the feelings of tension and conflict that signify them. But the upkeep of the humanity of mankind, both collective and distributive, requires the past's alteration. As Disraeli remarked somewhere, "The man of experience is one who repeats the errors of his forefathers"; yet, as Santayana observed a generation later, "Those who forget the past are doomed to repeat it." Such is mankind's peculiar plight; it may neither forget the past nor repeat it. To achieve a human future it must retain and recall yet change its past. If the change prospers as it proceeds, then the old and the new have suffused one another, in such wise as to form a new harmonious configuration of knowledge and know-how; the two have become orchestrated to one another; the new has been naturalized in the communion of the old; a body of knowledge has been altered and transvalued.

Certain learnings, however, fail of that consummation. The tensions and the anxieties that are phases of the process do not get reshaped into a fresh, more comprehensive intimacy, warmth, and functional smoothness. The past becomes remoter and colder, but the future, though nearer, does not feel warmer; it does not suffuse and transvalue the past, as new learnings normally do. Although the learner now has acquired the new art or science, it is by contiguity, not by absorption and identification; he is an outsider using it, not an insider living it. It is a possession such as cramming for an examination achieves, and gets lost as soon as its purpose has been served. Its more extended role in his struggle for existence is unwillingly servile, not freely serviceable. He will earn his living with it, in whole or in part, but he won't live his life in it. The learning sequence has failed of consummation; it has been blocked in mid-passage.

Certain psychologists, philosophers, and theologians interpret this stoppage as the distinguishing characteristic of our awareness. They play variations upon a dialectical theme of G. F. W. Hegel's, which he argued in his *Phenomenology of Mind.* He spoke there of man's spirit as a divided, hence unhappy, consciousness, a nature doubled over and "merely contradictory," so an "alienated" soul. Karl Marx employed this notion to rationalize his revolutionary philanthropy, describing factory workers as victims of *entfremdung,* without ever inquiring whether or not many of them in fact felt alienated. But since his day, "alienation" has become a category of evil among all denominations of pundits and prophets deeply exercised over the plight of Western mankind and eager to guide them to safety and happiness. It happens, however, that the actual "alienation" of modernity's "common man" is not the stoppage they hypostatize; it is the phase of passage of future into past and which alteration of past consummates. Ongoing alteration is also "transcendence." The two words signify aspects of growth, animal growth in its stages, as well as human growth; they signalize selected human appreciation of the passage and perduration of time. Learning is alienation consummated as transcendence; as the passage of time, it is terminated by death. By and large, the "alienation" that our philanthropical pundits and prophets condemn bespeaks their own aversion to the modern's plight rather than his personal sense of his plight. They have to persuade him of it. His basic awareness is of transcendence. He looks and lives forward, strives toward a richer, freer future, not the recovery of an outlived past. Vis-à-vis modernity's "common man," the philanthropical alienists set themselves as Hegelian subject vis-à-vis Hegelian object; and subject does not enter into a pattern of participation with object, does not orchestrate object with its own Selfhood, but treats it as an alien identity, to be looked at, anatomized, worked *for* or *on,* even fought for, but not to be lived with. This would apply even more perfectly to the common men of Africa, Asia, and the islands of the Pacific who are eager to learn modernity and cannot, save by means of the hardships of alienation. In so far as an idea of mankind is implied by this notion of "alienation," it makes for aliency from the arduous and hopeful plight of the human multitudes.

Since education is not accomplished without alienation, without a turn from repeating the past to altering it, how colleges and universities do it becomes a consideration of major importance. Where learners are free or experience is the teacher, the learners learn to transform their past beliefs and behaviors into faiths and works whose consequences tend to be progressively more satisfying, more successful survival. Teaching, to them, is welcome, even vital, help toward this diversifying growth of their future, help affecting its direction, its shape, its ends-in-view, and its tempo. But the task that tradition or society or both assign the teacher is, directly and symbolically, to repeat in the pupils the doctrines and disciplines of their elders, and in such wise that they will also require the same of the teachers of *their* young. Teachers' assigned task is to form and fix the beliefs of their pupils. Let their philosophic faiths be what they will, the education they practice must be accomplished in two steps: the formation of the beliefs and the fixation of the beliefs that the culture of the group utters and embodies. They have succeeded when belief has become so fixed that the new believer's character and disposition are set and his life plan designed in such wise that he cannot help affirming and acting on those beliefs. He is then also apt to deny that anybody may differ from him as of right and not on sufferance and to penalize the different for being different in every way he can. The words "instruction," "inculcation," "indoctrination," "discipline" often signify such a fixing of belief. It is commonly the soft military training aims for. It is perennial in religious establishments—where Ignatius Loyola's "spiritual exercises" provides its most explicitly Western paradigm.

Currently, forming and fixing the future by transforming or suppressing the past from without, instead of suffusing it from within, has been called "brainwashing." It is an education that aims to confuse and upset an unwilling learner's psyche, by starving, soiling, embarrassing, shaming, and beating up his person for disagreeing, and by feeding and otherwise diminishing his sufferings in return for agreeing, until his beliefs are fixed beyond any unfixing. They have been committed to the death: *Ave, Imperator, morituri te salutamus.*

That presumption is, however, itself a belief that totalitarian authorities do not hold for infallible. If they did, they could dispense with the entire policy of persecution, coercion, suppression, terrorization, and slaughter of the different, which the record discloses as intrinsic to totalitarian culture. Their cultivation and use is postulated on the spontaneity and autonomy of differentiation, and this is confirmed by the sequences of defiances, heresies, defections, which totalitarian histories denounce. It is confirmed by studies of diverse "brainwashed," such as those of Robert Lifton,[3] and it indicates that the authoritarian doctrines and disciplines of the totalists and the inner conflict and alienation they end up with will soon or late fail of their purpose. Because they seek to suppress or annul the past, utterly to alienate it, rather than to suffuse and so change it, they succeed only in encapsulating it. Their creeds and codes are but superstructures and façades, not the foundations they want them to be.

In free societies, however authoritarian the tradition of schooling has been and however the winds of educational doctrine blow, the prevailing trend continues toward the treatment of learning as an inherently free enterprise that the content of even traditional programs of study—say, the "humanities" and the liberal arts or mathematics—points to. For all of it consists of present selections from the expressions, the discoveries, and inventions of earlier generations, whereof later ones give different values. As free enterprise, learning is a syndrome of looking, listening, handling, peeking, prying, breaking up, putting together, imagining, consuming, producing, all sorts of configurations, values, and existences—substantive, procedural, symbolical, emblematical—to form belief and

3. Robert Jay Lifton, *Thought Reform and the Psychology of Totalism* (New York: W. W. Norton & Co., Inc., 1960).

fix it or not, as the consequential give and take of the believer's experience decides. Because successful learning is such a syndrome, mankind discovers what already exists, creates what does not yet exist, and discards earlier discoveries and creations for later ones, which for the nonce sustain more satisfyingly the ongoing struggle to go on struggling that is human nature. As it proceeds farther and farther into the past, the once-future may or may not continue to satisfy; it lives on as antecedent ever under the test of new future consequences. Meeting the tests both alters it and keeps it a survival value, an article of faith to which the struggler more and more deeply commits himself. Commitment is a free man's closure of any process of discovery or creation, of innovation or development, that involves him. Commitment fixes belief for him.

Once so fixed, a belief goes over into actions that both channel and put it to trial; reproduction supervenes upon creation, repetition upon innovation and discovery. But the closure of commitment is not absolute closure; the belief is not fixed beyond all unfixing. Let it be the most reassuring his heart can desire or his head assent to, it is still a thing the believer bets on, even bets his life, but is still not a sure thing. His bet is a risk—which he will calculate as he can, with the risks calculation also creates. His commitment renders the belief a working hypothesis ever open to revision or displacement, ever subject to the competition of alternatives, ever being challenged and reconfirmed or not by consequences reproductive, repetitive, and contingent.

VI.

So with ideas of mankind. Each culture produces its own, and no one of them would all the schools of the world teach, or all the families assent to, not to say commit themselves to. Looking at the present plight of the world's populations, recalling what I have learned about their past, I believe deeply that the most comprehensive, the most positively consequential, identification of mankind, the one most likely to win global consensus, and perhaps efficacious global commitment, is the one that the claims and conduct of so very many power holders flout and nullify as they act on faiths whose works are cultural, creedal, and economic imperialisms which they advance by fraud and support by force.[4] That one is the unification of human diversity implicit in the Universal Declaration of Human Rights, already subscribed to be the greater number of "representatives" of the governments of the world's peoples. The Declaration recognizes that mankind consists of multitudes of persons and peoples, each different from the others and, as different, equal to the others in the right to live and to grow. It repudiates the ways of men that impose penalties or assume privileges because of their differences. It denies that these ways can have any ground in nature or any warrant in law. It postulates that wherever persons live together in societies, and for whatever purpose, they continue so, uncompelled, in the belief of each that he struggles on more freely, more securely, more satisfyingly, than by going it alone. The Declaration postulates that churches, states, businesses, all associations of persons, are moved by the same belief to commit themselves to alliances and organizations.

Thus the Declaration may be taken for a global profession

4. There is almost a global consensus to this effect. Thus, in December 1956 the United Nations Scientific and Cultural Organization (UNESCO) held a conference in New Delhi which declared: "The understanding necessary for peaceful cooperation between peoples can be based only on a deepened knowledge and appreciation by each people of the civilizations of other peoples." It laid particular stress on the need that Occident and Orient should develop reciprocal appreciation of each others' cultures. The conference disregarded the fact that such an understanding is also being sought to the ends of the war of all against all; that to will "peaceful cooperation" is a prior condition.

of faith; and it is true that the powers that profess it belie it
with their works. It is true that they all scheme and strive to
make of their international relations tools of their national interests; that they have rendered the United Nations Organization—which they covenanted for a means to global peace, freedom, and equal justice under law—but one more agency of the
war of all against all. It is true that they seem bent on keeping
the Universal Declaration from ever becoming other than a
substance of the thing hoped for, an evidence of the thing not
seen. Not even the more highly civilized of the members of the
most comprehensive international organization of mankind have
yet achieved an international mind, so that the forum of the
United Nations is most employed to exploit the blind parochial
interest of totalitarian imperialism and "neutralist" chauvinism.

All in all, the Universal Declaration of Human Rights and
the Charter of the United Nations Organization signify good
intentions to base evil actions on. They express compensatory,
not programmatic, ideals of mankind. The "human nature"
they bespeak is the Mephistophelean one of the Great Tradition,
which ever wills the good and creates evil. It displays itself today
in a man-wrought environment farther removed from its animal
heredity, far more authentically a reformation and development
of its cultural heritage, than any that the tradition remembers
and sustains.

This environment is a civilization wherein the temporal
and spatial distances between peoples have been so contracted
that the very continents are called neighborhoods, and their
human inhabitants seen as neighbors who could visit one another and learn from one another in ever-greater numbers, whose
neighborliness could become much that the faith of the Universal Declaration could eventuate in works as a free, co-operative, self-orchestrating society of societies of free men, as an

economy wherein all would assure to each his survival in equal liberty and equal security.

Unhappily, while temporal and spatial distances contract, psychic distances expand; nearness but facilitates conflict. Not only does modernity require a "moral equivalent of war"; it needs as well, and urgently, a moral equivalent of peace. The very agencies formed to develop and maintain ways of peace become fields of battle with words, ever on the edge of battle with weapons. Even the United Nations Educational, Scientific, and Cultural Organization has, in practice, tended to increase, not diminish, the psychic alienations. There, too, and much from the same motives, as spokesmen for UNESCO also recognize, the means fail of the end. According to the preamble of the agency's constitution, its aim is to educate "humanity for justice and liberty and peace," to strengthen "the intellectual and moral solidarity of mankind" by clearing away "ignorance and prejudice" and pursuing "objective truth" without let or hindrance. To achieve this the nations are to unite in a common work of education, science, and culture. The record does not indicate that the organization of the agency, its departments and projects, have employed the means or advanced the end with any better effect than the educational establishments that the peoples of the world diversely maintain. On its record, UNESCO is one more institution of higher learning added to those already existing, and as deficient as they in forming and fixing belief in "a world community," or educating, or helping to educate, the miscellany of mankind to live with one another as members of such a community.[5]

Moreover, on the record of them all, the consequential resistances to this consummation are worldwide and endemic.

5. A more optimistic opinion on UNESCO is expressed in the contribution by Dr. George N. Shuster, Chapter Three.

They begin in the immediacies of childhood experience and compound with the years, and it is those experiences that must needs be shaped into commitment to an idea of mankind as the self-orchestration—*e pluribus unum, in pluribus unum*—of the multitudes of cultures and the diversity of faiths and ways and works into a "world community."

But as the generations are presently educated, a young human who enters a college or university is a heart and a mind living forward from a past of commingled attitudes, ideas, images, preferences, and rejections that compose his personality. To form and fix belief in, and to commit himself to, the idea of mankind he would need so to learn it that his alienation from his past would come without external coercion or internal suppression; that his growth into the idea would be a self-transcendence achieving itself in a continuing orchestration of his immediate experiences with the symbolic presence of the absent singularities of the rest of humanity.

A course of study that has for its *terminus ad quem* so to achieve a free personal commitment to this idea of mankind would, of course, explore the idea side by side with its alternatives and rivals for intent, convincingness, and practical relevance. But it would also plan to bring the idea to bear on every branch of study, treating each on its record as an interest that associates many persons in many lands in common endeavors to advance and secure it, as an ongoing orchestration of their singularities into an international mind. Given their histories, there is no academic discipline, no art, no science that cannot be set in these perspectives. As fields of research, most of them do get so set, but rarely with any appreciation of the critical import of the setting.

That the formation and fixation in this wise of belief in a

world community *exit in pluribus unum* can lead away from the cruelties and bloodlettings of peoples' struggle for survival with one another and with their nonhuman circumambience is, of course, but a working hypothesis, a belief for peoples to bet their survival on. But since it is of record that they have not lived on because they won any bets on the belief's rivals and alternatives, that they live on in spite of having lost those bets, could they not well stake their future on this one?[6] May it not be that, as the beliefs of Galileo became consequential for physics and astronomy, the beliefs of Darwin and Pasteur for biology, so this conception of mankind, generalizing samples of the ways and means of people's actually living on, might displace the blind risks of the immemorial war of all against all by a reasoned, calculated risk? Recall Albert Einstein:

6. As that brave and dedicated soldier of humanity and martyr to its survival, Dag Hammarskjöld, declared in a message to the World Jewish Congress: "The quarter century since the founding of your Congress, witnessing the advent of both the nuclear and space age . . . has been one of unusual achievements and unparalleled risks. Following the second world war—the most destructive ever—peace has been neither won nor lost and is still to be made secure. On the other hand, the cataclysm of nuclear war, although often threatening, has been averted. These, surely, are dominating facts of these recent years. . . . It is becoming rather too sharply clear that a critical juncture has been reached in the world's quest for peace. The tendency in some quarters to sound alarums must be deprecated, but that does not preclude recognizing the dangers that do exist and recognizing facts, however harsh they may be. The greatest danger would be the failure to realize how utterly futile, how insane, resort to modern war would be. In this sense, it is beyond question that far greater effort than ever before exerted throughout the world will have to be brought to bear to safeguard peace. The point need not be labored that in these times of decision the United Nations is indispensable. Ironically, at this very time it has had to face a serious challenge. The United Nations, to justify the hope that has been placed in it, must be an Organization that by growing in strength and authority will become ever more effective in the works of peace and advancement. It must be active and dynamic in behalf of peace, using all the tried methods and tools now available to it, some of which, in fact, the United Nations itself has devised, as well as those new means which will undoubtedly develop in response to future need."

The supernational character of scientific concepts and scientific knowledge is due to the fact that they have been set up by the best brains of all countries and all times. In solitude and yet in co-operative effort as regards the final effect, they created the spiritual tools for the technical revolutions which have transferred the life of mankind in the last centuries—what hopes and fears does the scientific method imply for mankind? I do not think this is the right way to put the question. Whatever this tool in the hand of man will produce depends entirely on the nature of the goals alive in this mankind. Once these goals exist, the scientific method furnishes means to realize them. Yet it cannot furnish the very goals —if we desire sincerely and passionately the safety, the welfare and the free development of the talents of all men, we shall not be in want of the means to approach such a state. Even if only a small part of mankind strives for such goals then their superiority will prove itself in the long run.

Anyhow, since even totalitarians concede that it is no longer practicable for peoples to regard each other as they are used to, what have they to lose by committing themselves to this different idea of themselves and their relations, and jointly and severally betting their survival on it? At worst, they would be making Pascal's wager.

PART THREE

Perspectives Toward Mankind in Various Disciplines of Thought

8.

PAUL F. BRANDWEIN

Nature—Idea *and* Substance

Little do we see in Nature that is ours.
—WORDSWORTH

THE LAMENTING LINE is perhaps still true in Wordsworth's sense, but not so in the sense of *Naturwissenschaft*—science. The British, in custom and wisdom, call the organ of the British Scientific Society "nature"; the Americans, in their invention and wisdom, call the organ of the American Association for the Advancement of Science "science." In a real sense, scientists ask questions of Nature, seeking to construct and disseminate a meaningful world, nature entire.

These days, science is taught with the intent of giving the learner the tools by which he might discover, if you will, the *nature* of *Nature*. And, in so doing, those who would learn discover that nature and man are inseparable. The emerging planet spawned life out of matter. This planet became the home of plastic living things and man arose from them: man is the result of an inexorable mutation. Man and nature are inextricably one—one finds this in man's biology, or his chemistry, or his physics. Men may be divided politically, socially, economically, philosophically, but science sees man in a kinship with the living things from which he is derived, and, biologically, as one species.

189

Moreover, it sees man as seeking understanding of himself and his world, discovering its uniformities and its resources, and attempting to find ways of using these resources wisely. Not the least of these resources is man himself. Homo sapiens is become Homo *faber*.

Man as scientist does not seek experience blindly; he seeks experience in a search for meaning. Man, as a scientist, does not experiment flippantly; he seeks design. Man as scientist does not limit his aims; he seeks, although he rarely reaches, his ultimate concern, truth.

Because this is so, the scientist is the ever-learner, and those who teach science learn to learn. They are ever-learners not because facts are constantly changing, but because to see continuity through change one must perceive the continuous thread, the warp and woof of the scientific fabric. Viewed as a mass of facts, science is bewildering; viewed as an attempt to understand the way the world works, science is woven whole. The fabric of science, its pattern, its warp and woof are seen as *concepts*; its shuttle, its tools, if you will, are seen in the *way it confronts discrepancies* (sometimes this confrontation is called "scientific method").[1]

A scientist, in other words, has discipline and has a discipline. He is disciplined in his investigations; in turn his investigations arise out of what he is investigating. An astronomer investigates (he confronts discrepancies) differently from the physiologist, but both seek to discover what can be confirmed by others—in short, they seek what is stable and uniform within the variety of experience.

What is it, then, that we hope young people will see in

1. If we seem to show a distaste for the phrase "scientific method," it is because the phrase has been used to denote an inexorably successful way of problem solving (perish the term). The phrase "scientific method" either needs banishing, or appropriate use. Its use has value in historiography.

science, and come out a cubit taller? Two things at least, and perhaps at most: a unity within a seeming diversity and a way of learning.

We need, first, then, to look at the scientist's domain. Our purpose is to seek out this unity within diversity which, we believe, exists, and to focus on the way of learning which is, we propose, characteristic of the scientist's way of work.

Conceptual Schemes and the Curriculum

For the special vantage point of the teacher, who must apprehend the world of science so that the experiences of children have meaning, the world of science builds not institutions, but ideas. And it is these ideas, or vast conceptualizations of the way the world works, that are the heritage of young people. Technologies, the products of science, change; the conceptual schemes, explanations of the way the world works, remain fairly stable during a lifetime. They are the continuities through which change may be examined. These conceptual schemes have universal application, as true in open societies as well as those that remain closed for the historical moment; ignorance of these conceptual schemes in modern civilizations produces the backward state. As we shall shortly see, these conceptual schemes affect all areas of life—social, political, economic, religious. Scientists and their ideas do not affect science only.

So Darwin's studies did not affect evolutionary doctrine alone; witness their impact in the political and religious fields. Copernicus did not weld a new cosmogony only; he shook the foundations of the religio-political state. Einstein's formulation $E = mc^2$, one epitome of classical physics, shook political alignments. Conversely, falsification of the conceptualizations of science can produce, in the mildest of terms, social blight. The *Rassenkunde* of Herr Goebbels justified brutal repression and a murderous genocide unequalled in history. The genetics of Lysenko made it possible to inherit acquired characteristics; thus neo-Lamarckism served communist dogma.

It is thus useless to classify science as nonhumanistic—it is in the warp and woof of social, political, philosophical, economic thought and practice; its misuse brings as much misery as political repression; its wise use aids prosperity, and an understanding of its ideas leads to amplification of cultural opportunities. Snow[2] laments the two cultures and for good reason; two cultures are a luxury that mankind cannot afford. The major conceptualizations of science should at least be part of the intellectual equipment of all citizens who would consider *this* world their home.

It is, of course, almost the crudest kind of oversimplification to identify these conceptualizations as categories, but in the interests of the discussion, the categories may prove useful. Further, a reader accustomed to subtlety of argument, or proposition, will no doubt be disappointed. Farseeing, sophisticated individuals will perhaps see all of these conceptual schemes as subtended by the vast conceptualization: The universe is in constant change.

We deal, however, with vast conceptualizations, and we must order them in some reasonable scope and sequence, for the child progresses in schooling, in knowledge, from year to year. For instance:

The totality of matter and energy is conserved.

Organisms and their environment are interdependent.

Man is the product of a long evolutionary history.

But those who would develop a curriculum for schools must ask

2. C. P. Snow, *The Two Cultures and the Scientific Revolution* (London: Cambridge University Press, 1959).

in what form—in our present state of knowledge and educational practice—can schools, teachers, children apprehend these vast schemes; how best can they weave them into the time span and developmental sequences of the child? Can a child apprehend, in one intellectual swoop, the labor of ten thousand years embodied in the vast conception: *The totality of matter and energy is conserved?* How long did it take "mature" men and women to come to grips with the idea that man is the product of a long evolutionary history? Do not men and women still prefer to think of man as descended (fallen) from a complete man touched by divinity, rather than as ascended (raised) from the protean molecule?

It is in this that curricular inventions differ: a curriculum is a social invention designed to encompass that knowledge which is most useful, that knowledge which reconstructs man's experience in a meaningful way. Some would say that the best way is to consider what men do; they are geologists, chemists, physicists, biologists—hence, teach geology, chemistry, physics, biology. I shall not labor the point that this structure is wasteful of the school's time, and the time of children. It is repetitious: in geology we deal with the structure of matter; in chemistry, physics, and biology we must review the same matters in similar introductory vein once again—and again. If the curriculum were organized and interrelated, there could be an allocation of teaching time to a specific subject, and thereafter one could build on it. In practice this does not work, for the very reason that once we define a discipline, say chemistry, we assign it a curricular domain and isolate its teachers from other groups. And zealously do they guard this domain.

We must not be naïve. The proposal of any curricular structure does not mean its acceptance. Who was it who said that changing a curriculum is much like moving a cemetery? But the function of the scholar remains: he must go too far (assuming the ideas will carry him there), so that others may go far enough.

One task of teachers seems, then, to be the construction of a meaningful curriculum, which derives its meaningfulness from the world of *educational idea* and *educational substance*. The *ideas* stem out of the conceptual schemes of science (organized as a curriculum). The *substance* stems out of what children and teachers *do* to learn the conceptual schemes (devised as a method of learning science).

At least for the elementary school, the structure of the conceptual schemes proposed for consideration are these:

A. Organisms are the product of their heredity and environment.

Subsumed under this conceptual scheme are major concepts that are useful in understanding the development of living things. Thus, while genes carry the hereditary code, the fullest expression of this code is in a favoring environment. Like begets like, true—but genes and environment account for the idiosyncratic nature of individuals and their approach to life and living.

While differences in hereditary units (genetic codes) do exist, there is no denying that in all essential characteristics— anatomical, physiological, embryological, biochemical—men are one. Taxonomically, man is one species, Homo sapiens; by definition a species consists of a group of living things in continuous variation which interbreed. Varieties (races) of man exist, as do varieties of living things generally—but man is still one.

The development of plants and animals can be related to their environment; inadequacies may produce aberrances.

Whether these are deficiencies in the supply of chemical energy (food) or, for the primates especially, deficiencies in the psychosexual environment, the effects are often predictable. Lack of vitamin D may produce rickets, and lack of an education may produce ignorance.

This conceptual scheme—adequately understood and leading to responsible action—would not deny to men anywhere the basic elements—one might almost say, the bare elements—needed for respectable growth and development. Yet in certain parts of the world, men have a life span of seventy years; and in other parts of the very same world, in a medieval environment, men can afford only a life span of some forty years; they die before their prime.

Whose responsibility is it that some men die too soon, and that the knowledge to prevent premature death exists? Does the knowledge man has of the prevention of disease and degradation apply to all men?

B. Organisms and their environment are interdependent.

Green plants capture the sun's energy; herbivorous animals depend directly on green plants; carnivores indirectly on the autotrophic green plant. Organisms do not live alone; they live in communities; they are interdependent.

True, a pine forest is different from an oak forest; the veldt different from the prairie; organisms on a mountaintop differ from those on a glacier; the life of the sea is different from that of a pond; the steaming jungle houses different animals than does the northern tundra or taiga—but ecological principles remain constant. Food niches exist; in all communities there is a flow of energy and matter between organisms and their environment.

Primitive societies lived in close relation to the environment; they were, in a sense, in harmony with it. The coming of the cities did not free that particular animal, Homo sapiens, from his environment; it made him even more dependent on his resources. To safeguard his future he had to conserve, that is, to use wisely.

Whether we deal with nitrogen-fixing bacteria, dependent on nitrogen and the nodules of legumes, or the Yucca moth, depending for its reproduction on the flowering of the yucca, or the seal, dependent on fish, or man depending on cereal grains, we see interdependence. But now man depends on other men.

Except in the most primitive groups—fast disappearing because of Homo *faber*—men do not fabricate their own shoes, utensils, musical instruments, ships, shirts, nor do they grow their own food. A light bulb used in London may depend on its tungsten from China or Canada; the citizens of Geneva depend on the copper mined in the Congo, and perhaps on the oil of Kuwait. The atomic tests in Nevada or Siberia affect men who were never physically there, but the minds of men reflect sadly on what goes on there.

Animals and plants are interdependent; men are interdependent. Donne was not an ecologist, but he set forth a principle of human ecology as part of man's ultimate concern—the bell tolls, but for *thee*.

C. Organisms have descended from simpler organisms; organisms are related through descent.

In the light of evolutionary history, man has come very lately on the scene. Compress evolutionary history (prehistory) into a time scale of twenty-four hours, and man is found to exist for one second—the last second. If evolutionary history will be permitted to continue, then man, as species, is perhaps about to flourish.

Matter did not end with matter. It proceeded into a further organization—into the field of the living. Matter formed the templates of life; the first great leap was into molecular self-duplication—reproduction, if you will—then perhaps to a virus-type organism, to a "first" cellular organization, to a protista, perhaps, then to the multicellular aggregates, into aggregates with differentiated cells and primitive division of labor, into the pre-invertebrates, into the swarm of invertebrates, prolific and prolix, into the proto-vertebrates, to man. Whether man proceeded through the Australopithecines, or through another line, man has a long prehistory—or ascent, if you will. Men came from the *same* stock, over a long prehistory. This stock shared its genes; it shared a prehistoric environment. Men shared each other.

True, fitness to survive played its part; not all genes had survival value. But even a casual survey of man's prehistory shows not only struggle but collaboration; not only competition prepared man as animal for ascent, but co-operation prepared him for life as man.

Not man, but men, survive. Man as species *seems* to be evolving into man as mankind. The story is not yet finished. The past is but prologue.

D. Matter is particulate; fundamental particles comprise it. Matter changes its forms; only under extraordinary conditions is matter destroyed.[3]

Here are subsumed all chemical and physical changes; the periodic table proposes a certain unity in structure. Except for one form of hydrogen, protons, neutrons, electrons combine to

3. Whether we consider the destruction of matter on our planet as ordinary or extraordinary depends on interpretation of events. For the ordinary day, for the ordinary chemical action, matter, although changed, retains its conventional structure.

form the different elements; a basic structure is discernible. The field we know as chemistry bounds this area; the men we know as chemists have transformed the face of the globe.

The chemist has changed the face of society through his understanding of chemical reaction: thus we get aspirin, penicillin, quinine, atabrine, nylon, orlon, plastics, fertilizers, cement, steel, alloys, gasoline, solid rocket fuels. There are very few things made today that existed in that form in 1850.

But organisms, all organisms, are made up of matter, as are all nonliving things. The differences between life and non-life are clear when the organisms are as complex as a cell; not as clear when we examine the least complex viruses.

Nevertheless, as one studies the world of matter, it is clear that the nonrenewable resources are not distributed equally. There are have-not nations, and thus have-not peoples. The naïveté of assuming a common market for Western Europe and not a common market for the world must occur to anyone who plays with the numbers of an exploding population acting upon limited resources of matter and, as we shall see, energy.

Advances in technology being what they are, the world cannot continue as have-not and have—and emerge stable.

E. Energy changes its forms, but is not annihilated.

Whether we consider the potential energy of placid water changing to the kinetic energy of onrushing Niagaras, then to electrical energy (via generators) into light and heat energy, whether we consider uranium releasing its nuclear energy, we have examples of the most prosaic, if little understood, changes of forms of energy.

Bitter struggles have come from man's desire to change from man-power to beast-power to horse-power; and the prizes of the struggle have often been the fossil fuels, coal and oil. Freedom from back-breaking drudgery, the culture of the cities, advances in sanitation, health, leisure have accomplished advances in our understanding of the uses of energy. Now nuclear energy emerges in the role of jinni.

The physicist is interested in light, not light bulbs; nevertheless, he has combined forces with the engineer to speed human activity. Thus communication progresses from the speed of the horse to the speed of light; transportation approaches Mach 1, and soon transportation to other planets will exceed escape velocity. The internal-combustion engine has transformed the habits of the family, and while the automobile annually kills more people than were annihilated in the battle of Tarawa, men still court the ease it gives them.

It is no doubt more satisfying intellectually to consider only one conceptual scheme in the field of matter energy: the totality of matter energy is conserved. We are left with little choice intellectually, but, pragmatically, teachers have been trained along lines of understanding matter and energy as duality. Chemistry and physics exist as courses; chemists and physicists exist as individuals. Perhaps it is best, in the interests of an acceptable evolution of social invention, to permit the marriage to occur in time. Whether we do or not, $E = mc^2$ is established; light is interpreted generally not only as wave but particle; the atomic nucleus is matter, but generates in waves of different forms; solid matter, coal, is a source of chemical energy, as is the liquid, oil. Chemical actions and reactions are best explained not only as interchanges of particles but as evidence of change in energy levels. Matter and energy are clearly to be thought of in unity. Nations that lack material resources lack energy resources as well.

F. The universe is constantly in change.

Once it was reassuring to live in a postage-stamp universe —never changing, never ending. The universe was geocentric and anthropocentric.

But the universe uncovered by astronomers is much more satisfying. A man, one creature amongst billions, finds himself on one modest planet (of nine) around a modest star (of a million or so) in one galaxy (of a million or so). The universe is vast, and, furthermore, it is expanding (gentle word) or exploding (harsh and threatening).

Stars change; there are novae and supernovae; our star could change and, in doing so, might incinerate our planet. And the energy of our star is found to come from hydrogen fusion— duplicated by man on earth.

In trying to understand this profound change from the cosmos with which Copernicus, Bruno, and Galileo were confronted to one of such vastness exceeding comprehension, man achieves humility at last. Especially is this true if he contemplates the possibility—Harlow Shapley would say the probability—of the existence of other modest stars with other modest planets with optimum conditions for life. Then his planet is not the only one. Humility then will be prologue, if you wish, to understanding of others with compassion.

It is not enough, however, to apprehend these conceptualizations, that is, *to know*. We need to know *how* we know. And moreover, we need to know *how well* we know *what* we know.

For instance, the conceptual schemes we have been concerned with are constructs—structures, in a sense, which we build in the mind. But the concepts, the pattern of fact and observations, which in turn pattern the conceptual schemes, are of sterner stuff. They are verifiable and, what is more, self-correcting. The processes and techniques that enable us to verify and correct the body of concepts that we call science are too often captured by an abominable phrase, "the method of science."

We find the phrase "method of science" anathema, not because scientists use it with appropriate vagueness, but because the nonscientist uses it as if it existed and, moreover, in the assumption that it exists as a series of steps (called "problem solving"). Further, in my observations of schools over the United States, it is apparent that teachers, particularly those with least training in science, train their students in the "steps" of the scientific method. The dangers of this are apparent, aside from the pitiful oversimplification of an intensely creative act.

Some ninety per cent of all the world's scientists are now alive; one estimate has it that the "new" knowledge turned out every hour equals a book a thousand pages or so of the size of a conventional encyclopedia. Surely a way of work that accomplishes this must be a "successful" one. It is convenient to acknowledge that the conclusions that find their way into new knowledge must be the result of conclusive ways of gathering evidence, and of conclusive checks and balances. Conveniently, one sees problems being solved with inexorable success, and the stigmata of the "method," the scientific paper with its liturgical steps, are dogmatized as the steps of the method. So one reads a scientific paper with its logical exposition leading from problem to conclusion, and the unpracticed can see the steps—problem, hypothesis, design of experiment, checks, conclusion.

Our search for system method for cause and effect everywhere betrays us, and we find it even where it may not exist. Perhaps Percy Bridgman's[4] statement concerning scientific

4. Percy W. Bridgman, "Prospect for Intelligence," *Yale Review*, 1945, reprinted in *Reflections of a Physicist* (New York: Philosophical Library, 1950).

method—"Science means doing one's damndest with one's brain, no holds barred"—is nearer the truth. Science is an art. Beveridge[5] expresses this, and Bronowski[6] illuminates the scientist's quest by his suggestion that scientists, like artists, search incessantly for "the hidden likeness" in objects and in phenomena. A word about these two important aspects of the scientist's mode and manner: his search for hidden likenesses and the self-correcting devices he has built into his work.

The essential life of the scientist is the life of the mind, the life of thought: if this is accepted, it is perhaps not difficult to accept the idea that there is probably incessant preconscious mental activity. Wallas[7] has termed this activity "incubation" prior to moments of illumination. It is almost as if we were dealing with a vastly complicated computer activity, of magnificently miniaturized components, constantly self-programed.

This constant mental activity is purposive; it bears fruit. There is a constant confrontation of objects and events, and there are "flashes of insight"—the "Eureka's," the "Aha's." There is no stately procession of problem to hypothesis, to design of experiment, etc., to a final conclusion. What is thought of as a procession is in all probability a melee—a creative explosion of thought where past, present, and future of the creative act are "seen" in a "flash of light."

The essential problem is always the same: Is it true? Then perhaps there is a design of some device which will afford a systematic nature of proof. It is this systematic nature of proof that is then called "scientific method."

5. W. I. B. Beveridge, *The Art of Scientific Investigation* (New York: W. W. Norton & Co., Inc., 1950).
6. Jacob Bronowski, *Science and Human Values* (New York: Julian Messner, Inc., 1958).
7. Graham Wallas, *The Art of Thought* (New York: Harcourt, Brace & World, Inc., 1926).

True, the elaboration of the systematic nature of proof is a creative act, rationally developed as a device. But it is the "flash of insight" that is the creative act—the act of genius, or better, of genesis, that characterizes the scientist as it does the artist. The conceptualization (the conclusion), the problem, the hypothesis, the design of the experiment are wedded in the "flash." It is in this flash of insight that the scientist "sees" the hidden likeness, the unity within chaos; it is then he divines essential meaning for that corner of the universe he has made his own.

But if this were all to science, it would perish. The "success" of science, if the word may be used, is based not only on the unique, the idiosyncratic creative act, the almost "nonrational" flash of insight, not only on the insistence of a critique that scrutinizes the nature of the evidence and insists on a systematic demonstration of proof, but on its arrogating to itself a means of communication that in itself is a magnificent social invention. Except in those situations where the military and industrial establishments intervene, scientists communicate their discoveries to each other. Newton said he stood on the shoulders of giants, the better to see farther. Generally speaking, this system of communication does not exclude individuals because of breed or creed. Here and there we find attempts to intervene in this communication, but secrets in science are, in the nature of things, not possible. In time, the "new" knowledge so carefully guarded comes forth in a "flash of insight" in yet another mind, in yet another country.

Schools, then, need not only teach a body of conceptual schemes, with the patterns of facts that buttress them, but are bound to give youngsters an opportunity to discover for themselves. The laboratory as well as the library serves the mind and the hand. We do not mean by this the so-called laboratory exercise; these are calisthenics useful in building skills in using equipment and in developing a rational approach to problem doing. In problem doing the conclusions are known; what is learned then is the reduction of error, the mastery of technique in developing a systematic nature of proof. In problem solving what is *not* learned is how to face the blank wall of Nature; how to ask questions of Nature.

It has been demonstrated again and again[8] that young people can investigate, "no holds barred," if they are given the opportunity to design their own experiments, if they are not punished (marked down) for failure. Failure is an integral part of discovery; the scientist learns to fail intelligently or he leaves science. It has been shown that if young people are given the psychological safety necessary to the art of discovery, they can become discoverers. Of course, not all have the temperament or the desire. But just as an athlete practices in the gymnasium or in the football field; just as a painter paints; just as a musician composes or performs, so a scientist-to-be can practice science in the library, laboratory, and in his armchair.

The young people who will become scientists are stalwart in the necessary act of transforming men into mankind, free to discover and learn, yet easy contributors to the world community. Science itself, we have said, thrives on free communication amongst men. Science itself, it is clear, depends on methods of intelligence, of creation, which in turn depend on verification by others. Two scientists are necessary to confirm a fact, so that

8. Paul F. Brandwein, *The Gifted Student as Future Scientist* (New York: Harcourt, Brace & World, Inc., 1955); *Biological Investigations for Secondary School Students*, Biological Sciences Curriculum Study (Boulder, Col.: BSCS, University of Colorado); and *Guide to Working with Potential Biologists in the High School*, in preparation (Boulder, Colorado: BSCS, University of Colorado). See also the laboratory materials of the Physical Science Study Committee, 164 Main Street, Watertown 22, Mass., and the Chemical Materials Study Committee, Harvey Mudd College, Claremont, Cal.

a third may believe it, and a fourth may build on it, and a fifth may use it.

The scientist's business is to construct and disseminate a meaningful world. For whom does he build it? To whom does he disseminate it?

9.

ANNE ROE

The Behavioral Sciences

A PARADOX threatens when we begin to contemplate the idea of mankind. Mankind exists. We have only to read the newspapers to know that each of us becomes increasingly dependent upon it. Yet the more we try to grasp its reality and meaning, the more it escapes.

So we may begin with the more concrete, or with that of which mankind consists, with individual men. But, though on another scale, we are here confronted with a similar dilemma. The more we try to comprehend the human person, the more mysterious it becomes. However, here at least we meet an almost universal and constantly growing interest, as is evident by the torrent of articles and books about child care, mental health, personal adjustment, and interpersonal relations. Very few of these publications have come from research scientists themselves, even though a number have come from persons trained in one or another of the behavioral disciplines. But for the most part, these have come from popularizers of science or staff writers, and they tend to promise more than they can perform, and still not to promise enough.

Why have the professional behavioral scientists not done

more to meet this need more effectively? One of the reasons is that they have the same attitudes as other scientists. They concentrate on the problem and its technical and theoretical implications. But not every investigation produces results of immediate relevance to our everyday activities, and even those that do may not have been planned for this. Furthermore, although research directed toward improvement of techniques such as diagnosis or treatment of disturbed persons can be applied with some ease, the difficulty comes when the findings are applied by others than those trained in the discipline, and particularly when they lead to alteration of ways of thinking and feeling. In the field of public health, to give only one sample, a problem arose with the introduction of anesthesia for childbirth. The storm of opposition was largely based on theological considerations centering around the conception of original sin. There are many who still believe in original sin, but few of those now object to anesthesia for childbirth.

Behavioral scientists have been no more remiss than other scientists in communicating the meaning of their results and of these hypotheses to the general public. But with regard to the first, the present rather widespread ambivalence is particularly strong. On the one hand, people hope that we can help them with their most personal and agonizing problems; on the other hand, they fear that we will find out too much about them. This fear is not always connected with fear of misusing these findings, although often it is. Mainly it is quite simply fear of exposure, not to others, but to oneself. And the less one knows about oneself, the greater this fear is likely to be.

I remember my first visit to Paris, when I was a guest at dinner in a French home. My knowledge of French, if it can be dignified by that phrase, was as much as a couple of college courses, taught in the fashion of those days, had given me. In this intimate and gay group, one of the guests asked me, in words of one syllable, what I did. When I replied that I was a psychologist, there was a shriek, and then an appalled silence fell on the table. I was baffled until one of them said, "But you are reading our minds!" This was thirty years ago, but there has been little change in the public attitude, and I fear there will not be much change in many more years, unless we do something constructive about it, beginning with ourselves.

What is it that all of us fear to have exposed? Is it just the accumulation of feelings of inadequacy or the residual of guilt we all have from the fact that the socializing process has not removed many violent and unacceptable desires but only, to some extent, taught us to control them? I think there is more to this. It may well be an inevitable concomitant of the degree of conscious awareness that is unique to man, the perception of self as individual and distinct from all others. Although it may be vague, it is, nevertheless, powerfully felt. Its very formlessness makes its defense the more necessary and the more difficult. With this underpinning for all our other sources for guilt feelings, it is easy to see why we do not welcome exposure. And it is also easy to understand why such illogical and essentially irrelevant conceptions as original sin and the need for salvation have been so widely accepted. At what stage in the long history of man this hiding of the precious self developed no one can know, but it must have come early, as early as conscious awareness of self as distinct from others.

Perhaps it is this need for an inviolable place of one's own that has been a major factor in the enormously greater advance and earlier start of the natural than the social sciences. Woodworth[1] has discussed at considerable length what he considers

1. Robert S. Woodworth, *Dynamics of Behavior* (New York: Henry Holt & Co., 1958).

the failure of need-primary theories to predict any greater variety of motives for humans than for animals, since both have the same "needs." He insists that the primary drive in behavior is the necessity to deal with the environment, and that the distinctively human interests (art, science, government, etc.) have their source in the combination of this drive with the special human capacities. Others concerned with problems of motivation have talked of exploratory drives, curiosity, and so on as among our—and other animals'—basic energizers. But whether or not it is the only one, there is no question but that the need to live in and with our environment is such a motivator and that it is very strong. But it follows that man's attention will be primarily turned *outwards,* and he will react to other persons as to other objects in the environment. (Even the Freudians, meaning interpersonal relations, use the term "object relations.") This basically outward-directed attention, whose survival value is obvious, combined with the need to protect the self from discovery, has over the centuries brought it about that man knows more of the world outside him than of the world within.

It is not necessary to belabor the point that the crisis of the present is man's capacity to destroy himself, or, rather, his incapacity not to destroy himself. Today, as a species, he is no longer at the mercy of the environment; he can control it sufficiently and adapt to it adequately, but in order to survive and to become mature, he *must* now control himself more than ever. Social scientists and humanists are not the only ones who see this. It was Einstein who said:

We can only sound the alarm, again and again; we must never relax our efforts to rouse in the peoples of the world, and especially in their governments an awareness of the unprecedented disaster which they are absolutely certain to bring on themselves unless there is a fundamental change in their attitude toward one another, as well as in their concept of the future. . . . The unleashed power of the atom has changed everything except our ways of thinking.[2]

More and more, there are those who point out that since man can choose, he *must* choose, and that if he does not choose to control himself, there may be no man on the earth in a little while. Only man will care. Does he care enough?

Some believe that what is called for is essentially a new religion, and this is persuasively argued by many among the humanists.

Religion of some sort is probably necessary. But it is not necessarily a good thing. The emergent religion of the near future could be a good thing. It will believe in knowledge. It will be able to take advantage of the vast amount of new knowledge produced by the knowledge-explosion of the last few centuries in constructing what we may call its theology—the framework of facts and ideas which provide it with intellectual support: It should be able, with our increased knowledge of mind, to define man's sense of right and wrong more clearly so as to provide a better moral support, and to focus the feeling of sacredness on fitter objects. Instead of worshipping supernatural rulers, it will sanctify the higher manifestations of human nature, in art and love, in intellectual comprehension and aspiring adoration, and will emphasize the fuller realization of life's possibilities as a sacred trust.[3]

The reason for some religions is expressed by Peck and Havighurst:

This present state in which most of us find ourselves is in itself the chief obstacle to be overcome. The problem of achieving ethical rationality is this: the aligning and harmonizing of violently powerful emotional forces is a *precondition* for rational thought.

2. Albert Einstein, New York *Times,* May 25, 1946.
3. Sir Julian Huxley, ed., *The Humanist Frame* (New York: Harper & Brothers, 1961).

This harmonizing can *only* be accomplished through the intrinsically non-rational (not *anti*-rational) means of harmonious experiences with other people who have great emotional importance for oneself. The intellect can be used to select and arrange such an experience, but the crux of the interaction is an emotional experience which has little to do with rational thought.

Thus we come to the paradox that points to a solution: not *either* intellect *or* emotion, but intellect *and* emotion are essential components of rationality.

As a corollary, non-rational symbols and action systems, such as are a nexial part of most religions, may be essential to all of us, if we are to experience the *sensations* and *emotions* that represent and embody the ethical interaction. A rational theory of ethics would therefore have to provide for these kinds of non-rational experiences, while at the same time providing for regular, rational examination of the course and the moral consequences of one's actions. Perhaps this is one of the reasons why ethics and religion have always been intertwined.[4]

Whether or not a new religion is necessary, what is needed is a conception grand enough to be invested with the passion that man has given to other beliefs and which alone can provide the power that is required. There is only one possible focus for this and that is man, man the species. What is called for is enough people who believe passionately in man, and in his possible future, that they can turn him from his present course.[5]

But what is man? Man is a species whose history through recorded time is known in major outline beyond question. Year by year more of the details of that outline are gradually learned,

4. Robert F. Peck and Robert J. Havighurst, *The Psychology of Character Development* (New York: John Wiley & Sons, Inc., 1960).
5. Anne Roe, "Man's Forgotten Weapon," Presidential Address, Division 12, APA, September 1958, published in *The American Psychologist*, Vol. 14 (1959), pp. 261-66.

but they do not change the essential pattern, and we do not need more details to set our future course now. There have been other species of men, but all men now living are one species. This is the basic tenet for a faith and for a new pattern for human cultures. The second essential tenet is that it is good for man to survive.

What does the survival of Homo sapiens mean? It does not mean that any of his present institutions should or can survive. On the contrary. *All* of these must change if man is to survive. There are institutions, religious or political, that claim absolute truth or absolute authority, and whose followers would rather see the death of man than give up this claim. These institutions, too, must change. In fact they are changing, though slowly, too slowly, and they still show no signs of relinquishing their claim to absolutes.

But our stake is more than one in the survival of the species. *We want a species to survive that we are proud of.* The chances are that life, some life, would continue and evolve again into new and different species; but none would be man. The future I want for my species is a society of individuals each of whom plays a significant, and in some measure unique, role in that society. It is a society in which every man, as far as it is humanly possible, is free from outer and inner restrictions that would prevent the richest development of his unique combination of capacities. It is a society not without tensions, but one in which the tensions are those of creation, not of destruction. It is a society in which no man may fear his neighbor, and no man need fear himself. It is a world society that welcomes any number of cultural subdivisions, and counts them all of value.

No such society now exists, and none can exist unless the majority of the members of it are possessors of a kind of character structure that is not now common. What is needed, then, is a radical transformation of personalities, not in terms of modes of adjustment, but in terms of moral character. Nothing else will serve; but it is at first glimpse an almost hopeless task to undertake in the brief time we may have.

What do we know about the development of personality and character? Not very much, but enough to make a start. To begin with, we know practically nothing about the degree in which genetic elements may be involved, so that these must be left out of the discussion. What we do know is that, to a very large extent, our characters and personalities are conditioned by our early experiences, and these depend not only upon the general cultural patterns of the society into which we are born, but also upon the patterns of living and of personal interaction of the families into which we are born. The evidence comes from many longitudinal and cross-sectional and retrospective studies of the developing individual; from case histories of those in therapy; from cross-cultural studies. There is no conflict as regards the general picture, but precisely what kinds of experiences lead to precisely what kinds of character structure are not clearly known. Nor do we know what influences may be adequately counteracting to deleterious early experiences. We do know that remedial measures undertaken in adult life are laborious and uncertain of outcome.

Many studies of child development have concentrated upon the effects of specific training procedures with respect to such matters as weaning and toilet training. These have little to say regarding broader issues of character development. Other studies have concentrated upon disciplinary issues and the climate of the home. These have been more helpful. We know quite surely that, while punishment may be immediately effective, rewards are in the long run much more effective in bringing about persisting behavior patterns.[6] We know that thoughtful and loving and consistent parents who encourage their children to increasing independence rarely have delinquent children. How many such parents are there?

This is not an easy question to answer, but there is only one study that suggests an answer and has much else to say on these issues; this is reported in *The Psychology of Character Development*.[7] It is a part of a larger study, which was concerned with many aspects of life in "Prairie City"—selected as typical of communities between 5,000 and 15,000 population—as they affect the behavior, beliefs, and feelings of the growing child. This part of the study reports intensive work with 34 of the 120 children born in the city in 1933, and which were studied intensively from 1943 to 1950. This sample of 17 boys and 17 girls was selected so that they ranged evenly from the top to the bottom of the group in measures of character made in 1933. Because the group is small, generalizations must be made with due caution. But the manner of selection and the intensity of the study have made it particularly enlightening.

Character is defined in terms of powerful, emotion-laden attitudes, and action patterns that tend to become habitual. With due allowance for maturational changes, there seemed to be very little alteration in basic character structure in the years from ten to seventeen, at least. Basic character was defined in a series of five dominant types, arranged on an ascending scale of psychological and moral maturity, as shown below. All subjects could be classified by dominant type, although none were entirely of one type, and all had mixed motives.

6. Robert R. Sears, Eleanor E. Maccoby, and Harry Levin, *Patterns of Child Rearing* (Evanston, Ill.: Row-Peterson & Co., 1957).
7. Robert F. Peck and Robert J. Havighurst, *op. cit.*

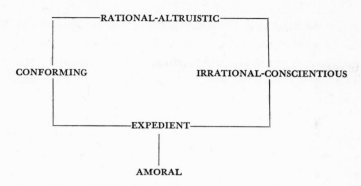

These types are described as follows:

Amoral: have the tendency to secure immediate gratification of impulse without regard for the welfare of others.

Expedient: have the tendency to secure maximal self-gratification with regard for the welfare of others only as a means to an end. Tendency to get what subject wants with a minimum of giving in return. Consistent behavior in disregard of others' welfare whenever it conflicts with subject's welfare as he defines it . . . subject may interest himself in others' satisfactions, but only if this brings him maximum gratification for his own wishes in the long run.

Conforming: have the tendency to conform to the patterns of behavior of the groups of which self is a member. . . . The important consideration is *why* he conforms, not whether he conforms. It is only if he conforms because he wants to conform, because he values conformity for its own sake, that he can be rated high. In general, there are two types of conformers. . . . The chameleon type of conformer seems to depend for guidance upon the outside social structure in which he finds himself, whatever it may be. The ritual conformer seems to have internalized the particular patterns more strictly, so that the immediate external structure may not be so much a source of rules as is his inner pattern if he finds himself in a new group different from the one in which he learned "the rules."

Irrational-Conscientious: having the tendency to behave in accordance with externally originated principles of conduct which have been introjected, operate autonomously to guide and criticize behavior, and are not subject to rational criticism by the self. . . . Tendency to do what the individual believes to be morally "right" in all situations. Tendency to judge others and often self in harsh, black-and-white terms (no middle ground, an act is either "right" or "wrong"), and to perceive others more as actors in expression of principles than as persons in their own right.

Rational-Altruistic: having the tendency to act with consideration of others and their ultimate welfare. This is carried out both in terms of the possible effects of action over a time-span and on any other people who might be concerned, and in terms of a rationally held body of principles as to what constitutes the greatest good for the greatest number. These principles may and perhaps must be originally derived from introjection. They have been modified and differentiated by conscious, rational assessment of their human significance. Perception of others primarily as persons rather than actors only. Willingness to let circumstances alter cases. Does not blindly impose his principles on persons and situations.

The Conforming and Irrational-Conscientious groups between them probably make up about half of the total population.

Who would pick the Amoral or Expedient as neighbors if he could choose, even if he were one of them himself? So long as there are no serious crises, or interpersonal pressures, the Conforming and Irrational-Conscientious groups may not do too badly, but the Rational-Altruistic type as described here is certainly the only one of these types that can develop the ideal society. Since above all things people of this sort are *not* dictatorial, they must be in much greater numbers than they were in this sample (less than a fourth) if we are to have any hope of attaining such an ideal. This is true even though it is suggested that the Conformers and the Irrational-Conscientious may make up as much as half of the total group, and even though they characteristically will "go along." But they will go along with old values, not with newer ones, until the new ones become majority values, and again they will not go on to still other—hopefully, better—ones.

How, then, did these particular children become Rational-Altruistic? On this point, the study is quite explicit:

Character . . . appears to be predominantly shaped by the intimate, emotionally powerful relationships between the child and the parents, within the family. Forces outside the family are not negligible nor irrelevant in their *indirect* effect on character formation, but it looks as though these forces operate mainly as they shape and guide parents' behavior, and as they reward or otherwise reinforce child behavior that follows the socially approved parts of the parents' behavior.

The distinctive common pattern of family experience that was unique to those who belong in the Rational-Altruistic group was one of consistent and strongly trustful and loving parents, who gave their children guidance but were lenient in punishment, and who also gave them the opportunity to experiment in making decisions and in developing and trading ideas without hesitation.

But the parents who treat their children in these ways are those who were treated in the same way by their own parents. If this were the only thing upon which we could rely, there would be little hope for the future: there is no assurance that such parents have more children than other parents—indeed, the contrary is far more likely—and even if they did, we could not wait enough generations for them to take over. We have no reason to assume that the proportion of people of this type is very different in this country now from what it was several generations ago.

This study did not investigate directly the effect of other institutions upon character development, but it did suggest strongly, as quoted above, that other institutions may affect parent behavior. They may also affect the child more directly. In a study of the adult adjustment of foster children whose own parents were variously alcoholic, psychotic, or normal, and some of whom had poor foster homes, Roe and Burks[8] concluded:

It seems very probable that residence in a home which is a respected part of the community, and the child's acceptance as a member of that community, make possible the formation of an organized ideal derived from the attitudes and forms of behavior of the community that can function as an integrating force, even in spite of unloving and harsh parents. It is conceivable that the basic assumption of our society, the assumption of the dignity and worth of the individual, is sufficiently pervasive that it may offer support even to the child whose dignity suffers attacks from his parents.

An important observation in the Peck and Havighurst study was that the Rational-Altruistic group were often selected as leaders by their age peers, and were generally accorded the highest regard. There was a high correlation between character maturity and school grades, and teachers did seem to mark down Expedient and Amoral children and to reward the others in terms of grades. But it is likely, here, that much of what was being rewarded by the teachers was conformity as much as anything else. The Rational-Altruistic group, because they are considerate, are unlikely to raise difficulties in a school situation.

8. Anne Roe et al., "Adult Adjustment of Foster Children of Alcoholic and Psychotic Parentage and the Influence of the Foster Home," *Quarterly Journal of Studies on Alcohol,* Memoirs of the Section on Alcohol Studies (New Haven: Yale University Press, 1945) Vol. 3, pp. 1-162.

There is disturbing evidence that teachers are more inclined to reward conformity than they are original thinking.[9]

We must make a *frontal* attack upon the development of more persons of high moral character than we can expect to have develop otherwise. The main institution in which this is possible is the public school. Private church schools are unlikely to be really helpful. This is because, although they profess to teach morality and ethical behavior, they do so always in terms of authority, and they come always, sooner or later, to doctrines that must not be questioned.

What people need most to learn is to reason about human behavior, their own and that of others. That human behavior has lawful, if complex, regularities is simply unknown to the vast majority of persons. Indeed, many refuse to believe it, lest this somehow diminish their self-image, or their feeling of having some control over their own destiny. There is a genuine paradox in this refusal, one that is difficult to resolve and one that I for one have not resolved, and so cannot usefully discuss. I recognize it, but I have learned to live with it, much as a physicist learns to live with the apparently mutually incompatible notions of light as particle and as wave.

But certainly one of the implications is that we must seriously try to concentrate on the resources of the behavioral science in developing educational programs for adults as well as for children; for teachers and parents and statesmen; for politicians and priests; for other scientists—and for ourselves. The aim is to find ways of increasingly deep and accurate self-

9. Jacob W. Getzels and Philip W. Jackson, "The Highly Intelligent and the Highly Creative Adolescent: A Summary of Some Research Findings," in C. W. Taylor, *The Third University of Utah Research Conference on the Identification of Creative Scientific Talent* (Salt Lake City: University of Utah Press, 1959; and F. B. Jex and R. M. Merrill, eds., *University of Utah Research Monograph* (Salt Lake City: University of Utah Press, 1958), Vols. 1, 2.

knowledge, which is the one essential for effective ethical behavior. (Because behavioral scientists are humans first, we do
not all possess as individuals such a degree of *self*-knowledge as
our studies might suggest. Nor do we always maintain toward
each other, let alone everyone else, that attitude of trust and
acceptance that is believed by many to be the basis for thera-
peutic change and for the development of a Rational-Altruistic
type of character. It is true, however, that, in my experience,
we mobilize fewer defenses against each other in social circumstances than do many other groups. But surely we should try
harder to put our knowledge to personal use.)

To apply such an aim to society generally, it is easiest to
see how to start in the schools, if only because the children are
there for many hours a day and quite literally at our mercy.
There are principles to be followed, and plans that have been
tried and tested.

Cronbach has summarized the possible roles of the school:

First, the school builds emotional readiness by making the
pupil secure. Second, it reinforces his desire "to be good." Third, it
teaches him to see ethical conflicts as problems to be solved intelligently. Then, while this growth is continuing, the school provides
opportunities to deal with such conflicts and gain experience in
solving them. Any school program presents some occasions for
ethical learning. The fifth aspect of building character is to translate
the experiences into conscious generalizations. The verbal summary
may be brief and simple with young children; with older ones there
will be occasions for discussing complex dilemmas. Out of this
thinking they will create properly complex philosophies of life.

Special thought needs to be given to covering the range of
important problems. For example, a program where students always
interact with the teacher, having no occasion to work in groups, will
confront them with none of the problems of settlement of disputes
or delegation of responsibility. Therefore, extracurricular activities

and student government are of special value because they introduce problems the school subjects do not.

A person who learns to reason about his conduct and learns what he holds most dear can adapt his character to new strains and new uncertainties. . . . Character begins to set almost at the time of birth. Some of the underlying fears and pleasures are firmly set before school entrance, and the later structure of character does grow around this framework. But a person can acquire new understandings and attachment to new ideals throughout his life, if at his core he likes the world, feels that the world likes him, and believes in the power of his own intelligence.[10]

There have been successful attempts at introducting into the elementary school curriculum modifications that lead to real understanding of human dynamics. Ojemann and others[11] have been doing extensive and careful work in this field, at the Child Welfare Research State of the University of Iowa, supported by a grant from the National Institute of Mental Health. It is pointed out that the usual content of social studies courses of all varieties is almost entirely descriptive, with very little causal material.[12] In junior high school texts in civics, for example, discussions of crime include statistics on the incidence of crimes, data on police forces, and other community agencies, but practically nothing on the dynamics of crime in the individual case. Similarly, history courses include dates of changing governments, boundaries, battles, population movements, and so on, and little or nothing of the effects of any government on

10. Lee Cronbach, *Educational Psychology* (New York: Harcourt, Brace & World, Inc., 1954), quoted in Peck and Havighurst.
11. Ralph H. Ojemann et al., "The Effects of a 'Causal' Teacher-Training Program and Certain Curricular Changes on Grade School Children," *Journal of Experimental Education*, Vol. XXIV, No. 2 (1955), pp. 95-114.
12. Frances S. Stiles, "Developing an Understanding of Human Behavior at the Elementary School Level," *Journal of Educational Research*, Vol. XLIII (1950), pp. 516-24.

the private lives of its citizens. Children are taught essentially what people do, but not why they do it, and furthermore, there is incorporated in much of the materials a judgmental approach without any suggestion that the judgment itself might be questioned. It may be remembered that Piaget[13] has shown that quite young children tend to hold that punishment should be relevant to the *intent* of any action as well as to the results of it. Our schools do not reinforce this, nor do they help the child look for intent in himself and others.

It was found[14] that a course in human behavior, introduced into an otherwise unchanged curriculum by likewise unchanged teachers is not an effective means for bringing about any genuine understanding of how the social environment operates. Ojemann and his group therefore set up a more comprehensive program, designed to help the child develop a "causal" orientation toward his social environment. By this they mean an understanding that human behavior is produced by many factors and that one can recognize and take these in account, as opposed to an orientation that considers mainly the overt form of the behavior. This program involved an intensive training of four teachers (one fourth, one fifth, and two sixth grade), the development of special teaching materials, and a study of the results in terms of pupil learning. The experimental design and statistical analysis were unusually sophisticated. Each of the experimental teachers was matched to two other teachers on appropriate variables. One of each pair of control teachers was at liberty to use any of the materials or none of them; the other could not use any of the materials. Pupil change was assessed in terms of responses on two tests: one, the Problem Situations

13. Jean Piaget, *The Moral Judgment of the Child* (New York: Harcourt, Brace & World, Inc., 1932).
14. S. L. Zelen, "Effect of a Causal Learning Program," Mimeographed Report, Preventive Psychiatry Project (Iowa City: State University of Iowa, 1954).

Test, which is a measure of the child's willingness to be *immediately* punitive in a hypothetical situation when no retaliation is anticipated, and the other, called the Causal Test, which "attempts to tap the child's awareness of the dynamic, complex, variable nature of human motivation, though it does not require that he have any specific knowledge of the causes of behavior themselves." About six and one-half months intervened between the pretesting and the post-testing. The classes of the experimental teachers showed marked changes in the appropriate direction on the two measures. These were significantly greater for all grades than the changes in either control group, which in fact were very slight. It appeared that the change was related more to the use of the specially prepared materials by trained teachers than to the materials themselves. The precise role of the materials is not clear, because the extent of their use in the control group in which they were permitted was highly variable, and not apparently related regularly to outcome.

The training program for the teachers must have brought about significant changes in them as well as in their specific teaching techniques and the way in which they handled specific problems. The preliminary intensive month-long study was followed during the school year by group conferences held every three weeks. The kinds of materials developed for the curriculum included:

1. Introduction to the causal approach by the story method: stories to be read by the pupils, to be followed by discussion of the reasons for the behavior described. A teachers' manual was prepared for this.

2. A series of workbooks which served as introductory units to social studies and health, e.g., How considering causes affects our reaction to behavior; and How past experiences affect methods people use.

3. A series of workbooks which served as introductory units to social studies and health, e.g., How considering causes affects our reaction to behavior; and How past experiences affect methods people use.

4. Revision of units in history and geography to incorporate the elementary principles of human behavior.

5. Units on the use of the room council for helping pupils apply this approach in room council discussions.

This experiment has been described in some detail because it brings us out of the realm of vague hopefulness and into the realm of specific action. Here is an action program already tried, and it works. Doubtless it can be much improved upon, but it introduces no great difficulties in training or in administration, it is unlikely to upset parents, and it is very broadly applicable.

In spite of the primary role of the teacher, we should not overlook the importance of the school guidance counselor in the development of greater self-understanding and, consequently, of understanding others.[15] For him to function in this way requires no changes of curriculum, no special teacher training. If these other things are being done, the guidance counselor can cap them in a meaningful way. There is no serious question raised about the importance of getting into a personally enriching and socially useful occupation. We know now that much more is involved in attaining this end than matching aptitudes to job skills. We believe now that the most important thing is to help the child to evaluate his own personal attributes, to understand wherein his major satisfactions and needs lie, to know what he can put up with in order to gain more important

15. Anne Roe, "High Hopes," Address to Annual Luncheon, NVGA, published in *Vocational Guidance Quarterly*, Vol. 8 (1960), pp. 195-201; and A. D. Biderman and H. Zimmer, *Manipulation of Human Behavior* (New York: John Wiley & Sons, Inc., 1961).

ends, and above all to know what kind of life will give him the greatest fulfillment. The better he understands himself, the better basis he will have for making vocational choices—and for making any other choice. Seen in this perspective, the function of the guidance counselor is not just jobs, and people to take them, it is primarily to increase the student's self-awareness and his awareness of the motivations of others—in short, to help apply the causal approach to a particular problem.

What can we hope for from such programs? More people who are capable of rational, independent reasoning. More people who are easily and more genuinely friendly. More people whose behavior is ethically motivated and controlled. The more individuals of this kind in the population, the more likely we are to have them in positions of national and international influence. If all the world's presidents and prime ministers were of Rational-Altruistic character, even though still in the minority in their own countries, if all the delegates to the United Nations were of this type, the face of the world would be changed. This does not mean that self-interest, that reasonable national interest, would be discarded, but that humanity's interests would become paramount.

In other terms, all men would belong finally to the same ingroup, however many other groupings each might also take part in. Indeed, these other groupings would be encouraged for the diversity they give, because diversity gives richness and greater possibilities for development in different ways. One feature of cultural evolution is the increasing number of roles that any individual member of the culture may be called upon to play. This is also true of his own individual history: he constantly assumes new roles without discarding old ones, although the old ones may change. No man need be less an American because he happens to be also a Coloradan; less a Coloradan because he lives in Denver. He need not be less a businessman because he is a member of a church, less a churchman because he is also a father, or less a father because he is also a son. So a man need not be less a man because he is also an American.

10.

VAN METER AMES

Aesthetics

ART IS LIFE arriving where it is going from the beginning: becoming more alive, aware, masterful; freer to make its own ongoing the goal. Life has come a long way from the ooze to man, and from man's weakness in the midst of enemies and hazards, monstrous and minute. With luck and developing skill, in spite of setbacks, plagues, and ignorance, men have reached the point where their remaining problem as a species is to get along with other men. From the cave paintings of the stone age, men have used art to help them recognize and realize what their life depended on. Prehistoric art seems to have been largely magic. Art still is magic in enabling men to do what all their achievements in science and technology cannot accomplish without art—that is, to give men the help they must have to imagine their situation, to imagine the disaster ahead if they do not wake up to the reality, and to imagine what life could be beyond the present crisis. Life without art, or without enough art or good-enough art, is blind. Art without life is empty, devoid of content, deprived of form. Art and life can go on well only together.

I.

For art to help mankind move on freely, art must be free. Yet as soon as art has an audience—most obviously in movies, radio, and television—it enters the market, and the market is not likely to be freer for art than for anything else. The economic limitation on freedom is not the only one, and may be less important than social and political restrictions. But only free art can be "the great instrument of moral good" that Shelley thought poetry was.

To keep art from communicating is not only to violate but to impoverish society. Censorship in various forms constitutes recognition that art has influence, that it communicates, not accidentally but surely. "It is when . . . men cut themselves off from one another as non-communicating sects, races, nations, classes and cliques that art is degraded to a cult and mankind becomes uncivil."[1] Freedom in art is bound up with freedom in general. Complete freedom might not be more conducive to good work than unmitigated coercion, but this is not the real question. The pertinent consideration is that the arts are recognized to be powerful agents in promoting self-consciousness and in opening up possibilities; that governments and commercial interests are tempted to use the arts, not to foster them, but to restrict them. Private sanctions are not likely to be better than public ones. Since the freedom of art may be abused, like any freedom, the best safeguard would seem to lie in a tolerant criticism that is publicly responsible, rather than in what may be merely private prejudice or sheer lack of aesthetic cultivation, which threatens to hold all art to an adolescent level. On

1. Horace M. Kallen, *Art and Freedom* (New York: Duell, Sloan & Pearce, 1942), pp. 907, 915.

the other hand, to suppress free criticism by persons or organizations would be tyrannical, too.[2]

Plato's case for state censorship was that art is too irrational and emotional to be trusted within a rational order. Talent that could be put to a socially valuable use could and would be perverted. He would forego the benefit of poetic ability in order to be safe from its abuse. He was thinking of the welfare of a small city-state. But there is the same problem in thinking of a large modern nation, or of mankind. Should people be free to enjoy art they like, regardless of its influence? Plato said in the *Laws* (Book II) that to make pleasure the criterion of artistic excellence was an intolerable idea, unless it was the pleasure of the best educated. His reasoning was circular, since for him education would begin with Apollo and the muses. So an educated person would be able to sing and dance well, though he must sing and dance what was good. There was no problem here for Plato, with his assumption that melodies which express virtue are good; those which express vice are not. For him, to say that the pleasure of the best educated should be the criterion of artistic excellence did not mean that the arbiter of taste must have had more training in art than other educated persons, but that he must be pre-eminent in virtue. That one might be truly virtuous and not be fairly familiar with the arts would not have occurred to Plato.

Yet he was on guard against art because he appreciated its creative and unpredictable nature. Art is inherently pitted against political and commercial conformism and the assembly line. The artist glorifies the human touch, the individual difference, not only in painting and sculpture. The poet, desper-

2. Cf. Bertram Morris, "The Arts Today," *The Antioch Review*, Winter 1960-61, pp. 474-75.

ately bent on being free, verges on or plunges into the irreverent, the mad—anything to be alert and intense, to jolt the reader out of complacency and conventionality, to make him pay attention. Before a successful page the reader will be startled by the aptness of what is said. He will see that the poet is out of patience with all that is merely traditional and official; that he is keen on what is lived and felt here and now, not learned or handed down but freshly experienced. New poetry is hard to understand at first because of its unfamiliar use of speech; the poet is always doing something unexpected with it, except when what would normally be said cannot be improved, then lets the language speak for itself. The poet will reject clichés, break syntax, mock departments of English, hark back to the vernacular, and print what had not been seen in print, so that eyes will get what ears knew. He will use what never was heard until struck off in the heat of a retort, a *tu quoque,* in a garage or a night spot or in the family circle. The poet keeps tradition and convention in mind, often to have fun with them and leave them in the lurch. The result will be hard-hitting, with no filling or coasting. It may be parodying or alluding to the newspaper, to murder, sex, and comics, with a crack at television; perhaps a serious facing of the world situation, even reverting with a different slant to the ancient theme of separation and loss.

In music also there is estrangement from custom, with violent insistence upon what is new and now. Composers explore the resources. It is not just a matter of atonality and the use of noise, but of experimenting with intervals and duration, perhaps with sound coming not only from in front but from behind, above, below, and working it all into the composition itself. The feeling is that music must break out of the established form, which has been vulgarized; to risk taking in chaos, with more and more that seems irrational and contrary to form, as it has been, while working out intricate structures that will baffle the performer as well as the hearer, short of prolonged effort and familiarity. The initial effect is shock. Creative musicians are reacting fiercely against the degradation of music in radio and television, with the exception of a few programs. If radical modern music seems unduly difficult and alien, it is not from being inhuman and antisocial, but from a will to achieve something genuinely social and significant rather than trite and cheap. The development of new music goes beyond both formalism and expressionism as they had been understood, rejecting an ideal of form that did no encouraging exploration of unused and unsuspected aspects of hearings, moving away from expression that could not express today's passion for personal freedom in an impersonal society.

A parallel trend in the novel is bringing to the fore neglected elements of the medium and trying new departures in technique. Here is the same feeling that what is established and official need not be binding. Notably, Nathalie Sarraute, Michel Butor, Claude Mauriac, Alain Robbe-Grillet, and Marguerite Duras find that fiction (and life) can be renewed through searching into what had been overlooked or unappreciated in the novel's former absorption in gross events too easily presented because relatively superficial. The casual and the commonplace, too subjective and incidental to figure on the world stage on the scale of recognized reality, may be what makes the world worth saving. Camus made such an observation in *The Plague,* in sympathy with absurd little eccentricities, the more human for being of no great pith or moment. In the face of mass production and massive waste, when whole buildings are thrown out like old shoes and nature is paved away for the wheels of progress, it is a brave stand of the merely human to cherish small things that no organization would make into merchandise, no computation include in the economy.

The existentialists have made much of the absurd as the absence of any overarching scheme, declaring that values depend upon the choice and decision of men who consequently are condemned to freedom. But Sartre and Camus can be seen evolving toward the position of the Italian existentialist Nicola Abbagano, who is not far from William James and John Dewey in holding that men can make constructive use of their freedom in a world that is still full of possibility. To the existentialist the freedom that all men have is exemplified in the artist who seeks to be creative in each stroke, never willing simply to repeat what he or anyone else has done.

This attitude is of crucial value now that a future must be worked out on a viable basis not given by the past. In looking at a finished work of art it is easy to suppose that the artist had the outcome clearly in mind when he began. *But what men need today is the confidence the artist must have that an unprecedented transformation of the given can be achieved.* Salvation may be in the lesson that true art, not being a repetition of anything already clear, must have recourse to sketches, models, notebooks, followed by a selective, corrective picking out and trying out to find what is clearly wanted; once it is found, surprising the artist himself along with others. Bursts of inspiration go with probing and groping, after disciplined preparation and followed by sheer persistence—if the problems are as complicated as they must be now, in art or the like.

II.

There has been a close relationship between art and life among primitive peoples in the civilizations of the Orient, and throughout Western history, except that in the nineteenth and twentieth centuries the Industrial Revolution has made much of life so ugly or boring that many artists have been alienated from society. Some advantage has resulted for humanity from this alienation as well as loss. Art has been freed to concentrate upon the sense of design, which has enriched the experience of art as relief from banality. Yet it has been hard on the artist to be isolated, and unwholesome for art to be used unduly as escape.

The truth is that the artist is simply doing what anyone does when impelled to organize the work he is doing or to reconstruct the situation he is in. If people were not doing this aside from painting, poetry, music, sculpture, and architecture, they would not do it there either. Art is just more of the refining that makes for any fulfillment in life. The trouble is, and the problem is, to bring all modes of production toward aesthetic quality. But men should be able to solve this problem. *It is not a block in the nature of things or in human nature but a further self-assignment of the sort that men have been at home with since they took the road toward mankind by more and more purposefully remaking their world and themselves.* As John Dewey saw, art tends to be escape or decoration in a fragmented and frustrating society. In a better order all production and activity could invite and come to use the vision and the delight of art.[3]

The harm of the romantic conception of the artist as lonely genius is powerfully portrayed by Thomas Mann in *Doctor Faustus*. The composer Adrian sells his soul to the Devil for twenty-four years for creative work, which means that he must forego love and sanity. Paralleling his mad career as he destroys himself is that of Hitler destroying Germany. In a final revul-

3. See John Dewey, *Art as Experience* (New York: Minton, Balch & Co., 1934), pp. 80-81.

sion Adrian says that if art has become impossible without hell's help, there must be a better way. Art should have a more healthy relation to life.

Sartre condemns art that does not have a social justification. But writing can fight. So he contends, in his essay on "What is Literature?," that the prose writer must be engaged, must write for social influence. He holds that a novel is written to get the reader to use his freedom toward making the world. Although this may come close to a Marxist view, Sartre feels indebted to the Americans Faulkner, Hemingway, and Dos Passos, for showing how the novel can help people to face up to their actual situation. To the objection that a novel might discourage people instead of bolstering their morale, Sartre replies that a novel cannot have a bad effect, because he means by a novel a work that generates generosity.

The society with which the human (socio-psycho-physical) organism needs to have a constructive relationship is now nothing less than mankind. It is a large order for art to help here, where, as Dewey observed, the "gap between organism and environment" is almost final. To close the gap and make men at home in the world would bring a consummation no less aesthetic than vital, but so far beyond what has been human capacity as to be completely in doubt. Today it is not only a question of a better-ordered society for the sake of greater happiness, but of having a setting in which men can continue to be men at all. Not only the artist, or any man who wants to surpass himself, must do what has never been done, but mankind, not for fun or satisfaction, but for survival.

Unfortunately, though organization is rapidly increasing all over the world, it is not primarily for the sake of mankind as such. It is mostly external engineering of mechanical arrangements, as in planning the movement of airplanes and automobiles, in ways that happen to be ruining cities, risking lives, and not imagining what people are to do with their lives beyond hurrying from place to place and consuming more of what can be sent flying anywhere. No amount of going, getting in touch with the other side of the globe, and venturing into space can substitute for the experience of growing through doing and learning things that engage the whole organism, the whole person, in a whole life and in a whole humanity.

Works of art are on the way to such creative living, except when they themselves are distorted by the disorientation of the artist. So far as art can perform its historic office in this dangerous age, it will still work beyond the isolated achievements enjoyed by individuals here and there, toward remaking life in general—reworking it from what is merely natural or complexly and barrenly artificial, in the direction of truly human living.

However, this optimism is sobered by the reflection of cruel Renaissance despots with exquisite taste and countless virtuous persons without any, not to mention artists who flout community. Also sobering is the fact that virtue and taste have lost their supposed human universality and are considered relative. The good, the true, and the beautiful have become painfully controversial. Values can no longer be taken for granted, but call for theory, and no theory is accepted by all. The idea of laws of beauty and taste has been discredited.

More modest, yet perhaps more promising for the unity of mankind, is the task of inquiry, of gathering careful information about works of art and the ways of artists, critics, and art lovers, in relation to other aspects of culture. Moreover, a more scientific approach to art is already turning up data and insights providing better understanding than absolute laws and standards could give, even if transcendent guidance could be recovered now.

If fixed laws of taste are gone, so are most of the people who simply know what is best because they prefer it, and those of them who survive feel more obliged to support their dicta by appeal to names and reputations with market value. Evaluation does not have to be abandoned, but it will have to rest upon more investigation and comparison, with reasons given, open to confirmation or question by any who are interested and informed. At least this is the situation if a naturalistic approach to aesthetics is accepted. The alternative, to regard art as outside nature and society and unamenable to the kind of questing and testing applicable to other human interests and activities, has implications that make rational discussion almost out of the question. Appeal to intuition and absolute affirmation ensue, conflicting with the revelations of different cliques or cultures. Meanwhile, the naturalistic and humanistic approach is being justified by the way it works, the way it helps people to move out of prejudice and provincialism into a wider and freer world.

This new world—if we may take the optimistic point of view—may become really world-wide. Yet it need not—as many are afraid of when hearing about the emergence of mankind— abolish the cherished traditions of national groups. There are indications already that the universals of technology may be combined with concern for local demands and intimate needs. Even the modern multiple housing unit is coming to be not only technically efficient but concerned with age differences and individual preferences.

Impatient of all that holds back progress, men everywhere are on the road toward a more just situation for everyone, though there is no guarantee of going far enough, or of not going astray into forms of order that destroy the freedom they promise. It is clear now, except to the chauvinistic, that a good life at home cannot be safely attained or continued as long as people elsewhere are denied the amelioration of their lot that science now makes mandatory. One nation can no longer be isolated from other nations. Scientists are working together across national and ideological lines, despite being drafted into the secrecy of "security." People all over the world, whether formally religious or not, are sharing a common aspiration beyond all that divides them.

Whether democracy with science is better than authority and force, also with science, cannot be proved on paper. But democratic ways shine by comparison with the terror and suffering that come from totalitarian ways. Democracy is parodied and betrayed, however, by the adherents as well as by its enemies. Nowhere are the ideals of democracy achieved beyond doubt or compromise. How much chance has a way of life open and trusting, giving fair play to all, when this bares it to subversion? How can tolerance be protected against intolerance? Can Athens be safe from Sparta without becoming Spartan? If there is no guarantee that democracy and science will build a viable future, there is increasing reason to fear that no alternative can do it, or that one might succeed inhumanly. But art that can express democratic attitudes and be co-scientific need not stand aside, except as some withdrawal is an aid to vision.

The scientific approach in one field after another is showing the difference between better and worse ways of growing things, of making things, and of treating people; even if there is no one and only procedure that is best without qualification or need of revision. The close relation of art to human nature is being clarified by scholarly studies in the psychology of art, confirming the view that it is natural and important for people to have the benefit of art and of working somewhat as the artist does, and important that the artist take his place among the workers of the world.

Building a world fit to live in, let alone one that will hold together, is not a project separate from the process of developing the individual into a person who can live with himself and others with some imagination. Although art intended to stimulate international friendship may fail as art, art with no apparent humanitarian purpose may do something to save the world. Increasing freedom in handling the medium, leading to a more personal and intimate concern with very subtle experiences, can have social consequences through promoting sympathy with people who make or enjoy art that other people respond to, across all the divisions of time and distance, as Malraux has emphasized in his conception of the "museum without walls."

The break, in this century, from representing nature to new modes of expression, charging each work with more individual feeling, has brought not only more confidence in the self-sufficiency of forms and colors but a new sense of freedom. The importance of art today is again what William Morris felt: that here is the last stand of hand work in our culture, in contrast to the spreading division of labor that cuts a person off from the outcome of his effort. Lewis Mumford's hope for a rebirth of creativity through technology no longer has much appeal. There is felt instead a deep need for the individual to make things himself, to mark them with his own strokes, even with drips and slips that would have to be effaced from machine work but which testify to his active presence. The use of open forms, changing movements, all kinds of randomness, shows unconstrained activity throughout. The accidental is exploited, instead of being expunged as it must be in industry. The artist refuses to transmit anything already prepared and presupposed.

This makes communication difficult, but also makes it

worthwhile, because it calls for participation from "the other." It calls upon him to be a person, an appreciator responding to qualities freshly presented in their own right. There must be attention to what is attempted or accomplished, with some generosity of spirit, some willingness to contemplate and wait for an effect that may not be obvious but which comes with communion, in a meeting of minds that may depend upon going more than halfway in each, in a sharing of feeling and imagination that is humanizing, and rare apart from making and awaking to art.[4] So even abstract art turns out to have social significance precisely because of its personal importance. Hence modern art was condemned in Hitler Germany and Stalin Russia. Instead of emphasizing Nazi or communist notions, it was international and a free expression of the human spirit.

What is needed is not the imposition of one culture upon another but free cultural exchange, appreciation of the art of other countries without rejection of the home-grown. The United States must learn to make a good impression abroad culturally, instead of relying upon the standardized products of the mass media, which lack the creative ability that should be put forward. Sensitivity to unfortunate conceptions of American life in the minds of foreigners, fostered by cultural isolationism, might be acquired through more interest in what others have to offer. We cannot afford to entrust our image mostly to commercial enterprises that do not seem at all guided by what people think and feel, aside from what they can be made to buy. It is no wonder that, in the eyes of the world, American society is too materialistic to care about art except when priced out of reasonable reach.

4. Cf. Meyer Schapiro, "The Liberating Quality of Avant-Garde Art," *Art News*, Vol. 56, No. 4 (Summer 1957), pp. 36-42.

The fact remains that art, in addition to providing entertainment and auctions, gives the closest approach to understanding what is behind the news and the statistics. There is a flood of information, but most of it is too impersonal and indirect for men to realize in vivid human terms what people have done to other people and are preparing to do, what they are getting ready to do to us, what we are all in the process of doing to ourselves and to our children. *We are in desperate need of words, visions, warnings that only art can devise, to save mankind from what we know will happen unless we all wake up in time.*

Only lack of imagination can explain that, despite the fate now faced by man if he cannot or will not join the human race, it is far from certain that he will join. His rivalries and jealous local loyalties make it doubtful. Science and technology, with globe-circling communication and transportation, make it physically possible if not imperative for a world community to develop. But tribalism continues, turning the new resources and techniques into dreadful weapons instead of into ways and means of peace, except incidentally. Even the social sciences, which promise to give man self-control comparable to the mastery that the other sciences have gained for him over surrounding nature, are perverted into methods of taking advantage of other people. Religion, too, is used for national as well as sectarian ends. So, to hope that art will bring the brotherhood of man when science and religion fail, is optimistic. Art is constantly used to exalt exclusive interests. National anthems are not hymns to universal harmony, any more than flags gallantly streaming. But there is the flag of the United Nations now, and art can help progressive tendencies. Realism and faith do not need to exclude each other.

III.

Art has always expressed the situation and interests of a time and place. Allowing, as it does, for confused influences, and for irreducible originality, it would seem that, in addition to the difficulty of interpreting the past through art, there is not much chance of relying on art to shape the future. Art reflects more than it molds the human condition. Nevertheless, in the process of registering and reinforcing attitudes in its own period, art must have some aftereffects, whether of reaction or acceptance. Significant is Arnold Hauser's recognition of the repeated reaching out of artists, and of their admirers, in various epochs, toward a way of life felt to be better than theirs, as they idealize it—as in pastoral poetry, from Hellenism on, in Brueghel's painting of peasant life for the court, and in Watteau's yearning visions of quiet joy. People in the envied state may be envying those who envy them. This does not mean that all idealizing rests upon illusion. If the psychiatric finding is accepted—that something like the happiness of childhood is what man misses—then the freedom from the daily toil of adulthood, provided by the advance of technology, should bring a really better life for everyone (though only if the general intelligence is high enough to use the opportunity for turning leisure away from boredom to interesting and innocent activities). Then most of the art of the past can be interpreted as already showing the road to mankind. The goal is not impossible to imagine, or to indicate, if it is already there in happy childhood hours, and in the hours when adults live in the spontaneous enjoyment of their own doings. The attraction of the life of uninhibited instinct for Freud has been called his Rousseauism. But Rousseau knew that getting rid of repression called for more, not less, civilization. In *The Social Contract* he did not urge a return to nature, but wanted an advance beyond the faults of conventional society. He saw that men cannot lessen repression without recognizing the rights of other men. They must head for utopia or ruin. The ideal and the practical must converge. There is only one road ahead.

It is in the direction of making the benefit of art, as science, available to all. Too often, art has been only of and for a few, expressing a way or ideal that could not be for all. If art cannot mean what it could for everyone, the hope is that appreciation will develop in every class. When art ceases to be concerned with the interests of normal human beings, it is nearing a dead end, or they are. Much of modern literature has led away from reality, through romantic aestheticism and on from impressionism and symbolism to the destruction of a self that could be at home in society, in Baudelaire, Rimbaud, Verlaine, Mallarmé, and, after them, to Kafka and Beckett. Now that no sensitive and reflective person can help feeling alien in a violently disordered world, such writers mean more to more people than could have been anticipated. But their revulsion is not enough, no matter how perfectly worded. Subjectivity is not enough, subtle as it may be. *There must be art that is large, public, and grown-up.* It will have to be complicated to be equal to the time. The people will need to be educated to appreciate it, but it will be for them, and will help to educate them. They will see that the freedom to appreciate and benefit from art is not free of the structure of society. Conditions conducive to the creation and enjoyment of great art are now the same as are basic to a life worth expressing in art; a life worth saving, able to go on making life and art inseparable, not for a small minority, not for aesthetics, but for mankind.

What is finally needed, behind or beyond what can be

found out in study or worked out in science, is the courage, the morality, to believe in the better, to believe it can be made appealing and compelling enough to be extended, shared, and made world-transforming. Ethics and aesthetics come together if Dewey was right:

. . . that art is more moral than moralities. For the latter either are, or tend to become, consecrations of the *status quo,* reflections of custom, reinforcements of the established order. . . . Art has been the means of keeping alive the sense of purposes that outrun evidence and of meanings that transcend indurated habit.[5]

The artist is likely to do better if it is not his purpose to save civilization. He is bound to be helpful in enabling men to realize their world more keenly, while giving the example of combining freedom and order in all of his work that comes off. In the very effort to do his work in his own way, the artist naturally gets down to a depth where all men are brothers. Men find in modern art a fascinating reflection of, and differentiated reaction toward, the impact of science and technology upon age-old ways of living, thinking, and feeling. By having their values expressed for them men are helped in taking stock of their situation and in proceeding more knowingly into the unknown. Art is not called for upon a blueprint of the future or for a new code of conduct. The theater can be a teacher only when felt not to be one, when it does not tell people what to think but leaves them something to think about. The same seems to be true of all art, even including the art of teaching.

What can be taught, in the sense of direct telling or pointing out, will soon not be taught but programed for self-instruction lessons, reduced to training and conditioning with the

5. John Dewey, *op. cit.,* p. 348.

help of machines. What will still demand thought or creative effort will then call more clearly for the indirection, the stimulus and suggestion, of art.

IV.

Art is the evidence that men can use the materials and energies of nature to expand their life. Art, instead of being apart from life—as it seems to be when set aside in museums and associated with the past and the remote—is a way of recovering the feel of a live situation, in which men are alive as healthy animals, as children are, with the senses alert and attention on the qui vive. It is a stretch of keen living that men like to remember, to live again and hope for more of it, unless they are tired or ill. Art celebrates momentous experiences and enhances them with imagination, through one medium or another, providing situations that never were on land or sea. To say they are "out of this world" is blasphemous. Understandably, people talk that way when their lives are stunted and aborted, not worth living. When life is fresh and expectant, something to write home about because it is not just an old story but new and wonderful, it is not out of this world; it is the best of this world. That is what Dewey calls having an experience that is *an* experience.

Dewey not only relates art to ordinary human living; he goes deeper to find the source and force of art in the rhythm of the organism, the live creature in the environment:

Life itself consists of phases in which the organism falls out of step with the march of surrounding things and then recovers unison with it—either through effort or by some happy chance. . . . If the gap between organism and environment is too wide, the creature dies. . . . For only when an organism shares in the ordered relations of its environment does it secure the stability essential to living. And when the participation comes after a phase of disruption and

conflict, it bears within itself the germs of a consummation akin to
the aesthetic. . . . To grasp the sources of esthetic experience it is,
therefore, necessary to have recourse to animal life below the
human scale.[6]

When art and life, imagination and reality, are not
wrenched apart by a divided society and a corresponding theory,
there is no problem of getting the poles together. People come
to realize that an artist in their midst expresses not only their
time and place but something of the human lot in general. Some
of the most neglected and unappreciated artists, who seemed too
experimental or advanced for the public, were accepted and admired when it was understood that in expressing themselves,
they were speaking for their fellows, too. Biographies of Van
Gogh's life and his letters would not have had the same interest
without his work. Taken with his work, they show what it means
and what it may cost to live thoroughly aroused, with everything
thrown into question. It was a critical situation whenever one of
his paintings was in process, even as considered technically. He
had to hold on to the relevant and reject the rest quickly enough.
He had to dive at the palette, mix and jab or swipe, seize another
brush, look, size up, place and relate, transpose, decide and exe-
cute, consider and strike again, before the light or his mood
changed. It is exhilarating to see a man striving to create and
capture values, or to see that he did and how he did it, alone and
driven, if not going mad. Out of the passing day-by-dayness, Van
Gogh gave special importance to a table, a bed, a field, a post-
man, a pair of shoes.

Sunflowers, trees, peasants bending to the field need only
to be rendered as Van Gogh saw them when he struggled to
see what they really were for him, to be *important for mankind.* One might doubt the value of putting an old pair of shoes

6. *Ibid.,* pp. 14, 15, 18.

on canvas before seeing them there, and seeing that they were
not just shoes. Then one's sense impressions are not just that, and
form is more than arrangement of sense data. It is alive with
human striving and arriving. The shoes were worn by countless
steps; they were used; and it was a comfort to take them off. They
were owned. They belonged to humanity as much as the faces
and worn hands from the same palette.

It may seem easy to dismiss such painting as appealing to
sentiment. The test comes with abstract or nonobjective work,
as devoid as possible of familiar associations. Here there is, with
whatever else, a reaction against sentimental representation in
favor of form that seems to have nothing to do with the familiar
affairs and emotions of life.

To explain devotion to supposedly pure form, the theory of
Einfühling, or empathy, was developed. The idea was that form
is receptive to activity projected into it by a subject; that form
is found beautiful when "feeling into" it is to experience agree-
ably a manifold as a unity—ugly when unity is not found, in-
sipid when unity is reached too easily. The trouble with this
theory is that for it, not the real human self, which is biological,
social, and psychological, but only an abstract self, concerned
with nothing but unity and variety in the abstract, is projected
into the art object. So empathy turns out to be only another ver-
sion of the separation of life and art, instead of an aid to getting
them together.

When life is disappointing, there may be relief in art that
tries to get away from life. But along with abstract art, naturalistic, or representational, art has held its own and is now taken
more seriously again. Formalists themselves never really limited
themselves to "pure form." Clive Bell spoke of form as "significant," and Hanslick had a place for feeling, while ostensibly re-
ducing music to a structure of tones and their relations in his

violent rejection of Wagner. A formalist may feel that content is of no importance when form is perfected; but it is impossible to ignore for long the demand for humanly significant content. Some aestheticians at the turn of the twentieth century were working free of the nineteenth-century separation of art from life, which found justification in the idea of art for art's sake. They saw that form, as it had been understood after Kant, could not be enough without something more. But if form in art cannot be purified of associations with life, and cannot suffice without the perspectives of experience, any more than art can be emptied of sensuous elements, then the form into which an artist puts his best effort will be imbued with human significance, whether regarded as abstract or not, if the result is to be admired as art by more than an elite with their own reasons for finding value where others do not.

The social potentialities of art are belied and travestied by the flashy trash and dismal junk oppressing any sense of beauty on the way in or out of a modern city. But the ugliness with which man has surrounded himself, like the frightfulness he is stockpiling, should be regarded as a complex problem to be solved rather than a fate to be accepted. If madness, horror, and utter dreariness are expressed by art, in oblique honor to life through denunciation of its betrayal, artists will not stop suggesting what it could mean to live more sanely and gaily, more richly and simply, whatever their own failures and disappointments. They venture into the unexplored, varying their methods and experimenting with approaches. Artists are akin to scientists in search of further knowledge and command of the energies in man and his environment. Art makes use of what the sciences achieve, while expressing the sense of what is ever beyond; giving form to the joy of life that is more ancient than science, and to the suffering and sadness that men still have to share or bear alone, no matter how smoothly and swiftly things are made to run; and not only by perfecting form but scrapping form in search of more effective expression.

Arnold Hauser sums up his impressive study:

All art is a game with and a fight against chaos: it is always advancing more and more dangerously toward chaos and rescuing more and more extensive provinces of the spirit from its clutch. If there is any progress in the history of art, then it consists in the constant growth of these provinces wrested from chaos.[7]

Through art, and thanks to art more than to anything else, men became men. Expression and communication ever culminating in art distinguish humanity as made up of beings who can know themselves, know what they are doing, learn how to do it better, and even see where they are going. Beings capable of art not only become self-conscious and group-conscious, but can, if they will, become human enough to go beyond merely going along, or in twos and threes, families and clans, teams and crowds, troops and nations, *to bring men together*. Then a future becomes possible in which men will share art that is not for everyone, as people now have their own loved ones, homes, and ways, while also moving in larger circles. When men are members of mankind, they will be freer than they are now to cultivate differences along with all that they have in common.

7. Arnold Hauser, *The Social History of Art* (New York: Vintage Books, 1958), Vol. 4, p. 246.

11.

ROBERT ULICH

The Humanities

Science sans conscience n'est que ruine de l'âme.
—RABELAIS

I.

ONE CAN look at the enterprise of learning as a gigantic theater, with thousands of actors playing with, and sometimes against, each other. Observe a modern university with hundreds of lecture halls, libraries, laboratories, and hospitals, or the school system of a modern nation, from elementary, secondary, and vocational schools to supergraduate institutions and the research centers connected with government and industry. And consider that each of these institutions, whether consciously or not, works no longer within a merely national framework but under the continuous impact of discoveries, inventions, intellectual exchanges, and political aspects of increasingly international character. Even in elementary schools conscientious teachers are today aware that sooner or later their pupils will be confronted not only with the concerns of their community and their nation but with the concerns of all mankind, who, crowded on one planet, may soon explore the life of other planets. And it will depend on the imagination and moral courage of the younger generation, whether this gigantic expansion of our horizons will

249

be the culmination of mankind's evolution toward ever higher achievements or its final disaster.

In view of the multitude of tasks and duties of education, this book offers but a few suggestions. Even within its limited scheme it would be incomplete if it did not contain a discussion of the relation of one of the oldest areas of scholarship, the humanities, to the past and future of mankind.

As with all cognitive pursuits, the humanities are motivated by that unique quality of man to which several contributors have already referred, the capacity of self-transcendence, or man's tendency to reach beyond his immediate physical and mental habitat into wider areas of life, always with the hope to reap from them fresh harvests of experience. One may just as well speak of man as the insatiable gatherer, engaged in the passionate, though never completed, attempt of overcoming the limits of personality within time and space through a vicarious participation in the achievements and failures, and the joys and sorrows, of his race.

This process of gathering is much more than a desire for mere acquaintance with the immensity of separate ideas and events occurring on the visible surface of history. It is a process of "orientation," in the deepest sense of the word, motivated by the want to be somewhat secure and at home in an overwhelming universe. It is a way of meeting the threat of loneliness by becoming one with life and living. Call it the search for meaning. Without doubt, our Western tradition has assigned the humanities a major role in this great inquiry.

Paradox though it seems, the more man is enraptured by his interest in the mysteries of life and living—in other words, the more he is in a state of curiosity that psychologists would call near-obsession—the more he feels that he is also in a state of inner liberation. He rises above the narrowness of his ego and the accidents of his environment. The vision of the vastness of the universe renders him humble as he realizes his finiteness and infinitesimality. But he also considers himself privileged because nature has endowed him with the gift of systematic reflection on the wonders of the cosmos. He is not only thrown into it, as the existentialist Heidegger says, but he participates. Instinct and wild passion are still with him, but he also possesses reason; the cruel battle for survival is still his lot, but he also has hours of grace when he can lift himself above the pure necessities of life and sense the dignity that lies in contemplation and understanding.

Hence all cultures except the dominantly militant and—as our culture threatens to become—the dominantly military and technical have professed a deep admiration for the reflective and contemplative life. Originally, this was identified with religion. The guru among the Hindus was loved because he renounced the goods of the earth for a life of devotion. Many of the Jewish rabbis, earning their bread as carpenters, held the faithful together during the diaspora because they interpreted the Talmud. And medieval man bowed before the scholarly priest. Even modern totalitarian regimes must try to find a *modus vivendi* with the transcendent urge in man. Apparently, there remains a sufficient number of people with the sense of reverence for the ultimate and for the men who helped them to venerate it.

But raising the contemplative element in human life above the ordinary does not require the assistance of a supernatural halo. The men whom Plato wanted entrusted with the guardianship of the state were not priests, but the doers and thinkers who had learned the art of dialectics. The *uomo universale,* or the "gentleman" of the Renaissance, was required to be a philosopher of a sort. The liberal theologian Schleiermacher, in his memorandum concerning the foundation of the University of Berlin (1809), somehow preserved the sacred tradition by calling the new type of scholar the "priest of truth," but he definitely suggested a secular institution, which subsequently became a model of humanistic and scientific studies.

Once contemplation has divided itself into the religious on the one hand and the secular on the other, it is the latter that will emphasize the virtue of the humanities. Doubting or even rejecting the idea of a life beyond, and no longer finding his higher criteria in a divine revelation, secular man will inevitably turn his gaze toward the sources of energy—wisdom and enjoyment, which he discovers in the deeds and thoughts of his fellow mortals.

Thus one could make a good case for the statement that the humanities received their full stature only when man took the risk to turn destiny from heaven into his own self, countering the threat of loneliness and isolation by deriving his inspiration from the ideas and ideals of his own making. To phrase it somewhat aphoristically, the humanities began to flower when theology was deposed as the "queen of the sciences" and had to be content with being a lesser pretender within the academic hierarchy.

It is therefore—to move from the theoretical into the social spheres—entirely within the logic of history that the early socialist-worker movements on the European continent, in their despair of any help from the churches, fastened their faith on "knowledge"—not primarily in the scientific and technical sense (they destroyed and hated the machines), but on knowledge in a humanistic sense. As a young man I saw inscribed over the doors of the meeting halls of the German socialist workers "Knowledge is power" or "Knowledge makes free." Marx was revered, not as an economist, but as a humanist savior.

Also, the early adult-education movements—Christian and anti-Christian—indicate that the common and often suffering man had an almost utopian belief in the humanities.

Historically, of course, the "humaniora," often identified with the "free" or "liberal" arts, connoted first a class distinction; they were the studies reserved for the free and privileged. But even in the Middle Ages the liberal arts—in contrast with the "mechanical" arts of the craftsmen—received a universal and ethical meaning: no longer the arts that were reserved *for* the free, but the arts that *made* free, because they opened the gates of the cosmos of mind and nature. The fact that the higher studies were, and to a degree are, a symbol of social distinction does not alter their essential role.

II.

In order to recognize the situation of the humanities in our present world of learning, let us join a college president who comes from the field of history and must defend before the visiting board the continuation of Greek and Latin and other highly nonutilitarian fields of the humanities. He might first explain that by the term "humanities" one should understand, not merely a bundle of more or less speculative and aesthetic interests, but history with its almost endless ramifications (for everything can be regarded under an historical perspective), philosophy, and the fine arts. He would assess the function of directing the minds of youth in such a way that they develop a genuine appreciation of all that is human and humane in man. The humanities should ever remind the student of Juvenal's famous sentence, *"Nihil humani mihi alienum est."* But our president should also emphasize that the humanities will help

young people to differentiate *what* within the wide and sometimes highly immoral realm of the *humanum* is desirable and
what is not.

Someone might challenge the president, arguing that many
of the administrative leaders in higher education come from
business or military careers and would not know, much less care,
whether Juvenal was a Roman or an Indian. Such nice and noble
ideas about college education they would consider a vestigial
"genteel" and "polite" tradition at a time when more scientists
and engineers are needed. To this the president could answer
that there is nothing particularly "genteel" or "polite" in a true
study of the humanities and especially of history. "What does"—
so he would say—"such a study, if taken seriously, ask the student to live with? With human situations profound and heroic,
but also tragic and disillusioning. He will find dogmatic and
superstitious opinions embraced as the embodiments of God's
will, apostolic self-deception of the honest and still more of the
dishonest, visions of heaven and of heavenly love and the fiery
clouds of hatred often in the same soul, nationalism and the lust
of conquest to the degree of self-destruction, revolutions, coun-
ter-revolutions, and cruel revenge. Where could one learn more
about the human race than in studying the origins, reaching far
back into early centuries, of the influence of men such as Mus-
solini, Hitler, and Stalin over large parts of the population,
which ultimately led to the most cruel wars in history? Even a
second Shakespeare could not lead us further up to the heights
and deeper into the abysses of the human soul than we might
achieve through the study of history."

In principle, the professors of the humanity departments
would agree with their president. Only, so they would tell the
visiting committee with a slight touch of departmental jealousy,
if history has that quality of realism and universality, their spe-

cialties also have it, provided they are properly taught. This, of course, so the critical visitor would interject, is often naïvely assumed as a matter of fact. He might refer to humanity courses both in high schools and college that led him to think any good course in a business school might tell a student just as much about mankind as a course on Plato taught by an unplatonic teacher.

The visitor might even touch on a more general problem and ask the professors how many students really developed "a philosophy," in the sense of an ordering system of thought and life, from the many conflicting opinions taught in a required survey course on the history of philosophy. Whereupon the professor of philosophy might answer that he does not intend to give his students "a philosophy," but that he hopes to teach them the art of philosophizing and of arriving at conclusions based on convictions instead of persuasions and conventions. To understand contradictions as expressions of the human quest for meaning should be considered one of the noblest tasks of an academic education. And whereas, so he would add, two or three decades ago one could sense a certain indifference on the part of the students, they now flock into the classrooms of professors who dare go beyond the formality of scholarship and invite them to participate in modern man's quest for new integrations in our dangerously disintegrating civilization. "Yes," the committee member will reply, "I agree with the professor. A certain degree of bewilderment is good—or beneficial. One cannot understand the struggle of mankind and always preserve one's peace of mind. One has first to be pulled out of his old mooring, and steered into the open sea with the winds of the world around one's ears. But no one wants to live forever in the midst of a stormy ocean. Unfortunately, I have met too many young college graduates in my business whose humanist teachers did not give them what the president and I hoped they would achieve, a sense of great horizons together with a sense of belonging. You must combine the two things, openness of mind and also faith, for only people with standards can understand and judge themselves and each other, and thus undertake the enormous tasks of present humanity."

"I admit," so the president would answer, "that the humanities have not always done what I consider their primary function, namely, to help the human soul to preserve its authenticity in our age of political, cultural, and spiritual turmoil. Many instructors have indulged in criticism as an end in itself, thus helping to produce a certain complacent relativism and a phobia for finding a hierarchy of values within the present welter of uncertainties. It is, to give but one illustration, a sad experience to discover, even among well-trained students, a widespread ignorance about the fundamental elements of our Greek-Roman and Judao-Christian tradition. Whatever one's position concerning problems of religion and *Weltanschauung,* one should at least know something about them. Otherwise one can neither defend nor reform them, and both seem necessary. I need not emphasize" —so the president would continue— "how much I loathe such slogans as the armchair scholar and the ivory tower. But, observing the indifference of some of our most erudite men with regard to the great decisions and responsibilities of modern men, I understand how these slogans have come about."

If the visiting committee had sufficient patience, the president could prove that up to the eighteenth century and even later the tradition of the humanities was not at all one of scholarly aloofness, but, in many respects, relevant and heroic.

For what other purpose did Spinoza write his *Tractatus Theologico-Politicus* but to lead the nations of Europe out of superstition and tyranny toward a world of freedom? In the two words *"libertas philosophandi"* (the freedom to think) he formulated the idea without which a modern university could not maintain its true purpose.

Locke's essays on government and on tolerance paved the way toward democracy. And when the eighteenth century's French rationalists, or *les philosophes,* investigated the relations between men and men, men and government, and men and religion, they did so not merely for historical reasons. Nor did they elevate speculation as a value in itself. Rather they believed in reason as the means given to man for the progress and happiness of mankind. For understanding society they tried to use the same methods that Galileo and Newton had used for understanding of nature. They were impetuous progressives, punished, as so many of their contemporaries in other countries, by churches for their heresies and by governments for their defense of justice.

Condorcet's *Outline of a Historical Description of the Progress of the Human Mind* is perhaps the best example for France. The English and French soon were rivaled by the Germans, although on different metaphysical grounds.

In the miraculously productive seventeen eighties, when German poetry and philosophy suddenly climbed to unforeseen heights, the poet-philosopher Lessing wrote his *Education of Mankind,* in which he asserted that the great religions, because but participants in the spiritual progress of humanity, cannot claim finality. The theologian Herder wrote his *Philosophical Ideas Concerning the History of Mankind,* in which he developed the concept of the evolution of the human race as being in harmony with the evolutionary principles inherent in nature. Intuitively, he anticipated here the work of Darwin and Spencer.

During the same decade Kant wrote his *Idea for a Universal History with Cosmopolitan Intent,* in which we find the great words:

The history of mankind could be viewed on the whole as the realization of a hidden plan of nature in order to bring about an internally —and for this purpose also externally—perfect constitution; since this is the only state in which nature can develop all the faculties of mankind.[1]

In 1793 Kant wrote his deistic *Religion within the Limits of Reason Alone,* for which he was reprimanded by the Prussian government, and two years later his prophetic essay *Eternal Peace.*

These and similar works culminated in the lectures that Hegel, in the eighteen hundred and twenties, delivered at the University of Berlin and which his disciples edited under the title *Philosophy of History.* In these lectures he interpreted history as the self-expression of the ever-creative and evolving World Mind, which uses mankind as its instrument for self-perfection.

Even Kant's *Critique of Pure Reason* (1781) can be classified under the category of fighting humanism. For the author's insight into the central problem of the relation between man and his universe, the problem of cognition, led in the wake of Descartes, Locke, and Hume to an increasingly clear and radical delineation of the boundaries between demonstrable knowledge on the one hand and religious and metaphysical speculation on the other. Thus he freed humanity of the earlier claims of the Christian clergy that the ultimates of their dogma could be based not only on revelation but also on the certainty of human reason. Not without justification—from their point of view—was Kant

1. Carl J. Friedrich, ed., *The Philosophy of Kant* (New York: The Modern Library, 1949).

named "the great destroyer" by reactionary minds. But with more justification was he called "the great liberator" by searching men.

On a secular level, all these philosophers repeated what St. Augustine had sought on a theological level a millennium and a half before them. They attempted to lift time and history above suspicion that they may be nothing but an eddy of accidents. Deeper forces, so they thought, operated within mankind's struggle for a better life. They did not expect salvation from a supernatural miracle, but from man's increasing understanding of the inner logic of events.

Rightly, the empirically minded and therefore sceptical historians of the nineteenth century protested in the name of objective scholarship against what they considered the abuse of the past for the display of metaphysical *a priories,* existing merely in the minds and hopes of men.

But even the overpowering influence of the German historian Ranke, who insisted on telling how things had *really* happened (*"wie es eigentlich gewesen"*), could not circumscribe historical speculations on the destiny of mankind. When the great attempts of the Enlightenment of idealism and romanticism to write sense into history were revealed as relativities turned into absolutes, then substitutes appeared that were no better. While more exact in detail, they also had underlying philosophy. Often they were maimed by nationalistic chauvinism, and thus ethically inferior to the daring projects of earlier times. Even world histories that purported to picture the history of mankind depicted merely a variety of national events. They were sectional in interpretation even more than in content.

Yet despite all failures and disappointments, some men feel that historical knowledge has increased to such a degree that the venture of synthesis can be undertaken under improved auspices.

As in the eighteenth century, so also now, the ineradicable layman demands that some historians behave unacademically and
give him some guidance through the torrents of history.

This helps to account for the interest in Spengler's *Decline
of the West* before and after World War I, and explains why
Toynbee's *Study of History* captured the public's attention during and since World War II. It makes no difference whether one
wants to name these books "philosophies of history" according to
Hegel's example, or just histories. They provide the same challenge to the humanities that the medieval mystics provided to
dogmatic theology. These mystics spanned the gulf between the
established discipline of church theology and related the human
soul directly to the divine. And who of our contemporaries,
when laying aside the works of Spengler and Toynbee, cannot
help but contemplate on the nature and destiny of man though,
perhaps, on a more empirical level?

III.

But in pursuing our imaginary president's trend of thought
about the dynamic occupation of the humanities with broader
concerns of man, we have neglected one factor. Of course, some
geniuses possessed an admirable capacity for interrelating a wide
variety of interests and disciplines: the Descartes and Pascal, the
Newton and Locke, the Leibniz and Kant. But the more they
extended their curiosity from theology to mathematics, from
metaphysics to politics, from the classics to the natural sciences,
and from regional and intolerant prejudices to the true concerns
of mankind, the more they added to the progressive differentiation of the content and method of scholarship. Although this
process of differentiation was characteristic of every step in the
understanding of man and nature, it also contributed to the
ever-increasing diversification and specialization of knowledge,

and has endangered even the unity of the humanities. Are they still able to give us a sense of cultural integration, of answering our quest for meaning, and of leading men beyond his immediate environment toward the doors of humanity? Or are they just an enormous conglomeration of diverging interests, a unity so loose that it does not deserve the name, a labyrinth instead of a house where the mind of man may dwell?

Many would answer this question in the negative. Thus, indeed, we may sometimes indulge in sentimental feelings about the medieval *artes liberales,* with their orderly sequence from the studies of the mind (grammar, which originally meant literature, logic, and rhetoric) to the study of measure and nature (music, arithmetic, geometry, and astronomy). But then one should look into the primitive encyclopedias, which, during and after the migration of the nations, transmitted some of the knowledge of antiquity to the medieval schoolmen, or even into the far-advanced *compendia* at the end of the Middle Ages. Then one will admit the value of precise and painstaking research motivated by your modern methodological conscience and the mass of details it has produced. *Embarras de richesse* is still better than poverty. And when we remember the filth, hunger, and disease of the early centuries, we will be grateful for modern science and think more realistically about the "blessings of the Middle Ages." Even then spiritual unity was a dream. Life was full of conflict.

In comparison with this transformation of a world of class distinctions and miracles into a world when man looks for social justice and thinks according to causal relations, the religious changes of the Reformation were sectional, despite their metaphysical depth and the heroism and the bloodshed that went with them.

Today we live again in such a momentous state of transformation. There is, in this essay on the humanities, no need to speak of the present revolution in the natural sciences. But we must speak of the changes in the humanities themselves, provided we understand them to be not a circumscribed number of traditional disciplines, but the whole body of studies concerned with the inner and social life of man.

Certainly the most important change in the scope and character of these studies is the development of the so-called social sciences. From the point of view of the historian of learning, should they be described merely as an expansion of trends already existing within the humanities? Or have they brought about such fundamental changes in the approach to the human problem that they deserve a special place on the *globus intellectualis?*

Many psychologists, anthropologists, and sociologists would answer this latter question in the affirmative. They would insist on difference and categorical separation. To explain their position, they might picture a dual world of scholarship—onesidedly, they would admit, yet useful as a device of argument.

On the one side, so they would say, there are the traditional humanities, with their libraries, their quiet studies, their contemplative mood, their reliance on intuitive insight, justified to a degree because the world they want to explore is essentially their own—a world of values and evaluations, of freedom and accident, of feelings and of emotions.

On the other side, they would picture the scientists in their laboratories, awaiting anxiously the results of their sometimes extremely costly and even dangerous experiments, suspicious of intuition and subjectivity, and disturbed when an element of chance and freedom enters into their world of physical properties—a world where there is no room for such concepts as good and evil, justice and injustice, love and hatred. Only disciplined

intelligence, patient observation, and reduction of phenomena
to quantitatively definable models will determine the quality
of the work.

It is from their world, not from the humanities, so the social scientists would say, that they have derived their methods
of research. However gratefully they might acknowledge the contributions of the great thinkers from Aristotle to ibn-Khaldun,
Giovanni Battista Vico, Kant, Hegel, and Comte and Spencer,
still more important are the contributions of Darwin and his
successors, the men who developed modern statistics and genetics, and the physiologists who have shown the interaction between mind and body. The social scientists could point to the
considerable amount of guesswork among famous humanists
even at a time when the scientists knew better, including Bacon
—although the humanists could retort by revealing the naïveté
about religious and philosophical issues of well-known scientists
sailing under the illegal flag of empirical exactness. See, e.g., the
Riddles of the World, by the German Darwinist Ernst Haeckel,
so widely read about 1900. However, if one needs an example of
the immature state of sociology and anthropology even as recently as one hundred years ago, one may examine the book *On
Women* (*La Femme*), by the Frenchman Jules Michelet, famous
during the nineteenth century as one of the more scientifically
minded historians. He has profound insight into the psychology
of the sexes, on adolescence and on education, and should not
be blamed for a certain bourgeois sentimentality characteristic
of his time, for no scholar can think in an historical vacuum.

But what would a modern scientist say if even one of his
younger students wrote the same nonsense about racial inter-
marriage and national differences as did Michelet—even though
a considerable number of our social scientists lent their services
to forms of nationalist propaganda that were anything but sci-

entific and more dangerous than Michelet's sociological adventures? Even the humanities themselves have profited considerably from modern comparative methods, anthropology and sociology, and it is characteristic of the present situation that the historian William L. Langer, in his presidential address to the American Historical Society,[2] suggested that his colleagues pay attention to the possible contributions of psychoanalysis to historical understanding.

At least a partial explanation for the animosity of the humanists against the social scientists lies in the naïveté with which the latter often applied the quantitative methods of the natural sciences to the problems of man. Whether intended or not, this quantitative approach easily created a mechanistic interpretation of man. For it emphasized one-sidedly the physical level of his existence, instead of advising him that not only there, but also in its cultural pursuits, should mankind find its bond of unity. Realism about man's nature is necessary to avoid the inevitable frustrations ensuing from pseudo-idealistic illusions and delusions, but if obscuring the view of the wholeness of the capacities of the human person, realism is not realistic but degrading. It is collectivistic, antidemocratic, and reactionary in essence.

The most undesirable result of the separation of the social sciences from the matrix of the humanities—of the desirable ones we will speak soon—occurred exactly in a field in which the future of mankind is most decidedly at stake, in the field of education. We still have psychologists who believe that one cannot become a good teacher without a course in animal psychology. But however much we may be impressed by the ingenuity of rats (which are not even the wild and aggressive, but laboratory rats), and however much we may enjoy our dogs and sometimes think that on the moral level they are preferable to certain ex-

2. *American Historical Review*, January 1958.

emplars of the human species, there is between them and humanity a decisive qualitative difference. Men can have ideas, write
them down, subject them to logical argument, and discuss them
silently even with partners in mind who lived many hundred
years ago.

An unfortunate historical coincidence widened the gap between the older humanities and the social scientists, especially
those interested in education. The latter acquired a sense of
independence exactly at a time when many admired natural
scientists were hostile to anything that reminded them of idealistic philosophies, metaphysics, and religion. But the warranted
disgust at the intellectual backwardness of pious dogmatism is no
justification for a determinism totally inadequate for the interpretation of the cognitive, ethical, and aesthetic values of civilization. As we now know, it is inadequate even for the explanation
of nature. And certainly the social scientists are no exception to
the rule that people who refuse to investigate the hidden premises in their own belief generally end with a very bad metaphysics. A most doubtful mythology often grows out of theories that
refuse to recognize their own myths.

Students have been ridiculed because they believed that the
great philosophical and religious traditions might still have
something to contribute to the guidance of man. Needless to say,
such a comprehensive and transcendent idea as that of mankind
and of mankind's freedom could not grow in such an atmosphere
of spiritual regression and "adjustment to the constantly changing environment." Whereas the older humanistic aims of education were related to the concept of a fully lived life in all of its
various dimensions, the prevailing concepts in education became, even in the American democracy, more and more partial
and, as a consequence, contradictory. "Needs" or "felt needs,"
without any definition of what kind of needs, were regarded as

the agents of education; growth, and self-realization, without sufficient understanding of the complexity of the self, these were proclaimed as compatible with co-operative living, adjustment as compatible with the necessarily selective nature of a free society, and the cult of the average as compatible with the progress of democracy. And if "mobility" and "efficiency" become ends in themselves, finally, and perhaps too late, the desperate question may be asked: "Toward what" and "for what?"

But no one should blame the social sciences as such for the despiritualization and dehumanization of the past decades. They participated in a process that traversed our whole Western civilization, including the humanities themselves. Perhaps it was here that the greatest nihilists were to be found. We were overwhelmed by a syndrome of unheard-of scientific and technical developments, the dissolution of time-honored, but disused and misused, absolutes, often passing under the name of religion, and by a false certainty as to the superiority of Western empiricism over any other form of cognition, until a void was created that had to be filled at any price. For men living in this mental constellation, solitude became loneliness, devotion was mistaken for surrender, and the divine gift of reason was reduced to mere intelligence, which for lack of higher criteria and a transcending impetus, perpetually gyrated within itself.

Furthermore, the new social sciences could hardly be expected to deviate from the historical rule that every novel movement of thought overestimates its inclusiveness. Many early Christians refused to recognize the value of Greek philosophy, nor did the scientific and liberal movements of the past centuries always understand their limitations. Every enthusiasm engenders one-sidedness. But it was just the one-sidedness that impressed and still impresses the public at large, for it feels more comfortable with simple than with complex answers.

Of course, in addition to novels, some good and many cheap, the daily press, the radio, and television are the main agents for creating modern opinion. But it is probably no exaggeration to say that many of the modern men of our urban civilization formed their philosophy of life and humanity more on the basis of psychological best sellers than on the religion they nominally professed. For a while, perhaps, Spengler and Toynbee were equal in influence among the more sophisticated. But again today, many of the most widely read books in the non-fiction section belong to the social sciences, though they are often not appreciated by the scholarly critic because of their slogan character. There, nevertheless, remains the eminent influence, and consequently also the eminent responsibility, of the social scientist for the formation of the modern character.

Fortunately, the picture we have given here about the one-sidedness of the social sciences is itself one-sided. True, the fascination of the natural sciences misled many among their representatives. But the men most maligned by the professors of the humanities, the "testers," who invented the intelligence quotient and other devices have, in spite of an early period of clumsy methods and hasty conclusions, contributed more to human welfare and understanding than most of us realize. To-day their pupils assist our physicians in the hospitals, the officers in the army, the managers in the plants, the teachers in the schools, and the parents in their decisions about the future of their children. They are part and parcel of a society in which the human person is respected.

The quantitative method when conscientiously applied to the human being inevitably creates the qualitative concern. It leads the investigator into the depth where the mind of man and its values, hopes, and frustrations merge into the eternal mysteries of existence. Even Freud resorted to mythology in order to explain the strange twists of the human psyche, and his disciples, to mention only Otto Rank and Carl Gustav Jung, joined the anthropologists and the historians of religion in their interest in man's early symbols and intuitions. Furthermore, the activist tendency, so characteristic of the social scientists, did not allow them to stay long in a mood of cool scientific aloofness. There is not only an analyzer of persons in every psychologist, and an analyzer of societies in every sociologist, but also a healer. Thus, it became evident to the best social scientists—as to every good statesman after a revolution—that the methodological premises needed examination. They realized that the early warnings of such men as Heinrich Rickert against the inconsiderate fusion of quantitative and qualitative, generalizing and individualistic, methods, though outdated in many respects, contained a considerable measure of truth. There is today as much soul-searching among the social scientists as among modern theologians, the whole work of Gordon Allport being one of the outstanding examples.

And if further proof is needed of the essentially humanistic character of the social sciences of today, it can be found in all contributions to this book that deal with their realm and range of interest. But it should be added that none of these essays could have been written by the mere application of the older humanist forms of research. And it would be difficult to find a more persuasive combination of the scientific-activist with the philosophical-humanist trend among the social scientists than the following paragraph taken from an address by John R. Seeley to the American Orthopsychiatric Association:[3]

It would be entirely wrong to think of a society as an aggregate of persons, though I know that this view is in common. The society *is* —it extends as far as it lives and moves and has its being—in the

3. Thirty-ninth Annual Meeting, Los Angeles, March 21-24, 1962.

shared definition of situations. At the center of that network is—as for the person—its self-definition. Now whatever else the social scientist does, he *redefines* and thereby and in so far alters the society. . . . So the social scientist is—in the very performance of his social role—a social actor, a crucial actor, a mover and shaker, parallel in function to any formally designated politician, and probably eventually more powerful. . . .

Certainly there is much truth in C. P. Snow's well-known book *The Two Cultures and the Scientific Revolution*.[4] But, however wide the distance between the humanities and social sciences, ultimately they prove the wisdom of Pope's famous line that "the proper study of mankind is man."

And it is a perfect definition of the goal that finally unites the humanities with the social and natural sciences when Paul Brandwein says in his essay "Nature—Idea *and* Substance," contained in this book:

Men may be divided politically, socially, economically, philosophically, but science sees man in a kinship with the living things from which he is derived, and, biologically, as one species. Moreover, it sees man as seeking understanding of himself and his world, discovering its uniformities and its resources, and attempting to find ways of using these resources wisely. Not the least of these resources is man himself.

As a historian of education I cannot help but remember the answer that one of the last educational statesmen of Europe, Anatole de Monzie, gave to French educators who, like their colleagues of other European countries, were passionately fighting for or against a greater place for the sciences in the dominantly humanistic curriculum of the secondary schools. The French philosopher Henry Bergson had even gone so far as to assert

4. C. P. Snow, *The Two Cultures and the Scientific Revolution* (London: Cambridge University Press, 1959).

that the abandonment of Latin would cause the loss of the *"esprit de précision"* and thus have a disastrous effect, not only on the cultural mission of France, but also on the design and production of its jewelry.[5]

Anatole de Monzie then said that it was not the *content* that preserved *"culture générale"*—which we may translate here as a sense for the universal values of humanity—but the *spirit* in which subjects were taught and interpreted.

Thus we arrive here at the conclusion that, essentially, the traditional humanities have no prerogative over any other area of scholarship in their claim of sensitizing man to the *humanum* that we seek in mankind. It is done wherever and whenever the spirit moves a thinker to apply his findings to the universal problems of the race, even though he may not speak expressly about it. We would paraphrase De Monzie's statement by saying: It certainly matters *what* we teach and learn and that we culti-vate in ourselves and our students a clear sense for the methods appropriate to the various disciplines of thought. But it also matters *how* we teach and learn. We have to refine not only the tools of research but our awareness to what degree they help mankind in understanding itself. If this principle applies, we cannot say who helps the future more: the historian who writes the biography of a great statesman, the social scientist who tries to understand the horizontal and vertical relationships between men, or the biologist who tells us about our place in the material creation. We must go deeply into our field of specialty, other-wise we are condemned to amateurishness; but without a sense for the general we cannot fully use our specialty for the benefit of man. A metaphor urges itself on the mind. The various

5. Henry Bergson, "Les Etudes Greco-Latines," Address to the Academie des Sciences, *Revue de Paris,* May 1923.

disciplines of knowledge can be imagined as resting on the circumference of a circle. Each of them exists in its own right, has its specific topic, method, and purpose, and extends its research into different expanses of the ever-widening universe. Yet we also sense a deep inner unity.

First. Whatever a person's ultimate faith, whether dualistic or monistic, for the scholarly investigator the universe is one. He must believe that it is a cosmos and not a chaos, otherwise his search would have no meaning.

Second. All our systematic inquiries are connected with each other by their position on the line of the circumference. None is completely without some relation to the others. For through each of them runs the thread of rationality and logic, which is one and the same in spite of all the differences. Furthermore, the old separation of subject matter has broken down. Each scholarly interest discovers ever-new relations to so-far-distant areas of study. It is a paradox. The greater the expanse, the greater also the sense of affinity and the need for mutual help. Every creative scholar lives today in a painful and at the same time joyful dilemma. He cannot cultivate his own field without borrowing seeds from other fields that are not really his own.

Third. From all positions on the circumference, a line can be drawn toward the center of the circle, and this center is *mankind*—mankind with its endless curiosity about itself, its nature and its purposes, and its sense of togetherness despite all its conflicts. There is no virtue and no crime, there is not one human face, however unusual through its beauty or through its ugliness, through which there does not shine the countenance of humanity. And there is no scientific discovery that, through its proper or improper use, will not eventually elevate or degrade all of us.

IV.

But if we believe this to be true, where then, to pose the question once more, is the justification for teaching the humanities at the time of astronauts and nuclear fission, of rising national, international, and economic problems which we cannot understand without time-consuming information?

By no means is this an idle query. There are many who consider a department of the humanities more or less a luxury, aside from being useful for teaching foreign languages as a somewhat glorified Berlitz School, and for teaching a smattering of "general" education. For one does not need the help of specialists—so they will say—to appreciate a good book on the history of one's country or a literary or artistic masterpiece.

Such an opinion is not even entirely wrong. The arts are not created for experts, and up to the middle of the nineteenth century a gentleman who had studied the classics and mathematics in college had no need for, nor had he much respect for, the academic parvenus who pretended to teach him how to read a great play or novel, even in another language. Actually, the classics were the great timesavers of earlier education. Moreover, many of us leave a concert with a feeling of inner enrichment without ever having attended a class in harmony.

In order to look at the whole problem from another perspective, we might ask if one is necessarily a philistine if he believes that the useful may also have some value for the individual and for the soul of mankind. Unless the vital, the intellectual, and the spiritual are seen as parts of a whole, the human being will never be fully understood.

What answers could the humanist now offer? In view of our previous discussion he should, of course, confirm that his study has no exclusive privilege in helping the student to understand his role within humanity, but rather represents a specific emphasis and mode of thinking.

While unfolding before our eyes the picture of mankind's struggle for civilized living, he helps us to understand what man is and of what he is capable, reaffirming Plato's famous statement in the *Apology* that the unexamined life is not worth living. He combines the horizontal level of continual expansion of knowledge with the vertical dimension of ever-deeper self-understanding. He drives man out of his isolation into the agora, where people meet and exchange ideas. He invites him to wander through foreign lands and to project himself into their works of art and thought, into the motives and decisions of their statesmen, into the graces of their peace, and the heroism and shame of their wars. But while he helps him to live more sympathetically with the others, he might also help him to live more sympathetically with himself, or to become a person. Going outward should also mean going inward. And both processes may even lead beyond mankind and challenge us to ask the question as to our place within the gigantic universe of being. Are human essence and existence, and are the fleeting phenomena of our life, embedded in a greater truth? And what is the nature and validity of the symbols that man has created to express his search for ultimate verity and meaning? In confronting man with the immense span of human history, the humanities should give him a sense of proportion for what is trifling and transient, and what is important and enduringly great.

The humanities exemplify the dialectic without which all human enterprise would be doomed to sterility. On the one hand, they preserve the sense of continuity against the powerful impact of change. On the other, they push the mind into the flux and flow of concrete occurrences. They help us to believe in the value of tradition and in the value of renewal, in the abiding and evolving, in the necessity of faith and the necessity of criticism, and in the continuous interplay between the polarities of the sustaining and the impetuous, which are part of our life just as much as birth and death, inhaling and exhaling.

We also learn from the humanities that any civilization, however proud of itself, plays but a partial role in the evolution of human history. It can grow in depth, and even in size, only through continuous interaction with other groups and cultures. No nation's uniquely productive, or "classical," period resulted from ingrowth. Rather it resulted from a confluence of many streams of thought and action, national and international. People without the courage to risk their tradition will never renew it; nor will they produce a work of interest to mankind.

In our time of mechanization and competition we should lead youth into the treasure rooms of the past in order to strengthen their resistance against the temptation to establish false criteria with regard to the future. The criterion of mechanization is that things tick and click; the machine provides the standard. Therefore we hear now, even in the democracy of the United States, such a term as "social engineering." Adolf Hitler's Minister of Propaganda (propaganda ministries are also a modern invention) liked the word "streamlining" (*Gleichschaltung*). Not only the political machinery, but also the arts and sciences and, of course, the conscience of the people, had to be streamlined.

The criterion of competition is success. If taken out of the natural wholeness of life it engenders haste, jealousy, and unfair practices. No wonder that exactly in the most prosperous and busy countries nervous diseases increase.

As an antidote against the restlessness of our time, the humanities should provide a deeper sense for the relation between time and being than we have today. Our immersion in the thought of men who lived long ago teaches us the immortality of great ideas. Where ideas prevail, time is no longer the great destroyer; it becomes the great preserver. The knowledge of continuity protects us against the insane exaggeration of the value of change. Even scholars are today astonished to hear that change is a meaningful concept only if at the same time we have the notion of an abiding order. Without it, change would turn into chaos. This applies—and this should be one of the most urgent lessons of the humanities—not only to things, but also to minds. The logic we use in the process of thinking is not of our own making, nor does it emerge and disappear with the individual thinker. Consequently, there is something like truth in contrast to transient opinions. There is theoretical as well as ethical truth, although the limitations of our reason may not permit us to comprehend truth in its absoluteness. But take away this and mankind will lapse into barbarism.

In our admiration of the effectiveness of science we often forget what the great scientists know all too well, namely, that the generalizations at which they aim are hypotheses that will be replaced or, at least, corrected. The evolutionary theory, however useful, is still an incomplete explanation of the course of nature. Just as was the case with the Ptolemaic system, one day it too may be replaced, whereas the great intuitive guesses of the human soul, though also suffering from the inadequacy of the human language and from dogmatic accretions, have eternity so far as that term can be used within the framework of history. The plays of Aeschylus, the Bhagavad-Gita, and the dialogues of Plato will be admired as long as the flames will burn on the altars of civilization.

This leads us to another dilemma in the scientific procedure, the ambiguousness of definitions. Definitions are necessary for general and scholarly progress as the white corpuscles in the human blood. But the red corpuscles are just as necessary, the red stuff of immediate experiences and events from which the generalizations and generalities are derived. The humanities —not just learned, but truly assimilated—help us to understand the passions, the instincts, the dreams, and the utopias without which the human mind would become uncreative. The practitioners of the seemingly useless are just as necessary as the practitioners of the useful; and never mistake play for laziness! It may be the deepest source of re-creation. Those who have lost play, have lost childhood, and with it the access to the grounds of imagination where a cave dweller who decorated his walls and a modern painter will meet.

A productive, as well as a crucial, polarity has permeated the history of man; here, too, we need the wisdom of the humanities. This is the polarity between the individual and the community. Neither can exist without the other. Yet one of the two is always eager to destroy the balance. In certain periods individualism and its companion, liberalism, must assert themselves against the devouring Leviathan of a coercive community, represented in our Western tradition primarily by the state or the church or by both. And there is the continual threat of dried-out conventions against men and ideas with the spark of excellence.

In other periods the community may have to guard itself against the disruptive forces of the cult of personality and egotism, often hiding itself behind the thin shield of originality. It might be good to remind a certain type of bohemian and fringe dweller, proudly despising the *misera plebs,* that they themselves could not indulge their individualism without conventions by which a society is held together. But there are no prescriptions that could tell us how far to go toward one side or the other. Only the richness and maturity of disciplined imagination, which should result from the love for the humanities, can guide us. For, as we have already said, the humanities interpret to us man's continuous battle with himself and his fellow men and acquaint us with the ideas and creations by which great thinkers, statesmen, and poets have tried to reconcile the conflicting forces in humanity.

To be sure, the fact remains that all too many are insensitive to ideas, even if they can talk about them. Every teacher has sometimes been frightened by this empty kind of intelligence, where ideas remain inert because they fail to create commitment. And it seems that in the ever-widening circles of obligation that characterizes an expanding civilization, the commitment to mankind is the last and most difficult. Even this last commitment would become another sterility, or, worst of all, the excuse for a despotic attempt at world conquest by a gigantic power, if it did not place itself under the judgment of these infinite and, as many would feel, ultimately religious criteria, such as reverence for life, dignity, love, justice, and mutual responsibility. Whether or not one believes that they are reflections of an overarching cosmos, they nevertheless represent the order without which there can be no civilization. And all this —to revert to the issue of individuality versus community—all this can never be felt in a group or in a nation unless it is, first of all, felt in persons strong and numerous enough to impress even the indifferent by their steady example and persuasiveness.

Here appears to be the most remarkable feature in this book. The contributors who have given much of their time to writing on this topic come from a great variety of studies and, in all likelihood, also from a variety of *Weltanschauungen*. Yet they agree on one fundamental tenet. In our shrinking world we have only one alternative. Either we live forever in a state of anxiety and of that painfully felt imperfection that always comes when men know the challenge without meeting it, or we convince ourselves and those who want to listen that we will only then save and promote human civilization if we realize that today, more than ever, mankind as a whole is involved in every people's thinking and doing. The French writer Albert Camus has written the following wonderful words:

Great ideas, it has been said, come into the world as gently as doves. Perhaps, then, if we live attentively, we shall hear, amid the uproar of empires and nations, a faint flutter of wings, the gentle stirring of life and hope. Some will say that this hope lies in a nation; others, in a man. I believe, rather, it is awakened, revived, nourished by millions of solitary individuals whose deeds and works every day negate frontiers of the crudest implications of history. . . . Each and every man, on the foundation of his own sufferings and joys, builds for all.[6]

Very few sentences could be added to Camus' words. Certainly, a sensitive and creative person is solitary exactly in his most creative hours. Yet there are turning points in human history when individuals and their ideas can no longer stand their loneliness but burst forth in movements and actions. As we say, then the time is ripe.

After two world wars and the danger of a third, we live again in such a time. We may feel that the international organizations that have arisen during the past decades are inefficient, although we may also be optimistic. Nevertheless, they are symbols of a new conscience of humanity. And if they do not work as we hoped, it may not be their fault but ours. For

6. I first discovered them in an editorial by Norman Cousins in the *Saturday Review*, March 25, 1961. The original is to be found at the end of Albert Camus' *Discours de Suede* (Paris: Gallimard, 1958).

organizations live not by themselves but by the spirit that feeds them.

And so do even the "millions of solitary individuals" of whom Camus speaks. They all support each other by the mere feeling of their presence. Moreover, however much they have formed themselves by their own labor, and however much they may even have rebelled against their schools, they have also been educated by them. Otherwise, there would not be "millions." But many more of these who "live attentively" are needed.

This is the conviction that has brought the writers of this book together. We know there is much groping in these essays (as there was much groping when our ancestors conceived the ideas of democracy and freedom). And there are here no fanfares and global programs. But we also know that our highly intellectual, perhaps overintellectualized, civilization can hardly advance beyond the present state of dividedness toward a state of mutual understanding unless the schools, from the early stages up to the universities, prepare our youth for a new form of thinking and existing, which alone can meet the gigantic responsibilities of the future. If you want to be pessimistic, you can say that this is impossible. But you can also be optimistic and say: "We must try, and, if we do, we are already on the way."

Some recommended books:

Howard Mumford Jones, *One Great Society. Humane Learning in the United States* (New York: Harcourt, Brace & World, Inc., 1959).

The University and World Affairs, Report of the Committee on The University and World Affairs (New York: The Ford Foundation, 1960).

Norman Cousins, "The Human Commonwealth," in C. Scott Fletcher, ed., *Education: The Challenge Ahead* (New York: W. W. Norton & Co., Inc., 1962).